# *The* MYSTERY *of* FAITH

MYSTERY LIGHT

# The MYSTERY of FAITH

*An Introduction to the Teaching and Spirituality of the Orthodox Church*

## HILARION ALFEYEV

Edited by
Jessica Rose

ST VLADIMIR'S SEMINARY PRESS
Yonkers, New York
2011

LIBRARY OF CONGRESS CATALOGING-IN-PUBLICATION DATA

Ilarion, Hieromonk.
  [Tainstvo very. English]
 The mystery of faith : an introduction to the teaching and spirituality of the
Orthodox Church / Hilarion Alfeyev ; edited by Jessica Rose.
    p. cm.
Originally published: London : Darton, Longman & Todd, 2002.
  Includes bibliographical references (p.      ) and index.
  ISBN 978-0-88141-375-5
  1.  Orthodox Eastern Church--Doctrines. 2.  Spirituality--Orthodox Eastern
  Church.  I. Rose, Jessica. II. Title.
  BX320.3.I4313 2011
  230'.19--dc22                                              2011014672

St Vladimir's Seminary Press
575 Scarsdale Road, Yonkers, NY 10707
1-800-204-2665    www.svspress.com

Copyright © 2002 Hilarion Alfeyev

First published by
Darton, Longman and Todd, Ltd.
London, UK
2002

ISBN 978-0-88141-375-5

All Rights Reserved

PRINTED IN THE UNITED KINGDOM

# CONTENTS

# Contents

# Contents

# Contents

# FOREWORD

It gives me great joy to welcome the English edition of Bishop Hilarion's book *The Mystery of Faith*. First published in Russian at Moscow in 1996, it has already appeared in French translation in 2001. Here is an introduction to Christian doctrine, prayer and worship that is admirably suited to both Orthodox and non-Orthodox readers. It is profound yet clear, Patristic in spirit yet written in the language of today, loyal to tradition yet open to the future.

In writing this book, Bishop Hilarion has been able to draw upon a wide personal experience – pastoral, academic and ecumenical. Born in Moscow in 1966, brought up from childhood in the Russian Orthodox Church, he was ordained priest at the early age of twenty. After parish work at Kaunas in Lithuania, he then taught during 1991–3 at the Moscow Theological Seminary and Academy. The next two years (1993–5) he spent at Oxford, where I had the good fortune to be his university supervisor. How much I learnt from our conversations together! Never before or since have I had a pupil so single-minded in his dedication to research, and so swift in completing his doctoral thesis. It was later published under the title *St Symeon the New Theologian and Orthodox Tradition* (Oxford University Press, 2000). While at Oxford he also studied Syriac with Dr Sebastian Brock, and this led to the publication of a second work in English, *The Spiritual World of Isaac the Syrian* (Cistercian Studies, 2000). Significantly both Symeon and Isaac are mystical authors; for Bishop Hilarion has a special love for mystical theology, as readers of the present work will quickly discover.

Returning to Russia, Bishop Hilarion worked for six years (1995–2001) at the Department for External Church Relations in the central offices of the Moscow Patriarchate. This involved regular journeys abroad to participate in inter-Christian conferences. During this time he continued to write substantial theological works on such subjects as St Gregory the Theologian

– for this he was awarded a doctorate by the Orthodox Theological Institute of St Sergius in Paris – and the descent of Christ into hell. Consecrated to the episcopate in January 2002, he has recently been appointed head of the representation of the Moscow Patriarchate to the European Union at Brussels, with the title Bishop of Podolsk. The great hierarchs of the early Church, such as St Basil the Great and St Augustine of Hippo, succeeded in combining their administrative and pastoral duties with a life of scholarly study and writing; may the same prove true of the newly-consecreted Bishop Hilarion!

*The Mystery of Faith* is written in a generous, holistic spirit. For the author there is no separation between theology and spirituality, between dogma and personal experience, between faith and prayer; all of them form together a single, undivided whole. Bishop Hilarion agrees with the saying of the Desert Fathers that the theologian is the one who prays. He is not concerned merely to provide a factual description, in an abstract 'scholastic' style, of what it is that Orthodox Christians believe. He wants to present doctrinal teaching in personal, practical, dynamic terms, as a *way of life*. The great Metropolitan of Moscow in the nineteenth century, St Philaret, used to say that the Creed belongs only to those who live it. Such is exactly the spirit in which the present work is written.

One of the most attractive features of this book is the way in which the text is illustrated by frequent quotations from the Fathers and from contemporary authors. Bishop Hilarion sets before us the tradition of the Christian East in all its richness and creative variety.

True theology, so Bishop Hilarion insists, is impossible without a sense of wonder. He cites with approval the words of Albert Einstein, 'The person who has lost the ability to be amazed and to revere is dead.' May the present book evoke in many readers this lifegiving capacity for awe and astonishment.

Kallistos Ware
Bishop of Diokleia

# AUTHOR'S NOTE

The Russian version of this book was written during Great Lent 1992, at a time when I was lecturing in Dogmatic Theology at the Moscow Theological Seminary. The English translation is the work of several people. I wish to express my deep gratitude to Father Christopher Hill, Dr Dimitri Conomos and Jessica Rose, through whose efforts this version now sees the light of day.

The subtitle of this book is 'An Introduction to the Teaching and Spirituality of the Orthodox Church'. It is, however, neither a systematic exposition of the dogmatic theology of the Orthodox Church, nor a comprehensive analysis of Orthodox spiritual tradition. It is rather a personal commentary by an Orthodox priest on the dogmas of the Orthodox Church as they relate to spiritual life. Thus the book poses questions rather than giving answers. It is intended for a wide readership, interested in the teaching of the Orthodox Church both in its historical development and in relation to contemporary problems. In order to give the reader an opportunity to listen to the living voice of the Church's teachers and some of her leading theologians, I have included extracts from their writings on the teaching of the Church. Each chapter of this book is followed by a short collection of texts, mostly patristic, which illustrate the subject discussed in that particular chapter. I have borrowed this form of exposition from Bishop Kallistos Ware's *The Orthodox Way*, which has become a classic introduction to Orthodox theology and spirituality.

# INTRODUCTION

# WHAT IS DOGMA?

'*Dogma*' is a Greek word meaning an unchangeable truth, accepted by faith and binding for Christians (its basic meaning is 'law', or 'resolution'). In modern usage, the words 'dogma' and 'dogmatic' have acquired negative overtones, implying something frozen and lifeless. In Orthodox tradition, however, dogma has positive connotations, referring to the fundamental tenets of the Christian faith.

Dogmas are revealed by God and are based on Scripture, even though they may have received their definitive formulation at a later time. They are the inheritance of the whole Church as formulated by her collective mind. Opposed to dogmas are heresies, from the Greek word *hairesis*, which means 'taking out', or 'selection'. Heresies, then, are theological opinions taken out of the context of the Church's teaching and opposed to it. Dogmas were formulated in response to heresies that had arisen because of misunderstandings on basic points of teaching. From the beginning, the history of Christianity has been characterised by a continual struggle against heresies. It was through this struggle that the Church's consciousness was strengthened, formulations were made more precise and theological thought developed. The dogmatic theology of the Orthodox Church thus arises out of the two-thousand-year history of Christianity.

In our own day there is a widely held view that belief in religious dogmas is not obligatory: even if they still have a certain historical value, they are no longer vital for Christians. Moral and social agendas have become the main preoccupation of many Christian communities, while theological issues are often neglected. This dissociation between dogma and way of life, however, contradicts the very nature of the religious life, which presupposes that faith should always be confirmed by deeds, and vice versa. Thus, in the Epistle of James we find: 'Faith apart from works is dead' (Jas. 2:26). St Paul, on the other hand, claims that 'a man is justified by faith apart from works of law' (Rom. 3:28). The 'works of law' here means the Old Testament rites and sacrifices which are no longer necessary after Christ's saving sacrifice. Good deeds are necessary and essential, yet when separated from faith they do not in themselves lead to salvation. We are justified by faith, but only by a faith which informs the way we live.

No less alien to Christianity is the dissociation of dogma from mysticism, or of theology from the spiritual life. There is an essential interdependence between dogma and mysticism: both lead to knowledge of truth, but in different ways. 'And you will know the truth, and the truth will make you free', says the Lord, who himself is the only Truth, Way and Life (John 8:32; 14:6). Every dogma reveals truth, opens up the way and communicates life, while each heresy puts us at a distance from truth, closes off the way to salvation and renders us spiritually dead. The struggle for dogma which the Church has conducted throughout her history is, as Vladimir Lossky demonstrates, a fight for our being to be brought into the true Life, for our union with God and deification:

All the development of the dogmatic battles which the Church has waged down the centuries appears to us, if we regard it from the purely spiritual standpoint, as dominated by the constant preoccupation which the Church has had to safeguard, at each moment of her history, for all Christians, the possibility of attaining to the fullness of the mystical union . . . The main preoccupation, the issue at stake, in the questions which successively arise respecting the Holy Spirit, grace and the Church herself – this last the dogmatic question of our own time – is always the possibility, the manner, or the means of our union with God. All the history of Christian dogma unfolds itself about this mystical centre . . . The theological doctrines which have been elaborated in the course of these struggles can be treated in the most direct relation to the vital end – that of union with God – to the attainment of which they are subservient. Thus they appear the foundations of Christian spirituality.[1]

Life in Christ is a spiritual fire, while theology constructed mainly on rational deductions is like straw which may be scorched and destroyed by the flames of true religious experience. It is from this perspective that we may recall the 'father of scholasticism', St Thomas Aquinas. His *Vita* tells us that he had a vision of Christ shortly before his death. After this vision, to everyone's surprise, he ceased his literary activities, leaving his *Summa Theologica* unfinished. 'After what I saw, all that I had written seemed like straw to me', he told his disciples.[2] These words reflect a breach between religious experience and theological reflections based on human reasoning, between speculation about God and living with God. This breach was to become characteristic for the medieval Christian West. In the Orthodox East, and in the ancient undivided Church, however, theology was not divorced from life in Christ, nor was dogma separated from spirituality. Dogma and mystical experience are two sides of the same coin, or rather, they are fundamentally one and the same, namely the revelation of God to the human person and the union of the human person with God. Mystical experience was in fact the driving force behind the theological reflections of the Church Fathers, whose genuine encounter with God prompted them to write even more, rather than to stop writing as Aquinas did.

It is not perhaps mere chance that in Orthodox theology there has never been a complete and exhaustive collection of dogmatic truths such as the *Summa Theologica*, which was an attempt to systematise all Christian teaching in the form of questions and answers. For many centuries Aquinas's work determined the development of theological thought in the West, which became increasingly rational and scholastic. In recent centuries, for historical reasons, Orthodox theology has fallen under the strong influence of Western 'school theology'. This is reflected particularly in certain nineteenth-century Russian and Greek dogmatic textbooks, which divorced theology from genuine spiritual life and assumed the rationalistic approach characteristic of the 'school theology' of the Roman Catholic Church up to the Second Vatican Council. Only in the twentieth century, through the works of theologians such as Vladimir Lossky, Father Georges Florovsky and others, has the scholastic captivity of Orthodox theology been brought to an end. The general direction of the subsequent theological quest was worked out under Florovsky's slogan: 'Forward, to the Fathers!'

Theology, it was maintained, must not contradict religious experience but proceed from it. This has been the approach of the Fathers of the Church for two thousand years, from St Paul and Ignatius of Antioch to Theophan the Recluse and St Silouan of Mount Athos in the nineteenth and twentieth centuries. The present work, based on the writings of the Church Fathers, takes into account not only what they have in common but also particular theological insights brought into the treasure-house of Christian teaching by individual authors. In the Orthodox tradition, the main criterion of theological rigour is the so-called *consensus patrum*, the consensus of the Fathers on basic questions of doctrine, a concept which derives from Cyril of Alexandria. It would be wrong, however, to view this *consensus* as something artificially constructed which ignores the personal contribution of each writer. Neither is it to be conceived as some kind of common denominator of patristic thought. We believe that the consensus of the Fathers means their common approach to that which is essential, while allowing for differences on individual points. Thus particular theological opinions of certain Church Fathers, even if not shared by all, do not contradict the *consensus patrum*. They are the fruits of the spiritual quest of men of faith inspired by God, and they ought not to be summarily dismissed in order to leave a simplified scheme or *summa* of theology.

Apart from the writings of the Church Fathers, this book includes extracts from the work of contemporary Orthodox theologians. Orthodox dogmatic teaching is not a monument to Christian antiquity. It requires a living understanding and modern commentary which by necessity includes the experience of life today. Consequently, it would be unthinkable in an exposition of this kind to ignore the views of such remarkable modern theologians as Metropolitan Anthony (Bloom) of Sourozh, Archimandrite Sophrony Sakharov, Father Georges Florovsky, Vladimir Lossky, Bishop Kallistos (Ware) of Diokleia and Father Alexander Schmemann. Each one, while remaining true to the patristic Tradition, has also succeeded in translating Orthodox teaching into the language of contemporary people and in giving answers to the burning questions of modern Christians. Orthodox dogmatic teaching cannot be reduced to a mere repetition of what was said in the early centuries of Christianity. In saying this, we do not seek to *redefine* dogma. Rather we seek to *understand it anew* in such a way that dogma becomes part of the experience of today's Christians.

It would be impossible to identify a moment in the history of Christianity when the development of dogmatic theology ceased. Orthodox theologians normally reject the idea of development of dogma as expressed in the nineteenth century by Cardinal Newman, regarding it as an attempt to justify dogmatic innovations. At the same time, the Orthodox would agree with the idea of 'the progress of the doctrine of God' advanced in the fourth century by St Gregory the Theologian. According to this theory, the dogma of the unity of God the Father was clearly revealed in Old Testament times, whereas the other two Persons of the Trinity remained somewhat in shadow. In the New Testament, the divinity of the Son was revealed, but the divinity of the Holy Spirit was not clearly articulated.[3] Gregory regarded his own epoch as the appropriate time to clarify the doctrine of the Holy Trinity with the solemn proclamation of the divinity of the Spirit.

Nevertheless, dogmatic thinking did not come to an end in the fourth century. Many christological dogmas were formulated in the fifth and sixth centuries, and it was during the following three hundred years that the veneration of icons was proclaimed as dogma. Again, in the mid-fourteenth century, the doctrine of the essence and energies of God was promulgated in the Eastern Church. In our own day, the teachings of the Church continue to be formulated, and ecclesiology has become the major concern of theologians. Development, therefore, has far from run its course. It is not, however, a question of introducing new dogmas, as Newman's theory of dogmatic development might seem to imply, but of *revealing* and *identifying* what was hidden or previously lay in shadow. The progress of the doctrine of God is continuous and unending.

Founded on spiritual experience, Orthodox theology is a living entity today no less than hundreds of years ago. The same questions have always confronted us: What is truth? What is the meaning of life? How can one find joy and peace of heart? What is the way to salvation? Christianity does not aim to dot all the i's by answering every question the human spirit asks. But it does open up another reality which transcends all that surrounds us in this earthly life. Once this reality is encountered, we leave behind all our questions and bewilderment, because the soul has come into contact with the Divinity and falls silent in the presence of the Mystery which no human word can convey.

*Easter 1997*

### Chapter One

# THE SEARCH FOR FAITH

## THE CALL

Faith is the path on which an encounter takes place between us and God. It is God who takes the first step: he fully and unconditionally believes in us and gives us a sign, an awareness of his presence. We hear the mysterious call of God, and our first step towards an encounter with him is a response to this call. God may call us openly or in secret, overtly or covertly. But it is difficult for us to believe in him if we do not first heed this call.

Faith is both a mystery and a miracle. Why does one person respond to the call while another does not? Why is one open to receive the word of God, while another remains deaf? Why, having encountered God, does one immediately abandon everything and follow him, while the other turns away and takes a different road?

As he walked by the Sea of Galilee, he saw two brothers, Simon who is called Peter and Andrew his brother, casting a net into the sea; for they were fishermen. And he said to them, 'Follow me ...' Immediately they left their nets and followed him. And going on from there he saw two other brothers, James the son of Zebedee and John ... and he called them. Immediately they left the boat and their father, and followed him.

(Matt. 4:18–22)

What secret hides behind the readiness of the Galilean fishermen to abandon everything and follow Jesus at first encounter? Why, on the other hand, did the rich young man, who also heard Christ's 'Come and follow me', not abandon everything for him but 'went away sorrowful' (Matt. 19:21–2)? Is it perhaps because the fishermen were poor, while the young man 'had great possessions'? The former had nothing other than God, while the latter had 'treasure on earth'.

Each one of us has treasure on earth, whether it be in the form of money or possessions, satisfactory employment or material wellbeing. But the Lord said, 'Blessed are the poor in spirit, for theirs is the kingdom of heaven' (Matt. 5:3). In St Luke's gospel this is put even more simply and directly: 'Blessed are you poor, for yours is the kingdom of God' (Luke 6:20). Blessed are they who realise that, while they may possess many things, they in fact own nothing. Blessed are they who realise that no earthly acquisition can substitute for God. Blessed are they who go and sell all their wealth in order to acquire the pearl of great price.[1] Blessed are they who know that without God they are poor, who have thirsted and hungered after him with all their soul, mind and will.

It has never been easy to hear the message of faith. In our day we are usually so engrossed in the problems of earthly existence that we simply have no time to listen to this message and to reflect on God. For some, religion has been reduced to celebrating Christmas and Easter and to observing a few traditions for fear of being 'torn away from our roots'. Others do not go to church at all because they are 'too busy'. 'He is engrossed in his work'; 'work is everything to her'; 'he is a busy man'. These are some of the best compliments that one can receive from friends and colleagues. 'Busy people' are a breed peculiar to modern times. Nothing exists for them other than a preoccupation which swallows them up completely, leaving no place for that silence where the voice of God may be heard.

And yet, however paradoxical it may seem, in spite of today's noise and confusion, it is still possible to hear the mysterious call of God in our hearts. This call may not always be understood as the voice of God. It may strike us as a feeling of dissatisfaction or of inner unease, or as the beginning of a search. For many, it is only after the passing of years that they realise their life was incomplete and inadequate because it was without God. 'You have made us for yourself', says St Augustine, 'and our hearts are restless until they rest in you.'[2] Without God there can never be fullness of being. It is therefore crucially important for us to be able to hear and to respond to the voice of God at the very moment when God is speaking, and not years later. If someone identifies and responds to the call of God, this may change and transfigure his or her whole life.

The divine call may be likened to an arrow with which God, the experienced archer, wounds the human soul. Bleeding and unhealed, the wound compels the soul to forget all and to seek a doctor. St Macarius of Egypt[3] states that the soul which has felt this call is overcome by an attraction towards God:

The soul's thoughts burn with a spiritual love and an unrestrained pull towards the even more glorious and radiant beauty of the spirit, yearn with unrestrained love for the Heavenly Bridegroom and . . . strive for the exalted and the great which cannot be expressed in words nor comprehended by human reason . . . Through great labours, endeavours, years of asceticism and perfect combat . . . such souls are always enraptured by the heavenly spiritual mysteries and captivated by the variety of Divine beauty, seeking with a great thirst the best and the greatest. For the Divine Spirit contains the varied and the inexhaustible, the ineffable and unthinkable beauty revealing itself to worthy souls for joy and delectation, life and comfort, so that the pure soul, yearning hourly with a strong and ardent love for the heavenly Bridegroom, no longer looks earthwards, but is wholly engulfed by attraction towards him.[4]

## MANY PATHS

Throughout the ages, people have come to God in diverse ways. Sometimes the encounter is sudden and unexpected, sometimes it is prepared by circuitous paths of searching, doubts and disillusion. Occasionally God 'closes in' on us, catching us unaware, while at other times we discover God and turn to him on our own. This conversion may occur earlier or later, in childhood or in youth, in adulthood or in old age. There are no two people who have come to God by identical paths. There is no way that has been followed by more than one seeker. I am a unique traveller; I must take my own road, to discover a personal God, to whom I can say, 'O God, thou art *my* God!' (Ps. 63:1). God is one and the same for all people, but he must be discovered *by me* and become *mine*.

The experience of St Paul is that of a sudden encounter with God. A devout Jew, Saul hated Christianity, believing it to be a harmful and dangerous sect. 'Breathing threats and murder', he went to Damascus intending to cause great harm to the Church. When he approached the city, 'suddenly a light from heaven flashed about him'. He fell to the ground and heard a voice saying to him, 'Saul, Saul, why do you persecute me?' Then the voice said, 'I am Jesus, whom you are persecuting' (Acts 9:1–5). Blinded by divine light, Saul lost his sight. For three days he could not see, and neither could he eat or drink. After Baptism, his sight was restored and immediately he followed the Christ who had appeared to him person-ally and who had become *his* God. He then 'more abundantly than all' laboured in preaching the Gospel.[5]

Another notable example is St Anthony the Great. While still a young man, he went to church and heard the words of Jesus being read: 'If you would be perfect, go, sell what you possess and give to the poor, and you will have treasure in heaven; and come, follow me' (Matt. 19:21). The Gospel message struck Anthony so intensely that he immediately sold all his property and gave the money to the poor. This was his direct response to what he realised to be God's call, a call which reached him through the word of Scripture. Anthony then went to a monastery and began to practise what was written in the Bible. 'For he had given such heed to what was read that none of the things that were written fell from him to the ground, but he remembered all, and afterwards his memory served him instead of books.'[6]

One of our contemporaries, Metropolitan Anthony of Sourozh, is a further example of a miraculous conversion. In his early youth he was a nonbeliever; nothing of what he had heard about Christianity elicited any sympathy from him. On one occasion he became especially indignant at the sermon of a certain priest and decided to verify for himself whether Christianity really was as unattractive as it was portrayed in cloying stories. He opened the New Testament, chose the shortest of the four gospels in order not to waste too much time, and began to read:

As I was reading the Gospel according to St Mark, between the first and the beginning of the third chapter I suddenly felt that on the other side of the table where I was sitting someone was standing invisibly yet his presence could be felt absolutely. I looked up and could see nothing or hear nothing, I could feel nothing whatsoever, yet I was *absolutely* convinced that Christ was standing at the other side of the table . . . From this moment onwards there was a complete change in my life . . . I felt that there can be no other task in life than to share with others the joy which transfigures life and which had been revealed to me in the knowledge of God and Christ. And then as a teenager, whether at the right moment or not, at school, on the underground and at children's camps I would speak about Christ as he appeared *to me*, as life, joy, meaning, as something so new that it renewed everything . . . I was able to say with St Paul, *Woe to me if I do not preach the gospel!*[7] Woe, because not to share this miracle would be a crime before God, this miracle that had happened, and a crime before people as well, who all over the world are thirsting for a living word about God, about themselves and life . . . [8]

The following conversion story is that of a Hassidic Jew who was once presented with a copy of the Bible by a friend. Obviously, he did not want to read the New Testament, a book about 'that man'. At the same time he could not throw the Bible away since it also contained the Old Testament, a book about God. So he wrapped the Bible in a sheet of paper, put it on a shelf, and for a long time completely forgot about it. Some time later he went to Jerusalem in order to become a rabbi. Among the books which he took with him from America was one wrapped in paper: inside the package, he was quite surprised to see the Bible. He then began to read St Matthew's gospel and soon realised that the man written about in the gospel was the very Messiah for whom the Jews were still waiting, and that Christianity, not Judaism, was the true heir to the Old Testament religious legacy. When he told his Jewish wife about his discovery, she said she would rather divorce him than live with an apostate. Eventually, however, she also converted to Christ and they were both baptised.

No less unexpected was the religious conversion of the French yachtsman Bernard Moitesier. Taking part in a round-the-world, single-handed yacht race, he confidently headed for the finishing line and had every chance of winning a great deal of money and international fame. A triumphant winner's reception had already been prepared for him in England. To everyone's surprise, he changed course and set sail for the Polynesian shores. It was only after several months that it became clear why he dropped out of the race. Finding himself alone with the ocean and the sky for such a long time, he contemplated the meaning of life ever more deeply. The goals that he was pursuing – money, success, fame – seemed increasingly unattractive. In the ocean he felt the *breath of eternity*; he sensed such a powerful *Presence* that he no longer wanted to return to the vanities of everyday life.

Conversion is always both a miracle and a gift, whether it is sudden and unexpected or gradual. Often a person searches for a long time before coming to God; yet it is not the individual who discovers God but rather God who captures the individual. Nevertheless, there may well be a connection between the endeavours and zeal of the seeker and the object of the search: encounter with God. St Augustine, for example, passed through many trials in the search for truth. He read many philosophical and theological books before coming to understand, in his thirty-third year, that he could not live without God. In modern times people often begin their search for an abstract 'truth' through books before coming to a revelation of the Personal God.

Some have come to Christianity in a roundabout way, through other religions or cults, others after experiencing a catastrophe such as the loss of a loved one, an illness, or a sudden collapse of lifelong expectations. In misfortune we feel our poverty very keenly, through the realisation that we have lost everything and have nothing else or nobody other than God. It is only then that we find ourselves crying to God *de profundis*, 'out of the depths' (Ps. 130:1), from the abyss of profound grief and despair.

Conversion may also happen as a result of meeting a true believer, a priest or a layperson. Christ said, 'Let your light so shine before men, that they may see your good works and give glory to your Father who is in heaven' (Matt. 5:16). If Christians shone with the divine light, if divine love were reflected in their eyes, this would be the best witness for God. One young man decided to dedicate his whole life to God after a priest became transfigured before him, shining with a heavenly light like Christ on Mount Tabor.

There is, finally, what appears to be the most natural way of reaching God: to be a child born into a religious family and raised as a believer. But here, too, faith received from our families must be thought through and suffered by each individual: it has to become a part of *our own* experience. There are many people from religious families who break with the faith of their ancestors: the miraculous encounter with God does not occur. How this happens, we do not always know. What we do know is that nobody is born a believer. Faith is a gift, though often it is given through the efforts of the person who has sought it.

## PHILOSOPHY IN SEARCH OF A SUPREME GOOD

For as long as human beings have lived on earth they have striven to find the meaning of their existence. In Ancient Greece the philosophers studied the universe and its laws. They investigated human nature and human reason, hoping to discover knowledge of the first causes of all things. The philosophers not only engaged in rational debate and logic, but also studied astronomy and physics, mathematics and geometry, music and poetry. A diversity of knowledge was in many cases combined with an ascetic life and prayer, without which it was impossible to obtain a *katharsis*, a purification of mind, soul and body.

In studying the visible world, philosophers came to the conclusion that there was nothing accidental in the universe, that every detail has its place and fulfils its role by being subject to strict laws: the planets never go out of orbit and satellites never abandon their planets. Everything in the world is so harmonious and meaningful that the ancients called it the 'cosmos', that is, beauty, order, harmony, as opposed to 'chaos' – disorder, or disharmony. For them the cosmos is a huge mechanism in which a single unbreakable rhythm is at work, a single regular pulse. But each mechanism must have been created by someone, just as every watch needs to have been constructed and sprung. Thus the philosophers arrived at the idea of a single Author of the Universe. Plato called him the Creator, Father, God and *Demiurge* (maker or craftsman).

All that has come into existence needs a reason for its coming into existence [writes Plato]. Of course, the Creator and the Father of this universe is hard to seek, and if we find him, we should not tell everyone about him . . . The cosmos is beautiful, and its Demiurge is good . . . The cosmos is the finest thing that has come into being, and the Demiurge is the finest of all causes. In being good, he cares for all visible things, which abide not in peace but in disharmonious and disordered movement; he has brought them from disorder into order.[9]

Plato (*c.* 428–*c.* 347 BCE) lived in a country where polytheism characterised religious belief. People divinised the elements and forces of nature and worshipped them. The philosopher did not formally reject the gods, but he did recognise a higher Reason. In Plato's cosmology the gods fulfil roles similar to those of angels in monotheistic religions. The Demiurge created them and issues orders to them, and they obey his will. Wanting to create people, the Creator turns to the gods and says, 'Gods of gods! I am your Demiurge and Father of all things, and all that has arisen from me will be indestructible, for that is my will.'[10] He then gives them the primordial matter from which they create people. In effect ancient philosophy, through its best representatives, moved beyond polytheism and arrived at the truth of the one God.

The Greek philosophers also spoke about the *Logos* (meaning 'word', 'reason', 'idea', or 'law'), which was originally perceived as an eternal and general law upon which the whole world is constructed. However, the Logos is not only an abstract idea: it is also a divine creative force mediating between God and the created world. This was the teaching of Philo of Alexandria (*c.* 20 BCE–50 CE) and the Neoplatonists.

Plotinus, a representative of the Neoplatonist school in the third century CE, emphasises the transcendence, infiniteness, limitlessness and incomprehensibility of the Divinity. No definitions can exhaust it, no attributes can be ascribed to it. In being the fullness of Being, the One, as Plotinus calls the highest Principle, God, engenders all other forms of being, of which the first is the Intelligence and the second the Soul. Beyond the confines of the circle of the Soul lies the material world, that is, the universe, into which the Soul breathes life. Thus the world is a reflection of the divine reality and bears within itself the marks of beauty and perfection. The

One, the Intelligence and the Soul comprise in total a Divine Triad. Through purification (*katharsis*) we can be elevated to the contemplation of God. However, the One still remains incomprehensible and inaccessible. He remains a mystery.

In Plotinus, philosophy is transformed into a religion: one can speak of his theology, spirituality and mysticism. There is a striking similarity between what he says of a person's mystical ascent to the highest absolute Being and what the Church Fathers write about the vision of and love for God, of ecstasy and deification:[11]

The soul in its nature loves God and longs to be at one with him in the noble love of a daughter for a noble father . . . Those to whom all this experience is strange may understand by way of our earthly longings and the joy we have in winning to what we most desire – remembering always that here what we love is perishable, hurtful, that our loving is of mimicries and turns awry because all was a mistake, our good was not here, this was not what we sought; there only is our veritable love and there we may unite with it, not holding it in some fleshly embrace but possessing it in all its verity . . . The soul takes another life as it draws nearer and nearer to God and gains participation in him . . . The man is changed, no longer himself, no self-belonging; he is merged with the Supreme, sunken into it, one with it . . . There is thus a converse in virtue of which the essential man outgrows Being, becomes identical with the Transcendent of Being. The self thus lifted, we are in the likeness of the Supreme: if from that heightened self we pass still higher – image to archetype – we have won the Term of all our journeying . . . This is the life of gods and of the godlike and blessed among men, liberation from the alien that besets us here, a life taking no pleasure in the things of earth, a flight of alone to the Alone.[12]

With these examples from Plato and Plotinus we can see that Greek philosophy comes very close to the truths that are finally to be revealed in Christianity: the one God, the Creator of the world, the divine Logos, the Holy Trinity (Divine Triad), the vision of God, the deification of the human person. This is why early Christian writers called the philosophers 'Christians before Christ'.[13] An early Greek Father, Clement of Alexandria, claimed that philosophy paved the way for Christ in the Greek-speaking world in the same way that the Old Testament prepared the Jewish world for the coming of the Messiah.[14] Some of the Church Fathers came to Christianity through the study of philosophy and many of them thought very highly of it, in particular Justin Martyr, Clement of Alexandria, Basil the Great, Gregory of Nyssa and Gregory the Theologian. In the narthexes of ancient Christian churches alongside the martyrs and saints, there would be portraits of Socrates, Plato and Aristotle as forerunners and heralds of the Truth.

## THE OLD TESTAMENT: DIVINE REVELATION

The majority of peoples in the pre-Christian world followed polytheistic beliefs and cults. If there were individual thinkers, such as the Greek philosophers, who were capable of finding their way out of the captivity of polytheism, their insights into the existence of only one God remained for the most part speculative. God the Creator appeared remote and abstract. Some even thought that God simply arranged the universe, put the mechanism into motion and no longer interfered in people's lives: he abandoned everything to the will of fate.

There was one chosen people, however, whom God entrusted with knowledge of himself, of the creation of the world, and of the meaning of existence. The ancient Jews knew God not from books, nor from the deliberations of wise men, but from their own age-old experience. Noah, Abraham, Isaac, Jacob, Moses, Elijah and the many righteous men and women of Israel did not simply contemplate God and pray to him – they saw him with their own eyes, conversed with him face to face, 'walked' before him.

The LORD appeared to Abram, and said to him, 'I am God Almighty; walk before me, and be blameless. And I will make my covenant between me and you . . .' Then Abram fell on his face; and God said to him, 'Behold, my covenant is with you, and you shall be the father of a multitude of nations . . . I will . . . be God to you and to your descendants after you . . .'

(Gen. 17:1–4, 7)

The Jews called God 'the God of our fathers', that is, the God of their ancestors, and they preserved in holiness the covenant entrusted to their ancestors.

Each of God's revelations in the Old Testament bears a personal nature. God is revealed to humanity not as an abstract force, but as a living Being, who can speak, hear, see, think and help:

And the LORD said to Moses, 'Lo, I am coming to you in a thick cloud, that the people may hear when I speak with you, and may also believe you for ever' . . . On the morning of the third day there were thunders and lightnings, and a thick cloud upon the mountain, and a very loud trumpet blast, so that all the people who were in the camp trembled ... And Mount Sinai was wrapped in smoke, because the LORD descended upon it in fire; and the smoke of it went up like the smoke of a kiln, and the whole mountain quaked greatly. And as the sound of the trumpet grew louder and louder, Moses spoke, and God answered him ... And God spoke all these words, saying, 'I am the LORD your God ... You shall have no other gods before Me ...' And the people stood afar off, while Moses drew near to the thick darkness where God was.

(Exod. 19:9, 16, 18–19; 20:1–3, 21)

The darkness and the cloud here signify a mystery: although God reveals himself to Moses, he nevertheless remains mysterious and incomprehensible. None of the people should ever approach Mount Sinai, 'lest they die' (Exod. 20:19), for 'man shall not see [God] and live' (Exod. 33:20). Moses saw God, but the essence of God remained inaccessible to human vision.

God takes a vital and active part in the life of the Israelites. When Moses leads the people out of Egypt into the Promised Land, God himself goes ahead of them in the form of a column of fire. God abides among the people, converses with them and lives in the house that they build for him. Later, when King Solomon completed the building of the Temple, he called upon God to live there:

A cloud filled the house of the LORD, so that the priests could not stand to minister because of the cloud; for the glory of the LORD filled the house of the LORD. Then Solomon said, 'The LORD has set the sun in the heavens, but has said that he would dwell in thick darkness. I have built thee an exalted house, a place for thee to dwell in for ever' ... 'But will God indeed dwell on the earth? Behold, heaven and the highest heaven cannot contain thee; how much less this house which I have built! Yet have regard to the prayer of thy servant and to his supplication ... that thine eyes may be open night and day toward this house, the place of which thou hast said, "My name shall be there" ... Whatever prayer, whatever supplication is made by any man or by all thy people Israel, each knowing the affliction of his own heart and stretching out his hands toward this house; then hear thou in heaven thy dwelling place, and forgive.'

(I Kings 8:10–13, 27–9, 38–9)

God, who abides in darkness, who is surrounded by great mystery, whom heaven and earth – that is, the visible and invisible world – cannot contain, comes down to people and lives where *they* want him to live, where *they* have set aside a place for him.

This is the most striking thing about the religion of revelation: God remains under the veil of mystery and yet at the same time he is so close to people that they can call him '*our* God' and '*my* God'. It is here that we encounter the gulf between divine revelation and the achievements of human thought: the God of the philosophers remains abstract and lifeless, whereas the God of revelation is a living, close and personal God. Both ways lead us to understand that God is incomprehensible and that he is a mystery; yet philosophy abandons us at the foothills of the mountain, forbidding us to ascend further, whereas religion leads us up to the heights where God abides in *darkness*, it draws us into the cloud of unknowing where beyond all words and rational deductions it opens up before us the mystery of God.

### 'Believe in the Gospels and in the witness of the Holy Church'

How happy are we Christians! What God is ours!

How much to be pitied are those who do not know God . . .

O, unhappy, erring peoples! They cannot know what true joy is . . .

But our joy is Christ. By His sufferings He has inscribed us in the Book of Life, and in the Kingdom of heaven we shall be with God for ever, and we shall see His glory, and delight in Him. Our joy is the Holy Spirit, so pleasant and delectable. He bears witness to the soul of her salvation.

O brethren, I beg and pray you in the name of God's compassion, believe in the Gospels and in the witness of the Holy Church, and you will, while still here on earth, savour the blessedness of Paradise. For the Kingdom of God is within us; with the love of God the soul knows Paradise. Many princes and prelates abandoned their thrones when they came to know the love of God. And this we can understand, because the love of God is a consuming love – it gladdens the soul to the point of tears by the grace of the Holy Spirit, and no earthly things can compare with it.

*St Silouan of Mount Athos*

### Philosophy paves the way to Christ

. . . Philosophy . . . is the clear image of truth, a divine gift to the Greeks; it does not drag us away from the faith . . . but rather, so to speak, by the use of an ampler circuit, obtains a common exercise demonstrative of the faith . . . Accordingly, before the advent of the Lord, philosophy was necessary to the Greeks for righteousness. And now it becomes conducive to piety; being a kind of preparatory training to those who attain to faith through demonstration . . . Philosophy was given to the Greeks directly and primarily, till the Lord should call the Greeks . . . Philosophy, therefore, was a preparation, paving the way for him who is perfected in Christ . . . The way of truth is therefore one. But into it, as into a perennial river, streams flow from all sides.

*Clement of Alexandria*

## The miraculous rise of Christianity

. . . Although a great many lawgivers were eminent among Greeks and barbarians, as well as numberless teachers or philosophers who promised they were declaring the truth, we remember no lawgiver so influential that he was able to inspire the minds of other nations with zeal . . . Therefore, no one was able to introduce and to implant what seemed to him the truth even in one nation in such a way that his knowledge or his belief should reach everyone . . . Nevertheless, in every part of the world, in all of Greece and in every foreign nation, there are numberless throngs of people who have left their ancestral laws and those they supposed gods, and who have dedicated themselves . . . to the discipleship and worship of Christ. And they have done this not without finding an immense hatred stirred up against them from those who worship idols, with the result that they are often afflicted with tortures by these people and sometimes are led away to death . . . Anyone can see in how short a time this religion has grown, making progress by the penalties and deaths exacted of its adherents, still more by the plundering of their possessions and by every kind of suffering endured by them . . . This word is preached throughout the whole world so that Greeks and barbarians, wise and foolish uphold the religion of Christ's teaching. Because of this it cannot be doubted that it is not because of human powers or abilities that the word of Christ Jesus grows strong with all authority and persuasion in the minds and souls of all.

*Origen*

## The way to Christianity through Platonism

At that time, after reading those books of the Platonists and being instructed by them to search for incorporeal truth, I clearly saw your invisible things which *are understood by the things which are made* (Rom. 1:20). Although pushed backwards in my search, I perceived what that was which, because of my mind's darkness, I was not permitted to contemplate. I was made certain that You exist, that You are infinite . . . that You are truly He Who is always the same . . . But I was too weak to find my joy in You . . . It was with the most intense desire that I seized upon the sacred writings of Your Spirit, and especially the Apostle Paul . . . I made a beginning, and whatever truths I had read in those other works I here found to be uttered . . . (But) the pages (of Platonic books) do not have this face of piety, the tears of confession, Your sacrifice, a troubled spirit, a contrite and a humbled heart (Ps. 51:19), the salvation of Your people, the city that is like a bride (Rev. 21:2), the pledge of the Spirit (2 Cor. 1:22), the cup of our redemption. In those books no one sings: *Shall not my soul be subject to God? For he is my God and my Saviour, my Protector. I shall be moved no more* (Ps. 61:2–3). In them no man hears Him calling to us: *Come unto me, all you that labour* (Matt. 11:28). They scorn to learn of Him because He is meek and humble of heart. *For You have hid these things from the wise and prudent, and have revealed them to little ones* (Matt. 11:25).

*St Augustine*

## The call

We know that in everything God works for good with those who love him, who are called according to his purpose. For those whom he foreknew he also predestined to be conformed to the image of his Son . . . And those whom he predestined he also called; and those whom he called he also justified; and those whom he justified he also glorified. What then shall we say to this? If God is for us, who is against us?

*St Paul*

## Everybody is called by God

Faith in Christ is new paradise. Thus God knew before the foundation of the world all who believed and will believe in Him, whom He called and will not cease calling until the end, whom He glorified and will glorify, justified and will justify; those, clearly, whom He reveals as conformed to the glory of the image of His Son through holy Baptism and the grace of the Holy Spirit. He makes them mystically all His sons, and establishes them as new out of old, immortals out of mortals . . .

*St Symeon the New Theologian*

### Chapter Two

# GOD

## THE WORD 'GOD'

The words used to refer to 'God' in different languages are related to various concepts. By analysing these, and how they relate to each other, we can develop our understanding of the nature of God. The peoples of antiquity attempted to find a word to express their notion of God or, rather, their experience of encounter with the Divinity.

In languages of Germanic origin the word *Gott* comes from a verb meaning 'to fall to the ground', to fall down in worship. This reflects an experience similar to that of St Paul, who was struck by divine light on the road to Damascus, and immediately 'fell to the ground . . . in fear and trembling' (Acts 9:4–6). As Metropolitan Anthony of Sourozh points out,

People who in ancient times tried to say something about God did not make any attempt to describe him, to say what he is in himself, but tried only to indicate what happened to a person when he suddenly found himself face to face with God, when he was suddenly illumined by Divine grace, the Divine light. All that the person could then do was fall down in sacred awe, worshipping the One who is incomprehensible and who at the same time had revealed himself to him with such closeness and in such a miraculous light.[1]

In the Slavonic languages and in Russian, the word *Bog* ('God') is related to the Sanskrit *bhaga*, which means 'dispensing gifts', and which in its turn comes from *bhagas*, meaning 'inheritance', 'happiness', or 'wealth'. The Slavonic word *bogatstvo* means 'riches' or 'wealth'. Here we find God expressed in terms of the fullness of being, perfection and bliss. These properties, however, do not remain within God, but are poured out onto the world, onto people and all living things. God dispenses the gift of his plenitude and endows us with his riches when we turn to him.

[ 14 ]

According to Plato, the Greek word for God, *Theos*, originates from the verb *theein*, meaning 'to run'. In ancient Greek religion this word was used to refer to a number of different 'gods': 'The first people who inhabited Greece revered as gods the sun, moon, earth, stars and sky. As they saw that all of this runs away, as it goes into rotation, the word they chose for them reflected their fleeting nature.' In other words, the ancients saw in nature and her cycles, her purposeful 'flight', indications of the existence of a higher reason which they could not identify with the one God, but could imagine in the form of many divine powers. It was only in the Septuagint (the first Greek version of the Old Testament) that the term *Theos* was applied to the one God, Creator of heaven and earth.

St Gregory the Theologian, one of the fourth-century Cappadocian Fathers, identifies a second etymology different from Plato's: he claims that the name *Theos* comes from the verb *ethein*, meaning 'to be set alight', 'to burn', 'to be aflame'.[2] 'For the LORD your God is a devouring fire', says the Bible (Deut. 4:24). These words are repeated in the epistle to the Hebrews, where God is described as capable of destroying and consuming all evil (Heb. 12:29). 'God is a fire warming and setting alight the heart and veins', said St Seraphim of Sarov in the nineteenth century. 'So if we feel in our hearts the cold which is from the devil, we shall call upon God; he will come and warm our hearts with perfect love not only for him, but for our neighbour. And it is from the face of this warmth that the coldness of the hater of good will flee.'[3]

Basil the Great, another of the Cappadocian Fathers, offers two more etymologies: 'God is called *Theos* either because he placed (*tetheikenai*) all things, or because he beholds (*theasthai*) all things.'[4] The latter interpretation is also accepted by St John of Damascus, who says that God is called *Theos* from *theaomai* ('behold', 'contemplate') 'because nothing escapes him and he watches over all, and because he saw all things before they came to pass'.[5] From the Greek *Theos* comes the Latin *Deus* and the French *Dieu*.

The Name by which God revealed himself to the ancient Israelites was *Yahweh*, meaning 'The One Who Is', that is, the One who has existence and being. It derives from the verb *hayah*, meaning 'to be', 'to exist', or rather from the first person of this verb, *ehieh* – 'I am'. This verb has a dynamic meaning: it does not simply denote the fact of existence, but signifies a living and actual presence. When God tells Moses 'I AM WHO I AM' (Exod. 3:14), this means 'I live, I am here, I am together with you'. At the same time this name emphasises the superiority of God's being over all other beings. He is the independent, primary, eternal being, the plenitude of being which is above being:

The God who is transcends everything by virtue of his power. He is the substantive Cause and Maker of being, of subsistence, of existence, of substance, and of nature. He is the Source and the measure of the ages. He is the reality beneath time and the eternity behind being. He is the time within which things happen. He is being for whatever is. He is coming-to-be amid whatever happens. From him who is come eternity, essence and being, come time, genesis, and becoming. He is the being immanent in and underlying the things which are, however they are. For God is not some kind of being. No. But in a way that is simple and indefinable he gathers into himself and anticipates every existence.[6]

Ancient tradition tells us that after the Babylonian captivity, the Jews refrained out of reverential awe from uttering the name *Yahweh*, the One Who Is. Only the high priest could do so, and this once a year on the day of Yom Kippur, when he went into the Holy of Holies to offer incense. If an ordinary person or even a priest wanted to say something about God, he substituted other names for *Yahweh*, usually the name *Adonai* (the Lord).[7] In script the Jews indicated the word 'God' by the sacred tetragrammaton YHWH. The ancient Jews knew well that there was no name or word in human language that could convey the essence of God. 'The Divinity is unnamable', says Gregory the Theologian. 'It is not reason alone that has demonstrated this, but the wise and ancient Jews. For those who revered the Divinity with special outlines and could not bear that the name of God be written with one and the same letters ... could they at any time have decided with a disparate voice to pronounce the Name of the indestructible and single essence?'[8] In refraining from pronouncing the name of God, the Jews showed that it is possible to be at one with God not so much through words and descriptions, but through a reverential and trembling silence.

## THE DIVINE NAMES

In Scripture we meet many names for God, each of which, while incapable of describing his essence, does point to certain of his attributes. A celebrated work of the fifth century, *The Divine Names*, attributed to Dionysius the Areopagite, is the first systematic exposition on this topic from a Christian point of view. Before Dionysius, it was also discussed by other writers, in particular Gregory the Theologian and Ephrem the Syrian.

The starting point for Dionysius is the namelessness of God: 'How can we speak of the Divine names? How can we do this if the Transcendent surpasses all discourse and all knowledge? . . . How can we enter upon this undertaking if the Godhead is superior to being and is unspeakable and unnamable?'[9] At the same time, God, being totally transcendent, is present in the created world and revealed through it. All creation longs for God, and we humans especially crave knowledge of him. Therefore God is to be praised both 'by every name' and 'as the Nameless One'.[10] Nameless in his essence, God is variously named by humanity when he reveals himself to us.

Some of the names attributed to God emphasise his superiority over the visible world: his power, dominion and royal dignity. The name 'Lord' (*Kyrios* in Greek) signifies the supreme dominion of God, not only over his chosen people, but also over the whole world. Appended to this name we find 'Lord of Hosts' (Hebrew *Sabaoth*), 'Lord of the ages' and 'Lord of lords', as well as 'Master', the 'King of glory' and 'King of kings':

Thine, O LORD, is the greatness, and the power, and the glory, and the victory, and the majesty; for all that is in the heavens and in the earth is thine; thine is the kingdom, O LORD, and thou art exalted as head above all. Both riches and honour come from thee, and thou rulest over all. In thy hand are power and might; and in thy hand it is to make great and to give strength to all.

(I Chron. 29:11–12)

The attribution 'Almighty', or *Pantokrator* in Greek, signifies that God holds all things in his hand. He upholds the world and its order: 'My hand laid the foundation of the earth, and my right hand spread out the heavens' (Isa. 48:13). God 'upholds the universe by his word of power' (Heb. 1:3).

The names 'Holy', 'Holy Place', 'Holiness', 'Sanctification', 'Good' and 'Goodness' indicate that God not only contains within himself the whole plenitude of goodness and holiness, but that he also pours out this goodness onto all his creatures, sanctifying them. 'Hallowed be thy Name', we say in the Lord's Prayer. This means: 'May thy Name be holy not only in the heavens, in the spiritual world, but here too on earth; may it be hallowed within us so that we may be as holy as thee.'

God is also called 'Wisdom', 'Truth', 'Light' and 'Life':

Wisdom as knowledge of divine and human things . . . Truth as the whole and not the many in essence (for the truth is whole, while the falsehood has many faces) . . . Light as the radiance of souls purified in the mind and life, for if ignorance and sin are darkness, then knowledge and divine life are light . . . Life, for he is the light, the bulwark and the realisation of all rational nature.[11]

'Salvation', 'Atonement', 'Deliverance', 'Resurrection': these are further names which Scripture ascribes to God. For only in him (in Christ) is accomplished humanity's salvation from sin and eternal death, and the resurrection to eternal life.

God is also called 'Righteousness' and 'Love'. The former emphasises Divine justice: God is the Judge who punishes evil and rewards good. This at all events is how the Old Testament perceives him. However, the Good News of the New Testament indicates that, while indeed being altogether just and righteous, God's standards transcend all our notions of justice. In the seventh century, St Isaac the Syrian wrote:

Do not call God just, for his justice is not manifested in the things concerning you. And if David calls him just and upright,[12] the Son revealed to us that he is good and kind. How can you call God just when you come across the scriptural passage on the wage given to the workers? . . . How can a man call God just when he comes across the passage on the prodigal son who wasted his wealth with riotous living, how for the compunction alone which he showed, the father ran and fell upon his neck and gave him authority over all his wealth? . . . Where, then, is God's justice, for while we are sinners Christ died for us! . . . Where is his repayment to be found in our works?[13]

The Old Testament notion of divine justice is complemented in the New by the doctrine of God's love, which transcends justice. 'God is love', says St John the Theologian (1 John 4:18). This is the best definition we can give of God, the most truthful thing we can say about him. As St Gregory the Theologian says, it is this name which is the most pleasing to God himself.[14]

In the Bible we also find a number of names for God that originate in the physical world and in human experience. These do not attempt to define his characteristics, but are symbols and analogies. God is compared with the sun, the stars, fire, wind, water, dew, cloud, rock and fragrance. Christ himself is spoken of as 'Shepherd', 'Lamb', 'Way', 'Door'. All these epithets, simple and concrete, are borrowed from everyday reality – but, as in Christ's parables of the pearl, the tree, leaven and seeds, we discern a hidden meaning that is infinitely greater and more significant.

The Bible also speaks of God as a being with human form having a face, eyes, ears, hands, shoulders, wings, legs and breath. It is said that God turns around and turns away, recollects and forgets, becomes angry and subdued, is surprised or afflicted; he walks and he hears. Fundamental to this anthropomorphism is the experience of a personal encounter with God as a living being, for which we have come to use earthly words and images. In the language of the Bible, there are almost no abstract concepts of the kind that play such an important part in the language of speculative philosophy. When indicating a particular length of time, biblical writers did not say 'epoch' or 'period' but 'hour', 'day', 'year' or 'age'. In referring to the material and spiritual worlds, they did not speak of 'matter' and 'spiritual reality', but of 'heaven' and 'earth'. Biblical language, unlike philosophical language, is of a definite, concrete nature precisely because the experience of God in the Bible is an experience of a personal encounter, not mere abstract speculative deductions. The ancients felt the real presence of God in their life – he was their King and Master; he was present when they worshipped, and at their festivals and gatherings. When David said, 'The LORD has heard my supplication' (Ps. 6:9), it did not imply that God had not heard him before but now did. God always hears us; it is we who are sometimes insensitive to him. The words, 'Let thy face shine on thy servant' (Ps. 31:16), are not a request for an absent God to appear suddenly, since he is always and everywhere present. They are rather a petition from someone who had not earlier noticed God to see, feel, know and meet him now.

The nature of biblical anthropomorphism becomes clear when one considers it in the context of divine condescension, or *oikonomia*. Here the incomprehensible and totally transcendent God clothes himself in the garment of human words, names and metaphors so that people can talk about him and come closer to him. God himself crosses the gap between the Divine and the human, the uncreated and created.[15] This 'incarnation' of God into human language was described in the fourth century by St Ephrem the Syrian:

> Let us give thanks to God
>> who clothed himself in the names of the body's various parts:
> Scripture refers to his 'ears'
>> to teach us that he listens to us;
> it speaks of his 'eyes'
>> to show that he sees us . . .
> He put on these names
>> because of our weakness.
> We should realise that,
>> had he not put on the names
> of such things,
>> it would not have been possible for him
> to speak with us humans.

By means of what belongs to us did he draw close to us:
He clothed himself in language,
    so that he might clothe us
in his mode of life.
    He asked for our form and put this on,
and then, as a father with his children,
    he spoke with our childish state.[16]

'Father' is one of the traditional, biblical names for God. His children are the people of Israel: 'For thou art our Father, though Abraham does not know us and Israel does not acknowledge us; thou, O LORD, art our Father, our Redeemer from of old is thy name' (Isa. 63:16). God's fatherhood transcends human fatherhood; it is steadfast even in the face of rejection by our ancestors. It also goes beyond our human understanding of male and female: 'From the womb before the morning star I have begotten thee' (Ps. 109:3–4, Septuagint). The Son, the second person of the Trinity, is begotten by the Father before creation. He is the Word (*Logos*) and Wisdom (*Sophia*) of God. The Hebrew word for the Spirit, who was present at the creation, is *ruah*, which is a feminine word. It is important, however, not to try to apply limited gender categories to God, for there is no gender in the Godhead.

The Orthodox, then, oppose modern attempts to change traditional God-language to make it more 'inclusive', referring, for example, to God as 'mother', and to the Son as 'daughter', or even using the generic terms 'parent' and 'child'. The name 'Father' was not imposed on God, but was chosen by God himself in his revelation to human beings. For the Orthodox, the full understanding of motherhood is embodied in the person of the Mother of God, yet motherhood itself is part of the created world, which originates in God. The veneration of Mary is not merely a cultural phenomenon, but a Church dogma and an essential element in Orthodox spirituality. It is not simply a cultural difference between the Orthodox and the Roman Catholics on the one hand, and most Protestants on the other, that the former venerate the Mother of God, while the latter may sometimes pray to 'God the Mother'. It is a serious *dogmatic* difference which cannot be healed until the veneration of the Mother of God is restored in those churches which, for one reason or another, have lost it. Moreover, it is not simply stubbornness on the part of the Orthodox to refuse to change biblical God-language, but rather a clear understanding that the entire spiritual, theological and mystical tradition of the Church undergoes irrevocable alteration when traditional divine names and images are changed. As Father Thomas Hopko says, 'What is required is not the replacement of these names and images, nor their alteration on the basis of historical circumstances and cultural conditions, particularly those of the contemporary world, especially the modern secularised West. What is needed is rather their proper understanding and application.'[17]

Indeed, any name can be applied to the Divinity, while none can describe it. All the names used for God in the biblical and Orthodox traditions are aimed at grasping the mystery which is beyond all names. Nevertheless, it is crucially important to remain within the tradition, and not try to replace it with new forms. All names for God arise from human experience. Yet there is a difference between biblical anthropomorphism, which is based on experience of the personal God in his revelation to the human race, and the pseudo-anthropomorphism of modern theologians who, by introducing the notion of gender into the Godhead, speak of God as 'He-She', or 'Our Mother and Father'.

## THE ATTRIBUTES OF GOD

It is difficult to speak of the attributes and qualities of him whose nature lies beyond the confines of words. Nevertheless, we can discern those qualities from the actions of God in the created world. According to St John of Damascus, God's attributes are as follows: he is uncreated, without beginning, immortal, boundless, eternal, immaterial, good, creative, just, enlightening, unchangeable, free from passion, uncircumscribed, uncontained, unlimited, indefinable, invisible, inconceivable, wanting nothing, having absolute power and authority, life-giving, almighty, infinitely powerful, sanctifying and communicating, containing and sustaining all things.[18] What is the biblical and traditional basis for attributing these qualities to God?

By saying that God is uncreated and without beginning we claim that there is no higher principle or cause of his existence beyond him; he himself is the cause of all things. God has no need of anything incidental. He is free from all outer constraint and influence: 'Who has directed the Spirit of the LORD, or as his counsellor has instructed him? Whom did he consult for his enlightenment, and who taught him the path of justice, and taught him knowledge, and showed him the way of understanding?' (Isa. 40:13–14)

Being infinite and boundless means that God exists beyond the categories of space and is free from all limitation or imperfection. He cannot be measured. It would be wrong to attempt to compare or to contrast him with anyone or anything. God is eternal, which means that he exists beyond the category of time; for him there is no past, present or future: 'I am the first, and I am the last' (Isa. 48:12); ' "I am the Alpha and the Omega," says the Lord God, who is and who was and who is to come' (Rev. 1:8). Having neither a beginning nor an end, God is uncreated – nobody made him: 'Before me no god was formed, nor shall there be any after me' (Isa. 43:10).

God is constant, immutable and unchangeable in the sense that in him 'there is no variation or shadow due to change' (Jas. 1:17). God is always true to himself: 'God is not man, that he should lie, or a son of man, that he should repent' (Num. 23:19). In his essence, actions and attributes he always remains one and the same.

There is no complexity in God, only simplicity; he is indivisible and not comprised of parts. The trinitarian nature of God is not a division of the one Divine Nature into parts: the three Persons are one God, and the essence of the Godhead remains undivided. Belief in the perfection of the Divinity excludes the possibility of dividing God into parts, since every partial being is imperfect. What does the simple nature mean in essence? asks St Gregory the Theologian. He answers by saying that if reason desires to investigate the infinite God, it will not find any beginning or end because the boundless extends further than either beginning or end, and cannot be located between them; and when reason surges upwards or downwards trying to find boundaries or limits to its concepts of God, it does not find them. The absence of all boundaries, divisions and limits is the simplicity abiding in God.[19]

God is described as immaterial and incorporeal as he is not a material substance and has no body. By nature he is spiritual. 'God is spirit', Christ tells the Samaritan woman (John 4:24). 'The Lord is the Spirit,' repeats St Paul, 'and where the Spirit of the Lord is, there is freedom' (2 Cor. 3:17). God is free from all materiality: he is neither somewhere nor nowhere nor everywhere. When the Bible speaks of the omnipresence of God, it is once more an attempt to express the subjective experience of humans who, wherever they may be, cannot cut themselves off from encounter with God: 'Whither shall I go from thy Spirit? Or whither shall I flee from thy presence? If I ascend to heaven, thou art there! If I make my bed in Sheol, thou art there! If I take the wings of the morning and dwell in the uttermost parts of the sea, even there thy hand shall lead me, and thy right hand shall hold me' (Ps. 139:7–10). Subjectively, we can experience God everywhere yet may not experience him anywhere. God remains beyond the categories of place.

God is indefinable, invisible, inconceivable. No matter how much we investigate God, no matter how much we speak about his names and his attributes, he nevertheless remains elusive to the mind as he transcends our every thought. 'To know God with the mind is difficult, and to speak about him is impossible', writes Plato.[20] St Gregory the Theologian, in a critique of this saying, writes: 'To speak about him is impossible, but to know him with the mind is even more impossible.'[21] Basil the Great adds: 'I know that God is. But what his essence is I consider to be beyond my understanding. So how am I saved? Through faith. And faith is content with the knowledge that God is (and not what he is) ... The awareness of the incomprehensibility of God is indeed knowledge of his essence.'[22] God is invisible – 'No one has ever seen God' (John 1:18) – in the sense that no one can ever contemplate God in his essence or grasp him by sight, perception or the mind. We can be in communion with God and can become partakers of him, but we are unable to comprehend God's essence.

This last point, the incomprehensibility of the divine essence, was especially emphasised by the Church Fathers of the fourth century in their polemics against the heresy of Eunomius. According to the latter, 'God does not know about his own essence more than we do.'[23] 'I know God in the same way as God knows himself', Eunomius claimed. This teaching was a sort of Christian rationalism, where nothing mysterious and mystical remained, nothing which would surpass the ability of the human reason. Long before Kant and Tolstoy, the attempt to create 'a religion within the boundaries of reason' was made by Eunomius and refuted by the Church Fathers.

The knowledge of God is a path which, according to Gregory the Theologian, leads only to the contemplation of God's 'averted figure', not of his essence:

I am running with a mind to see God and so it was that I ascended the Mount. I penetrated the cloud, became enclosed in it, detached from matter and material things and concentrated, so far as might be, in myself. But when I directed my gaze, I scarcely saw the averted figure of God, and this whilst sheltering in the rock,[24] God the Word incarnate for us. Peering in I saw not the Nature prime, self-apprehended – by 'self' I mean the Trinity – the nature as it abides within the first veil and is hidden by the Cherubim,[25] but as it reaches us at its furthest remove from God, being, so far as I can understand, the grandeur, or as divine David calls it *majesty*[26] inherent in the created things he has brought forth and governs. All these indications of himself which he has left behind him are God's 'averted figure'. They are, as it were, shadowy reflections of the Sun in water . . . the Sun overmastering perception in the purity of its light.[27]

One cannot know God as God knows himself: one can only know God through Christ and through reflecting on the visible world. Eunomius reduced the concept of God to something that could be comprehended by human reason, that is, the sum total of what human reason could attribute to the Divinity. For Gregory the Theologian, such an image of God meant nothing but an idol created by humans. A Christian should humbly recognise that God is a mystery beyond anything which might be attributed to him. A person who attempts to comprehend God's essence is, according to Gregory, like someone who runs after his own shadow: the faster he runs, the faster the shadow moves. The way towards God can never end with the comprehension of God's essence: its end is silent amazement before the mystery. In this state all discursive knowledge falls silent.

The heroine of the Song of Songs seeks her lover but cannot find him, pursues him and cannot reach him. The image of the pursuit has been interpreted in the Christian tradition, for example by Origen and Gregory of Nyssa, to mean the soul's pursuit of God, who eternally flees from her. The soul seeks God, but no sooner does she find him than she loses him again. She attempts to comprehend him, but fails to do so, endeavours to embrace him, but cannot. He moves with great speed and always transcends the soul's capabilities. To find God and to catch up with him would mean that we had become divine ourselves. The laws of physics dictate that if the material body were to travel at the speed of light it would turn into light. So it is with the soul: the closer she is to God, the more she is filled with light and becomes a bearer of light.

## CATAPHATIC AND APOPHATIC THEOLOGY

When discussing the names of God, we inevitably reach the conclusion that not one of them can give us a complete idea of who he is. To speak of the attributes of God is to discover that their sum total is not God. God transcends any name. If we call him 'Being', he transcends being. If we ascribe to him righteousness and justice, in his love he transcends all justice. If he is love, he is much more than human love: he is love beyond our understanding of love. God transcends all attributes that we are capable of ascribing to him, be it omniscience, omnipresence or changelessness. Ultimately we come to the realisation that we can say nothing about God affirmatively: all discussion about him remains incomplete, partial and limited. We have to admit that we cannot say what God *is*, but rather what he *is not*. This manner of speaking about God has received the name of apophatic theology (the way of negation), as opposed to cataphatic (affirmative) theology.

Apophatic theology is the negation of all that God is not in the sense that God transcends any language which can be applied to him. Reflecting on the apophatic approach of Dionysius the Areopagite, Father Georges Florovsky speaks of God who

is higher . . . than any limitation, higher than any definition and affirmation and therefore higher than any negation . . . The apophatic 'not' is the same in meaning to 'supra' (or 'outside', 'beyond') and signifies not limitation or exclusion, but ascent and transcendence . . . God is neither soul nor reason, neither imagination nor opinion, neither thought nor life, he is neither word nor idea . . . God is not the 'object' of knowledge, he transcends knowing . . . Therefore the way of knowing is the way of abstraction and negation, the way of simplicity and silence . . . We come to know God solely in the peace of the spirit, in the peace of unknowing. This apophatic unknowing is rather supra-knowing – not the absence of knowledge, but perfect knowledge, and hence incommensurate with all partial unknowing. This unknowing is contemplation . . . God is known not from a distance, not through rational discourse about him, but through incomprehensible union with him.[28]

The image of Moses ascending Mount Sinai to encounter God, surrounded in darkness,[29] inspired both Gregory of Nyssa and Dionysius the Areopagite to speak about the divine darkness as a symbol of God's incomprehensibility. To enter the divine darkness is to go beyond the confines of being as understood by the intellect. Moses encountered God, but the Israelites remained at the foot of the mountain, that is, within the confines of a cataphatic (affirmative) knowledge of God. Only Moses could enter the darkness; having separated himself from all things, he could encounter God, who is outside everything, who is *there where there is nothing*. Cataphatically we can say that God is Light, but in doing so we liken God to light perceived by our senses. It is said about Christ transfigured on Mount Tabor that 'his face shone like the sun, and his garments became white as light' (Matt. 17:2). The cataphatic notion of 'light' is used here symbolically, since the light of Tabor is the uncreated light of the Divinity that transcends all human concepts of light. Apophatically we can call the divine light the 'supra-light' or darkness. Thus the darkness of Sinai and the light of Tabor are one and the same.

Apophatic theology can be expressed in several ways. The first is by using the prefix 'not-', 'in-' or 'un-' (as in not-being, not-existent, invisible, incomprehensible, unspeakable). Another is by use of terms with the prefix 'supra-', meaning 'beyond', from the Greek *hyper*: such as supra-existent, supra-good, even 'supra-God', *hypertheos*, as in Dionysius the Areopagite. Thirdly, we can use concepts which are deliberately contrary to what we expect, such as 'divine darkness' instead of 'divine light', or 'unknowing' instead of 'knowing'. Finally, apophatic theology finds expression in oxymorons – phrases in which one word is opposed to another: 'to see the invisible', 'to comprehend the incomprehensible', 'radiant darkness', or 'wordless hymn'.

In one of the hymns ascribed to St Gregory the Theologian, apophatic terminology is used to emphasise the transcendence of God, who is the Source of everything, the only Goal to which all visible creation is striving, and who at the same time is beyond any created being or any human concept:

> O you who are beyond everything! For what else can be sung about you?
> What word can glorify you? For you are unutterable by any word!
> What intellect can gaze upon you? For you are incomprehensible to any intellect!
> You alone are inexpressible, for you have begotten all things that can be described in words.
> You alone are unknowable, for you have generated all that is knowable.
> Everything that has and does not have speech proclaims you.
> Everything that has and does not have reason venerates you.
> The desires and pains which are common to all
> Are directed towards you! Everything prays to you.
> Everything capable of understanding your commandment sends you a wordless hymn.
> All exists because of you alone. All in its entirety longs for you.
> You are the limit of all, you are both One and All, yet you are None,
> And you are neither One, nor All. O you who have all names! How can I name you, who alone are nameless?
> What heavenly intellect would be able to break through clouds that hide you? Be merciful, O you, who are beyond everything.

For what else can be sung
about you?[30]

In our understanding of God we often rely upon cataphatic notions, since these are easier and more accessible to the mind, but cataphatic knowledge has its limits. The way of negation corresponds to the spiritual ascent into the depths of God, where words fall silent, where reason fades, where all human knowledge and comprehension cease, *where God is.* It is not by speculative knowledge but in the depths of prayerful silence that the soul can encounter God, who is 'beyond everything' and who reveals himself to her as *in*-comprehensible, *in*-accessible, *in*-visible, yet at the same time as living and close to her — as God the Person.

## The mystery of God

This is a mystery hard to understand . . . It constantly moves ahead, fleeing from the person who thinks that he has already come close to attaining it. And yet God, located far from the person, moves closely around him. O ineffable wonder! 'I am the God who draws near — says the Lord — although in My essence I flee from your senses.' And this is indeed true. For under which name can the Uncreated draw near to that which He has created? And yet He surrounds us with His almighty power . . . constant in caring for us, constant in doing good works for us, leads us, enters into our presence and embraces us all equally. That is why Moses, convinced that the person cannot know God through his own wisdom, exclaimed: *Show Thyself to me* (Exod. 23:13). And he attempted to penetrate the darkness of the clouds where the voice of God resounded like thunder, that is, he tried to grasp the most profound and impenetrable ideas of being. But God does not exist either in a cloud or in any other place. He is beyond space, is not subject to any limitations of time, He cannot be surrounded by the properties of things . . . The heavens, although called His throne, do not embrace Him; He merely rests there, content with the creation of His own hands.

*Clement of Alexandria*

## 'God cannot be depicted by human speech'

'To know the Father and Creator of this world is no easy matter, and having done so you will still be unable to proclaim all you know of Him to everyone, for the mystery of His being, unlike other teachings, cannot be expressed in words', speaks the sincere friend of truth, Plato. It is certain that he had heard what had been said of Moses, in whom wisdom also resided — how he, in preparing to ascend the mountain to contemplate face to face this most majestic of mysteries felt by the mind, had to forbid his people to follow him in receiving these revelations that cannot be spoken of. And when Scripture says, *And Moses drew near to the thick darkness where God was* (Exod. 20:21), these words meant that for the person who has the capacity to understand God cannot be seen by the eye or depicted by human speech.

*Clement of Alexandria*

## *The ascent of Moses*

Since it is the Cause of all beings, we should posit and ascribe to it all the affirmations we make in regard to beings, and, more appropriately, we should negate all these affirmations, since it surpasses all being . . . It is not for nothing that the blessed Moses is commanded to submit first to purification and then to depart from those who have not undergone this. When every purification is complete, he hears the many-voiced trumpets. He sees the many lights, pure and with rays streaming abundantly. Then, standing apart from the crowds and accompanied by chosen priests, he pushes ahead to the summit of the divine ascents. And yet he does not meet God himself, but contemplates, not him who is invisible, but rather where he dwells. This means, I presume, that the holiest and the highest of the things perceived with the eye of the body or the mind are but the rationale which presupposes all that lies below the Transcendent One. Through them, however, his unimaginable presence is shown, walking the heights of those holy places to which the mind at least can rise. But then he breaks free of them, away from what sees and is seen, and he plunges into the truly mysterious darkness of unknowing. Here, renouncing all that the mind may conceive, wrapped entirely in the intangible and the invisible, he belongs completely to him who is beyond everything.

*Dionysius the Areopagite*

## *'God is beyond every assertion and every denial'*

So this is what we say. The Cause of all is above all and is not inexistent, lifeless, speechless, mindless. It is not a material body, and hence has neither shape nor form, quality, quantity, or weight. It is not in any place and can neither be seen nor be touched, It is neither perceived nor is it perceptible. It suffers neither disorder nor disturbance and is overwhelmed by no earthly passion. It is not powerless and subject to the disturbances caused by sense perception. It endures no deprivation of light. It passes through no change, decay, division, loss, no ebb and flow, nothing of which the senses may be aware. None of this can either be identified with it or attributed to it. Again, as we climb higher we say this. It is neither soul nor mind, nor does it possess imagination, conviction, speech, or understanding. Nor is it speech *per se*, understanding *per se*. It cannot be spoken of and it cannot be grasped by understanding. It is not number or order, greatness or smallness, equality or inequality, similarity or dissimilarity. It is not immovable, moving, or at rest. It has no power, it is not power, nor is it light. It does not live nor is it life. It is not a substance, nor is it eternity or time. It cannot be grasped by the understanding since it is neither knowledge nor truth. It is not kingship. It is not wisdom. It is neither one nor oneness, divinity or goodness. Nor is it a spirit, in the sense in which we understand that term. It is not sonship or fatherhood and it is nothing known to us or to any other being. It falls neither within the predicate of nonbeing nor of being. Existing beings do not know it as it actually is and it does not know them as they are. There is no speaking of it, nor name nor knowledge of it. Darkness and light, error and truth — it is none of these. It is beyond assertion and denial. We make assertions and denials of what is next to it, but never of it, for it is both beyond every assertion, being the perfect and unique cause of all things, and, by virtue of its pre-eminently simple and absolute nature, free of every limitation, beyond every limitation; it is also beyond every denial.

*Dionysius the Areopagite*

### Affirmation and negation

Thus it is clear that God exists, but what He is in essence and by nature is unknown and beyond all understanding . . . Only the Divinity is unmoved, and by His immovability He moves all things . . . Divinity is without a body. All this, however, is by no means indicative of His essence — no more than is the fact of His being unbegotten, without beginning, immutable, and incorruptible, or any of those other things which are affirmed of God and about Him. These do not show what He is, but, rather, what He is not . . . It is impossible to say what He is in His essence, so it is better to discuss Him by abstraction from all things whatsoever. For He does not belong to the number of beings, not because He does not exist, but because He transcends all beings and being itself . . . The Divinity, then, is limitless and incomprehensible, and this His limitlessness and incomprehensibility is all that can be understood about Him. All that we state affirmatively about God does not show His nature, but only what relates to His nature. And, if you should ever speak of good, or justice, or wisdom, or something else of the sort, you will not be describing the nature of God, but only things relating to His nature. There are, moreover, things that are stated affirmatively of God, but which have the force of extreme negation. For example, when we speak of darkness in God we do not really mean darkness. What we mean is that He is not light, because He transcends light. In the same way, when we speak of light we mean that it is not darkness.

*St John Damascene*

## Biblical anthropomorphism

In the Bible, God sleeps (Ps. 44:24), wakes up (Jer. 31:26), is angered (Ps. 79:5), walks (Gen. 3:8), and has a throne of Cherubim (Isa. 37:16). Yet when has God ever been subject to emotion? When do you ever hear that God is a bodily being? This is a nonfactual, mental picture. We have used names derived from the human experience and applied them, so far as we could, to aspects of God. His retirement from us, for reasons known to Himself, into an almost unconcerned inactivity, is His 'sleeping'. Human sleeping, after all, has the character of restful inaction. When He is alert and suddenly benefits us, that is His 'waking up' . . . We have made His punishing us, His 'being angered'; for with us, punishment is born of anger. His acting in different places, we call His 'walking' . . . God's swift motion we call 'flight' (Ps. 18:10); His watching over us is His 'face' (Ps. 4:6; 34:16); His giving and receiving is His 'hand' (Ps. 145:16). In short, every faculty or activity of God has given us a corresponding picture in terms of something bodily.

*St Gregory the Theologian*

## Divine attributes

What, then, is my God? . . . Most high, most good, most mighty, most almighty; most merciful and most just; most hidden and most present; most beautiful and most strong; stable and incomprehensible; unchangeable, yet changing all things; never new, and never old, yet renewing all things . . . ever active, and ever at rest; gathering in, yet needing nothing; supporting, fulfilling, and protecting things; creating, nourishing, and perfecting them; searching them out, although nothing is lacking in You . . . What have we said, my God, my life, my holy delight? Or what can one say when one speaks of You?

*St Augustine*

*Chapter Three*

---

# THE TRINITY

## THE MYSTERY OF THE TRINITY

Christians believe in God the Trinity – Father, Son and Holy Spirit. The Trinity is not three gods, but one God in three Hypostases, that is, in three personal beings. It is the only instance where I=3 and 3=I. The cornerstone of our faith is something that appears as an absurdity according to mathematics and logic. Yet Christians participate in the trinitarian Godhead not through logic but through repentance, through a complete change and renewal of the mind, heart and feelings (the Greek word for 'repentance', *metanoia*, literally means 'change of mind').[1] To touch upon the mystery of the Holy Trinity is impossible unless the mind sets aside a rational way of thinking and becomes illumined by divine grace.

The doctrine of the Trinity is not an invention of theologians, nor a teaching which gradually developed within the Church, but a divinely revealed truth. At the Baptism of Jesus Christ, God reveals himself in all clarity to the world as Unity in three Persons: 'Now when all the people were baptised, and when Jesus also had been baptised and was praying, the heaven was opened, and the Holy Spirit descended upon him in bodily form, as a dove, and a voice came from heaven, "Thou art my beloved Son; with thee I am well pleased" ' (Luke 3:21–2). The voice of the Father is heard from the heavens, the Son stands in the waters of the Jordan, and the Spirit descends upon him.

Jesus repeatedly speaks of his unity with the Father, and of being sent into the world by the Father.[2] He also promises to send his disciples the Spirit, the Comforter, who proceeds from the Father.[3] Sending his disciples out into the world to preach, he says to them: 'Go therefore and make disciples of all nations, baptising them in the name of the Father and of the Son and of the Holy Spirit' (Matt. 28:19), which becomes the baptismal formula of the early Christian Church.

In the Incarnation of the Word, God revealed himself to the world as One in three Persons. The ancient Israelites, who had preserved their sacred faith in the one God, would not have been able to accept the idea of a divine Trinity, as this would have been taken to mean polytheism. At a time when belief in many gods was universal, the mystery of the Trinity was hidden from human sight. It was hidden as if it were in the very depths, in the very heart of the dogma of the divine unity.

Nevertheless, in the Old Testament there are a number of passages which Christian tradition has understood as pointing to the plurality of the Persons in God. The first verse of the Hebrew Bible – 'In the beginning God created the heavens and the earth' (Gen. 1:1) – gives the name for God in the plural (the Hebrew *Elohim* literally means 'Gods'), while the verb 'created' is singular. The interplay between singular and plural in this and other passages of the Old Testament, which can, of course, be explained as something peculiar to Hebrew grammar, has often been taken in the Christian theological tradition as identifying both the unity and the plurality in God.

There are several instances in the Bible where God appears to be speaking to himself, as though the Persons of the Trinity were conversing. Before the creation of human beings God speaks as if in council: 'Let us make man in our image, after our likeness' (Gen. 1:26). With whom can he be in council, if not with himself? With the angels? Yet humans were not created in the image of the angels but 'in the image of God' (Gen. 1:27). Early Christian exegetes claimed that this verse identified the Persons of the Holy Trinity in conference. Similarly, after Adam has eaten of the tree of the knowledge of good and evil, God again speaks with himself: 'Behold, the man has become like one of us, knowing good and evil' (Gen. 3:22). And at the time of the construction of the tower of Babel, God says: 'Come, let us go down, and there confuse their language, that they may not understand one another's speech' (Gen. 11:7).

Certain events recorded in the Old Testament are also seen by Christians as symbolising not merely the plurality but quite specifically the trinitarian nature of God. The Lord appears to Abraham by the oak of Mamre:

He lifted up his eyes and looked, and behold, three men stood in front of him. When he saw them, he ran from the tent door to meet them, and bowed himself to the earth, and said, 'My lord, if I have found favour in your sight, do not pass by your servant . . . I [will] fetch a morsel of bread, that you may refresh yourselves, and after that you may pass on – since you have come to your servant' . . . They said to him, 'Where is Sarah your wife?' And he said, 'She is in the tent.' The LORD said, 'I will surely return to you in the spring, and Sarah your wife shall have a son.'

(Gen. 18:2–3, 5, 9–10)

Here Abraham encounters three Persons, but addresses them as 'my lord'. 'They said' is equivalent to 'the Lord said'; three is equivalent to one.

The prophet Isaiah describes his vision of God, around whom stood the seraphim proclaiming, 'Holy, holy, holy is the LORD of hosts'. This threefold 'holy' is understood as pointing mysteriously to the three Persons in the Godhead. Then the Lord says: 'Whom shall I send, and who will go for us?' to which the prophet replies, 'Here am I! Send me' (Isa. 6:1–8). Again there is an equivalence between 'I' and 'us'; again one is equivalent to three.

There are also texts in the Old Testament which are interpreted as identifying the divinity of the Son of God and his generation from the Father: 'The LORD . . . said to me, "You are my son, today I have begotten you" ' (Ps. 2:7), and 'The LORD says to my lord: "Sit at my right hand" . . . From the womb of the morning like dew your youth will come to you' (Ps. 110:1, 3). Each of these biblical texts, however, merely points towards the mystery of the Trinity without speaking of it directly. This mystery remains under a veil, which, according to St Paul, can be lifted only by Christ.[4]

## TRINITARIAN TERMINOLOGY

From the very first days of the Church, Christians have believed in and prayed to God the Father, the Son and the Holy Spirit. Many years passed, however, before the doctrine of the Trinity acquired a precise theological formulation. It became essential for the Church to develop an appropriate terminology to communicate the dogma of the Trinity to people educated in the classical tradition. There were many such Christian Hellenists in the fourth century. The simple and somewhat primitive language of the Gospel was inadequate for them to comprehend the mystery of Christianity: they demanded a more sophisticated explanation in the rationalised language of Greek philosophy. Are the three Persons of the Trinity equal, or is there subordination among them? Is the Son consubstantial with the Father, or does he have a different substance? Is the Holy Spirit God or not? In the fourth century these questions interested not only 'specialists' in theology but also a wide spectrum of ordinary believers. It is not easy for us today to understand how two friends meeting in one of the town squares of Constantinople, Alexandria or Antioch, or even at the crossroads of village streets, could abandon all earthly concerns and discuss whether or not the Divinity is 'one in essence' or 'in three Hypostases'.[5]

Appropriate language was also necessary for the Church because of the many trinitarian heresies that had sprung up within it. One which arose in the third century was that of Sabellius, who taught that although God is a single essence, the three Persons are three different manifestations of one and the same nature, as though there are three 'masks' under which God reveals himself (the Greek word for 'person', *prosopon*, denotes not so much the human personality as the mask of an actor). Sabellius believed that the same Monad operated at various times in three different modes: in the Old Testament God revealed himself as Father, in the New Testament as Son, and in the Church after Pentecost as Holy Spirit. According to Sabellius, God is 'Son-Father': unrelated to the world he is a silent monad; related to it he is the Logos-Word.

Virtually the entire fourth century was marked by the struggle with another heresy, Arianism, which had a great many followers. Arius was an Alexandrian priest, who taught that the Father is the only true God, and the Son his creature. The Son was created 'from out of nothing', but he was superior to all other creatures in that he was born before all ages. Arianism was a form of subordinationism, which viewed the Trinity as a hierarchical entity in which the Son is subordinated to the Father and the Spirit to the Son. This teaching gave rise to heated debates throughout the Christian East, and it was because of the sudden spread of Arianism that the First Ecumenical Council was convened in Nicaea in 325 to formulate the Orthodox doctrine of the divinity of the Son.

The Council of Nicaea spoke of the Son as being 'consubstantial' (*homoousios*) with the Father, that is, of one essence with him. However, the term 'essence' (*ousia*), borrowed from classical philosophy, had already acquired by the time of Christ a more everyday connotation, signifying 'property', 'estate' or 'money'.[6] The Church Fathers therefore preferred to use a different term – *hypostasis* (meaning 'existence'), which was originally synonymous with *ousia* ('essence'). Gradually, however, in the period following the Council of Nicaea, the word *hypostasis* also acquired a new meaning, that of personal existence, of a concrete individual being, while the term *ousia* was understood to mean being or existence in general. In particular, the great Cappadocians – Basil the Great, Gregory the Theologian and Gregory of Nyssa – played a decisive role in defining trinitarian terminology. They formulated the doctrine of the Holy Spirit as consubstantial with and equal in honour to the Father and to the Son.

Thus Orthodox teaching is traditionally expressed in the following way: God is one in essence, but he exists in three Hypostases. The formula 'one nature – three Persons' could still be interpreted as meaning there were three emanations or masks of one and the same essence, as in Sabellianism. Yet the formula 'one essence – three Hypostases', while confirming the ontological unity (that is, unity at the level of being) of the Divinity, at the same time emphasised the personal existence of each Hypostasis. Father, Son and Holy Spirit are three complete Persons, each of whom not only possesses the fullness of being but is also wholly God. One Hypostasis is not a third of a common essence; it accommodates within itself the entire plenitude of the Divinity. The Father is God, not a third of God. The Son also is God, and so is the Holy Spirit. We confess 'Father, Son and Holy Spirit, Trinity one in essence and undivided'.[7] In other words, the three Hypostases do not divide the one essence into three essences, neither does the one essence merge or mix the three Hypostases into one.

The Orthodox tradition speaks of God the Father as being the 'beginning' (*arche*), the cause of existence of both the Son and the Spirit. The Father is *unbegotten*, the Son is *begotten* from the Father, and the Holy Spirit *proceeds* from the Father. These 'personal attributes' are what distinguish the Persons of the Trinity from each other and at the same time express the relationships between them. The birth of the Son from the Father is eternal, as is the procession of the Holy Spirit: the three Persons are co-eternal. The generation and the procession are, according to St John of Damascus, different modes of coming into existence, but what the nature of this difference is, we do not understand. He emphasises, however, that no difference in essence or dignity between the three Persons is involved.[8]

The trinitarian doctrine of the Church is summed up by St Gregory the Theologian as follows:

It is essential to preserve faith in the one God and confess three Hypostases, or three Persons, each with his own personal attribute. It is my belief that faith in the one God is observed when the Son and the Spirit are attributed to the one Cause . . . Faith in the three Hypostases is observed when we do not invent any mixture or merging . . . The personal attributes are observed when we shall think of God as having no beginning and as the beginning, as the Cause, the Fount, the eternal Light, and the Son as not without beginning, yet as the principle of all things. When I say 'beginning', do not take this to mean time, do not place a barrier between the One who Begets and the

Begotten ... Thus the Father has no beginning as he has not taken his existence from anybody else, not even himself. And the Son, if you think of the Father as the Cause, is not without beginning, as the principle of the Son is the Father as the Cause, but if you think of the principle in relation to time, then he is without beginning because the Lord of time has no beginning in time ... Yet you ask: 'If the Son is born, how then is he born?' He who wants to see more and in greater detail will harm his eyesight more, and to whatever degree the object being viewed transcends the field of vision, then to the same degree will he lose the capacity to see, if he wants to see the whole object and not a part of it, which he could see harmlessly. You hear of birth: do not try to know what type of birth. You hear that the Spirit proceeds from the Father: do not be curious to know how he proceeds.[9]

## UNITY OF LOVE

Traditional Orthodox trinitarian terminology may sound strange to contemporary modern Christians without theological training. In ancient times it was formulated in order to clarify the teaching, whereas now it might appear to make it even more obscure.

The dogma of the Holy Trinity was, in fact, never easily understood, not even in the early centuries. In order to make it more comprehensible, the Church Fathers of that period sometimes resorted to analogies and comparisons. For example, the Trinity was compared with the sun. When we speak of the sun, we have in mind not only a material body, but also the light and warmth which proceed from the sun. While light and warmth differ from the material sun and from each other, they neither exist in isolation from the sun nor from each other. A similar instance is water, whose source and current cannot exist one without the other. All three are different things, yet all are water.

Analogies like these, however, may fall short of the true teaching about the Trinity. The sun's light, for example, is neither a person nor an independent being. One of the simplest ways of explaining the mystery is that reportedly given by St Spyridon of Trimithund at the Council of Nicaea. According to tradition, when asked how it is that Three can simultaneously be One, Spyridon responded by taking up a clay brick and squeezing it. From the soft clay in his hands a flame shot up while simultaneously water flowed downwards. 'As there is fire and water in this brick,' said Spyridon, 'in the same way there are three Persons in the one Godhead.'

Another version of the same story (or it may be a different story) is found in the Acts of the same Council. One philosopher argued long and hard with the Fathers of the Council, trying to prove logically that the Son cannot be consubstantial with the Father. Exhausted by long debates and eager to leave, the Fathers were suddenly confronted by a simple elderly shepherd (identified by some as St Spyridon), who announced that he was prepared to debate with the philosopher and disprove his arguments. Turning to the philosopher, the shepherd looked at him severely, and said: 'Listen, O philosopher, God is one, the Creator of heaven and earth, who has created all things through the power of the Son and the operation of the Holy Spirit. This Son of God became incarnate, lived among people, died for us and rose again. Do not labour in vain to seek evidence for that which is comprehended by faith alone, but answer me: do you believe in the Son of God?' Struck by these words, the philosopher could only say, 'I do.' The shepherd said: 'If you believe, then let us go to the church and there I will bring you into communion with this true faith.' The philosopher immediately stood up and went with the shepherd. On his way out, he said to those present: 'When people tried to convince me with words, I countered words with words; but when a divine power came forth from the mouth of this old man, then words were no match for this power, as man cannot contend against God.'

We face a similar problem when discussing the doctrine of God: human words cannot convey the divine reality. Similarly, God's enlightenment and grace are needed for us to comprehend trinitarian theology. No linguistic terminology is adequate to communicate the mystery of the Trinity. Yet the Christian faith is above all trinitarian, and it is crucially important for every Christian to partake as fully as possible in this mystery. The Trinity is not an abstract theological concept: it is a reality which is to be lived. The Trinity is someone to whom we pray, but it is also Community, the Communion of three in one, in whose image we build up our own human community.

At the same time, God the Trinity is not a frozen entity, not something static or lifeless. On the contrary, within the Trinity there is the fullness of life and love. 'God is love', says St John the Theologian (I John 4:8, 16). Yet there can be no love without a beloved. A monad in isolation can love only itself, and self-love is not love. An egocentric unit is not a personality. Just as we can only experience our personhood through relationship with other people, so in God there can be no personal being except through love for another personal being. God the Trinity is the plenitude of love, each hypostatic Person exists in a relationship of love for the other Persons.

The Trinity is therefore a relational entity. The relationships between the three Persons are relationships between 'I' and 'thou', or 'I' and 'he'. 'Thou, Father, art in me, and I in thee', says Christ (John 17:21). Concerning the Holy Spirit, our Lord says, 'All that the Father has is mine; therefore I said that he will take what is mine and declare it to you' (John 16:15). We read in St John's gospel: 'In the beginning was the Word, and the Word was with God' (John 1:1). The Greek text actually says 'and the Word was *towards* God' (*pros ton Theon*). This underscores the personal nature of the relationship between God the Word and God the Father: the Son is not only born from the Father, he not only exists with the Father, he is turned *towards* the Father. Thus each Hypostasis in the Trinity is turned towards the other Hypostases.

The icon of the Holy Trinity by St Andrei Rublev portrays three angels sitting at a table upon which is a cup, the symbol of Christ's redemptive sacrifice. Icons of this sort are known as 'The Hospitality of Abraham', their subject matter deriving from the encounter with the three angels at Mamre (Gen. 18). The three Persons of the Trinity are shown turning simultaneously to each other and to the cup. It is as though the icon is imprinted with the divine love which reigns within the Trinity, whose greatest manifestation is the redemptive act of the Son of God. As we shall see, Orthodox regard Christ's saving sacrifice as an act of love and self-emptying common to all three Persons of the Trinity. It is in this sacrifice that the love which exists within the Trinity was given and revealed to humans. In the words of St Philaret of Moscow, it is the 'crucifying love of the Father, the crucified love of the Son, and the love of the Holy Spirit triumphing through the power of the Cross'.[10]

### The faith of the Early Church

We believe in One God the Father Almighty, Maker of all things visible and invisible. And in One Lord Jesus Christ, the Son of God, Only-Begotten, born of the Father, that is, from the essence of the Father, God of God, Light of Light, true God of true God, begotten, not made, being of one essence with the Father, through Whom all things were made. Who for us and for our salvation came down from heaven, and was incarnate, and became man, and suffered, and rose on the third day, and ascended into heaven, and sits on the right hand of the Father, and shall come again to judge the living and the dead. And in the Holy Spirit. And those who say 'there was a time when the Son was not' and that He was created from out of nothing, or those who say that He is of a different hypostasis or essence, or those who call the Son of God convertible or changeable, the Catholic and Apostolic Church anathematises.

*Nicene Creed*

## 'Unchangeable, perfect and forever blessed Trinity'

If the Word is not co-eternally existent with the Father, then the Trinity is not eternal either, and before there was simply the One Who by being added to became the Trinity . . . And if the Son is not born from the essence of the Father but originated from non-being, then the Trinity too is comprised of non-being and there was a time when the Trinity was not . . . But this is not true. And never will it be true! The Trinity is not created. There is the eternal and one Godhead in the Trinity, and one glory of the Holy Trinity . . . Christian faith knows the unchangeable, perfect and forever blessed Trinity and cannot imagine that at any time the Trinity did not suffice . . . Christian faith worships the Trinity, preserving the indivisibility and unity of the Godhead.

*St Athanasius the Great*

## One in Three

If, it is asserted, we use the word 'God' three times, must there not be three Gods? . . . We have one God, because there is a single Godhead. Though there are three objects of belief, they derive from the single whole and have reference to it. They do not have degrees of being God or degrees of priority over against one another. They are not sundered in will nor divided in power . . . It is as if there were a single intermingling of light, which existed in three mutually connected Suns. When we look at the Godhead, the primal cause, the sole sovereignty, we have a mental picture of the single whole, certainly. But when we look at the three in Whom the Godhead exists, Who derive Their timeless and equally glorious being from the primal cause, we have three objects of worship.

*St Gregory the Theologian*

## The trinitarian doctrine

Thus the Holy Catholic and Apostolic Church teaches that the Father exists simultaneously with His only-begotten Son, Who is begotten from Him without time or change or passion, and in a manner beyond understanding, as only the God of all knows. They exist simultaneously, as does the fire with its light – without the light being first and the light afterwards, but both simultaneously. And just as the light is ever being begotten of the fire, is always in it, and is in no way separated from it, so also is the Son begotten of the Father without in any way being separated from Him, but always existing in Him. However, the light . . . does not have any individual existence apart from the fire . . . On the other hand, the only-begotten Son of God . . . does have His own individual existence apart from that of the Father . . . We likewise believe in the Holy Ghost, the Lord and Giver of life, who proceeds from the Father and abides in the Son; who is adored and glorified together with the Father and the Son as consubstantial and co-eternal with Them . . . (We do not say) that the Spirit is from the Son, but we call Him the Spirit of the Son . . . We also confess that He was manifested and communicated to us through the Son . . .

*St John Damascene*

### The mystery of the Trinity

This Unique Being is a nature in three Hypostases,
One divinity, one kingdom,
One power, for the Trinity is a Unique Being.
For my God is a Unique Trinity, not three beings,
Because the one is three according to Hypostases.
They are co-natural, one to the other according to nature.
Entirely of the same power, having the same essence,
United without confusion in a way that transcends any human
    intelligence.
Yet they are mutually distinct without being separated.
Three in One and One in Three . . .
In the One are the Three and in the Three are the One,
Or rather, the Three are as One to me and the One again is Three.
Thus, think of this mystery, adore and believe now and forever.
For this Unique Being that appears, shines forth, is radiantly splendid,
Is participating in, is communicating, is everything good.
For this reason we do not call Him by one name only but by several.
He is light and peace and joy,
Life, food and drink, clothing, a robe, a tent and a divine dwelling.
He is the East, the resurrection, repose and bath,
Fire, water, river, source of life and a flowing stream,

Bread and wine, the new delight of believers,
The banquet, the pleasure which we enjoy in a mystical way,
Sun, indeed, without any setting, star always shining,
Lamp that burns inside the dwelling of the soul.

*St Symeon the New Theologian*

# CREATION

## GOD THE CREATOR

A fundamental difference between the biblical and Hellenistic accounts of creation is that the latter never affirmed a creation *ex nihilo* (from nothing). Plato's Demiurge produces everything from primordial matter, but the biblical Creator makes the world out of nothing: 'Look at the heaven and the earth and see everything that is in them, and recognise that God did not make them out of things that existed' (2 Macc. 7:28). Everything that exists received its being from the free will of the Creator: 'For he spoke, and it came to be; he commanded, and it stood forth' (Ps. 33:9). God had no need to create the world. Even his love, which, like any true love, requires a beloved, could not constrain him to create. His love already found its perfection in the communion of the Holy Trinity where each Hypostasis is both subject and object, lover and beloved. God created the world because he wanted the superabundant life and goodness within himself to be shared by other beings who would become partakers of divine blessing and holiness.

Creation involved all three Persons of the Trinity: 'By the word of the LORD the heavens were made, and all their host by the breath of his mouth' (Ps. 33:6). The beginning of the fourth gospel speaks of the creative role of God the Word: 'All things were made through him, and without him was not anything made that was made' (John 1:3). The Bible also has this to say about the Spirit: 'The earth was without form and void, and darkness was upon the face of the deep; and the Spirit of God was moving over the face of the waters' (Gen. 1:2). The Word and the Spirit are, to use an image of St Irenaeus of Lyon, the 'two hands' of the Father,[1] an image of the co-operation of the three Persons. Their will is one, but each has a specific, different action. Basil the Great says, 'The Originator of all things is one: he creates through the Son and perfects through the Holy Spirit . . . Perceive these three: the Lord who commands, the Word who creates, and the Spirit who strengthens.'[2] In other words, in the act of creation the Father is the First Cause of all things, the Word (Logos) has the role of Demiurge or Creator, and the Holy Spirit brings to perfection all things that have been created.

It is not without reason that, when speaking of the creative role of the Son, the Church Fathers prefer the name 'Word' above all other names: the Word makes known the Father and reveals the Father to the created world. Like any word, the Word-Logos is addressed to someone, in this case to the whole of creation. 'No one has ever seen God; the only Son, who is in the bosom of the Father, he has made him known' (John 1:18). The Son has made the Father known to all creatures; it is because of the Son that the love of the Father has been poured out upon creation and has given it life.

From the time of Philo of Alexandria (*c.* 30 BCE–45 CE) the Logos has been seen as a mediator between God and creation, while the Christian tradition speaks overtly of the creative power of the Logos. It is in this sense that the words of the book of Isaiah are interpreted: 'My word . . . that goes forth from my mouth . . . shall not return to me empty, but it shall accomplish that which I purpose, and prosper in the thing for which I sent it' (Isa. 55:11). At the same time, the Logos is understood as the plan and law according to which all things are created, the rational foundation of things: it is due to the Logos that all things have purpose, meaning, harmony and perfection.

Created being, however, is of a different nature from God: it is not, as in pantheism, an emanation, a pouring out of the Godhead. Creation 'is not the least like its Creator in substance, but is outside of him', says St Athanasius of Alexandria.[3] The divine substance did not undergo any division or transformation or change in the creation of the world: it did not merge with creation or become dissolved in it. God is an Artist; creation is his picture in which we can discern his 'brush', his 'hand', and glimpse the radiant reflection of his creative mind. Yet the Artist does not disappear in his picture – he remains one and the same before and after creation.

Why then did God create all things? Patristic theology answers the question in this way: 'out of the abundance of his love and goodness'. 'Because the good and transcendently good God was not content to contemplate himself, but by a superabundance of goodness saw fit that there should be some things to benefit by and to participate in his goodness, he brings all things from nothing into being and creates them', writes St John of Damascus.[4] In other words, God desired that there should be something else taking part in his blessedness and partaking of his love.

## THE ANGELS

'In the beginning God created the heavens and the earth' (Gen. 1:1). Traditionally these verses are understood as indicating two worlds created by God – one invisible, spiritual and perceptible to the intellect, and the other visible and material. We have already remarked that there are no abstract concepts in biblical language and spiritual realities are often expressed by the word 'heaven'. Christ speaks of the Kingdom of heaven, and in the Lord's Prayer we say, 'Our Father who art in heaven . . . Thy will be done, on earth as it is in heaven' (Matt. 6:9–10). It is obvious that reference is not being made to the visible, material sky. The Kingdom of God is a spiritual not a material kingdom, for by nature God is Spirit. And when we read that he 'created the heavens', this means the spiritual world and its inhabitants, the angels.

God created the angelic world before the visible universe. The angels are incorporeal spirits who possess reason and free will. John of Damascus speaks of them as being 'ever in motion, free, incorporeal, ministering to God', of their rational, intelligent and free nature. Following Gregory the Theologian, he calls the angels 'secondary spiritual lights, who receive their brightness from the first Light which is without beginning'.[5] Located in direct proximity to God, they are sustained by his light and convey this light to us.

The Bible frequently mentions the angels, yet there are no detailed descriptions of them, and there is no mention of their creation (apart from the reference to 'heaven'). According to Isaac the Syrian, God created angels 'out of nothing all of a sudden', as

worlds on high without number, limitless powers, legions of seraphs of fire, fearful and swift, wondrous and mighty, which have the power to carry out the will of the almighty design, the simple spirits which are luminous and incorporeal, which speak without a mouth, which see without any eyes, which hear without any ears, which fly without any wings . . . They do not tire or grow feeble, they are swift in movement, never delaying in any action, fearful to look upon, whose ministry is wondrous, who are rich in revelations, exalted in contemplation, who peer into the place of the *Shekhina*[6] of Invisibleness, glorious and holy essences, who are arranged in ninefold order by the Wisdom which has created all . . . They are fiery in their movements, acute in intellect, wondrous in knowledge, resembling God insofar as that is possible.[7]

Angels are actively engaged in the unceasing praise of God. Isaiah describes his vision of God, around whom the seraphim stand and proclaim: 'Holy, holy, holy is the LORD of hosts; the whole earth is full of his glory' (Isa. 6:1–3). Yet the angels are also messengers sent by God to people (the Greek word means 'messenger' or 'herald'). They take a vital and active part in the lives of all people. Thus the archangel announces to Mary that she will bear a Son called Jesus;[8] angels come and minister to Jesus in the wilderness;[9] an angel supports Jesus in the garden of Gethsemane.[10] Christ himself indicates that we each have our own guardian angel[11] who is companion, helper and protector.

According to tradition, not all angels are equal in dignity and closeness to God: there is a hierarchy. In the treatise *The Celestial Hierarchy*, attributed to Dionysius the Areopagite, the author counts three angelic hierarchies, each of which is divided into three ranks. The first and highest contains the seraphim, cherubim, thrones; the second, dominions, powers, authorities; the third, principalities, archangels, angels. The names of all nine angelic ranks are taken from Holy Scripture and, to quote again from Isaac the Syrian, mean the following:

In Hebrew, Seraphim means those who are fervent and burning; the Cherubim, those who are great in knowledge and wisdom; the Thrones, receptacles of God and rest . . . These orders are given these names because of their operations. The Thrones are so called as once truly honoured; the Dominions, as those who possess authority over every kingdom; the Principalities, as those who govern the atmosphere; Powers, as those who give power over the nations and every man; Virtues, as ones mighty in power and dreadful in appearance; the Seraphim, as those who make holy; the Cherubim, as those who carry; the Archangels, as vigilant guardians; the Angels, as those who are sent.[12]

In this celestial hierarchy the upper ranks are illumined by the divine light and partake of the mysteries of the Godhead directly, while the lower ranks receive illumination only by devolution through the higher ranks. According to Dionysius, the angelic hierarchy finds its continuation and reflection in the ecclesiastical hierarchy of sacraments, clergy and the faithful. Thus, the ecclesiastical hierarchy partakes of the divine mystery through the mediation of the celestial hierarchy. Biblical tradition speaks of the number of angels in general terms: there are 'a thousand thousands . . . and ten thousand times ten thousand' (Dan. 7:10). The angels certainly outnumber human beings. Gregory of Nyssa sees the lost sheep of the parable as an image of the entire human race, while he takes the ninety-nine sheep who stayed in the hills to be the angels.[13]

## THE ORIGIN OF EVIL

At the dawn of creation, before God made the visible world, but after the creation of the angels, there was a great catastrophe, which we know about only by its consequences. Some of the angels, opposing themselves to God and falling away from him, became enemies of all that was good and holy. At the head of this rebellion stood Lucifer, whose very name, which literally means 'light-bearing', indicates that originally he was good. By his own will he changed from his natural state into one which was unnatural; he set himself against God and fell away from goodness into evil.[14] Lucifer, also called the devil (from the Greek *diabolos*, which means 'divider', 'separator', or 'slanderer'), belonged to one of the senior ranks of the angelic hierarchy. Other angels defected with him, as the book of Revelation tells us in a metaphor: 'And a great star fell from heaven, blazing like a torch . . . and a third of the sun was struck . . . and a third of the stars, so that a third of their light was darkened' (Rev. 8:10, 12). For this reason, some commentators say that a third of the angels fell away along with the morning star.

By exercising their own free will the devil and his demons found themselves in darkness. Every reason-endowed living creature, whether angelic or human, possesses free will: the right to choose between good and evil. Free will belongs to everyone so that we can, by practising what is good, become part of that good at the level of our being. In other words, goodness was never intended to be granted to us from outside but must become our very own possession. If God imposed goodness as necessary or inevitable, then no one could ever become a truly free person. 'Nobody has ever become good by force', say the Fathers.[15] Through unceasing growth in virtue the angels were meant to ascend to the fullness of perfection, to the point of utter assimilation to the God of supreme goodness. Yet some of them chose to reject God and thereby sealed their own fate and the fate of the universe, which from that moment onwards became an arena for the struggle between two principles and powers, opposed but not equal: the Divine and the demonic, God and the devil.

This teaching about the fall away from God deliberately provoked by the devil is a response to the eternal question in all philosophy about the origin of evil. It is a question that poses a particular challenge to Christian theology, which has often had to contend with explicit or implicit theories of dualism. These occur in different forms, but their general tendency is to perceive good and evil as two equal powers which have governed the world from the very beginning. At the end of the third century a powerful dualistic sect, the Manichees, named after their founder, Mani, attracted a large following in the East and continued to exist under other names (Paulicianism, the Bogomil heresy, Albigensianism) right up until the Middle Ages. This heresy combined various elements of Christianity with aspects of Eastern dualistic religions. The Manichees taught that the whole of being is made up of two realms which have forever existed together: the kingdom of light, filled with many good aeons (angels), and the kingdom of darkness, filled with evil aeons (demons). Spiritual reality is subject to the god of light, while the god of darkness (Satan) has unlimited dominion over the material world. Matter itself is, therefore, a sinful and evil entity, and humans should mortify their bodies by all means possible in order to be liberated from matter and return to the non-material world of good.

Christian theology viewed the nature and origin of evil differently. Evil is not a primeval essence that is co-eternal and equal to God. It is a falling away from good, a revolt. In this sense it would be wrong to call evil a 'substance', for it does not exist in its own right. As darkness or shadow are not independent beings but simply the absence of light, so evil is merely the absence of good.

Evil is not a living and animated substance, but a condition of the soul which is opposed to virtue and which springs up in the slothful because of their falling away from Good. Do not, therefore, contemplate evil from without; and do not imagine some original nature of wickedness, but let each one recognise himself as the first author of the vice that is in him.[16]

God did not create anything evil: angels and humans, as well as the material world, are all good and beautiful by nature. However, rational creatures, in possessing free will, can direct their freedom against God and thereby engender evil. This is precisely what happened. The light-bearing morning star (Lucifer), originally created good, abused his freedom, defaced his own virtuous nature and fell away from the Source of goodness.

Although it has no intrinsic substance or being, evil materialised into an active agent of destruction when it was 'hypostasised', that is, when it took reality in the form of the devil and the demons. Father Georges Florovsky explains this paradox of evil in the following passage:

One defines evil as nothingness. Certainly evil never exists by itself but only inside of Goodness. Evil is a pure negation, a privation or a mutilation. Undoubtedly evil is a lack, a defect ... But the structure of evil is rather antinomic. Evil is a void of nothingness but a void which exists, which swallows and devours beings. Evil is a powerlessness; it never creates but its destructive energy is enormous ... The problem of evil only takes on its proper character on the religious plane. And the meaning of evil is a radical opposition to God, a revolt, a disobedience, a resistance.[17]

Compared with the operation of divine being, that of evil is illusory and imagined: the devil has no power where God does not allow him to operate. Yet, being a slanderer and a liar, the devil uses falsehood as his main weapon: he deceives his victim into believing that great power and authority are concentrated within his hands. The truth is that he does not have this power at all. In the Lord's Prayer we do not ask God to deliver us from evil in general, but to deliver us from *the evil one*, from the evil-doer, a person that embodies evil.[18] This evil-doer, whose nature was originally good, is the bearer of that deadly non-being, non-life, which leads to his own death and the death of his victims.

Most assuredly, God has no part in evil, yet evil is somehow under his control: it is God who sets the boundaries within which evil can operate. As the opening of the book of Job shows, there is a certain direct and personal relationship between God and the devil.[19] We do not know, however, quite what the nature of this relationship is. According to the mysterious ways of Providence, and in order for us to learn, God allows evil to act as a means of setting people right. This is evident from those parts of Scripture where God is recorded as visiting evil upon people: thus God hardened the heart of Pharaoh;[20] God visited Saul with an evil spirit;[21] God gave the people 'statutes that were not good';[22] God gave the people up to 'impurity', 'dishonourable passions' and a 'base mind'.[23] In all of these instances it is not God who is the source of evil, yet in possessing ultimate power over both good and evil, he can allow evil to operate in order to transform it into a source of virtue and direct it towards good purposes. He can also use it to deliver people from a still greater evil.

The obvious question still remains: why does God allow evil and the devil to exist? St Augustine confessed that he could not answer this question: 'I am unable to penetrate the depths of this ordinance and I confess that it is beyond my powers', he wrote.[24] Gregory of Nyssa responded in a more optimistic manner: God permits the devil to act for a certain time only, yet there will come a time when evil will be 'finally obliterated by the long cycle of ages' and when 'nothing outside of good will remain, but the confession of Christ's lordship will be unanimous even from the demons'.[25] The belief in the final restoration of the demons and the devil into their initial state was also held by Isaac of Nineveh,[26] as well as by other Early Church writers, but it has never become a magisterial teaching of the Church.

The Church knows that evil is neither co-eternal with God nor equal with him. That the devil rebelled against God and even became the king and ruler of hell does not mean that his kingdom will last for ever. On the contrary, Christian eschatology, as we shall see, is profoundly optimistic and strongly believes in the final victory of good over evil, God over the devil, Christ over the Antichrist. Yet what this victory will entail and what the final outcome of the existence of evil will be we do not know. Pondering on this, the human mind once more falls silent in the presence of the mystery, powerless to delve into the depths of divine destinies. As God says in the book of Isaiah, 'My thoughts are not your thoughts, neither are your ways my ways' (Isa. 55:8–9, Septuagint version).

## THE UNIVERSE

According to the Old Testament, the visible world was created in six days. It is difficult to imagine that this refers to a conventional six-day period. We have already noted that the word 'day' in biblical language denotes an undefined interval of time, sometimes quite lengthy. The psalmist, for example, refers to the Israelites' forty years in the desert as 'the day . . . in the wilderness' (Ps. 95:8). In another psalm we read: 'For a thousand years in thy sight are but as yesterday' (Ps. 90:4). St Peter, too, speaks of how 'with the Lord one day is as a thousand years, and a thousand years as one day' (2 Pet. 3:8). From ancient times Christians have referred to the Kingdom of heaven and the age to come as the 'Eighth Day'. The biblical six days of creation are not, therefore, six ordinary days, but rather six consecutive stages gradually unfolding to reveal the epic picture of the great Artist.

The Genesis account of creation opens with the words, 'In the beginning' (Gen. 1:1), a phrase also used in John's gospel to describe the eternal existence of the Word of God (John 1:1). This is a 'beginning', therefore, that refers to existence before time. It is not yet finite time but infinite eternity, from which time is to be born.[27] The 'beginning' is that first reality which links time with eternity, since from the moment when time is set into motion the universe must subject itself to its laws. According to the laws of time, the past is already over, the future is yet to come, and the present exists as an elusive and forever fleeting second which ends when it has scarcely begun. And although time appears simultaneously with the universe, that timeless 'beginning' when the universe was poised to begin but had not yet done so is a pledge of the fact that creation is allied with eternity, and will once again become part of it upon the completion of its history.

Eternity is the absence of time, outside which there is no temporal being, but an eternal being, beyond being. The universe, called out of non-being into temporal being through the creative word of God, will not disappear at the end of time, nor will it slide away into non-being, but will become part of what is beyond being; it will become eternal. Plato said of the universe's temporal creation, 'Time arose together with the heavens so that, born together, they will disintegrate together, should disintegration come.'[28] Biblical revelation, however, puts the universe in the perspective of both time and eternity, so that even when time disintegrates the universe will remain. Time is an icon of eternity ('eternal nature is the prototype of time', said Plato)[29] and time will be sublimated into eternity, while the universe will be transformed into the kingdom of the age to come.

'In the beginning God created the heavens and the earth. The earth was without form and void, and darkness was upon the face of the deep; and the Spirit of God was moving over the face of the waters' (Gen. I:1–2). Other ancient translations of the Old Testament present the earth as 'empty and nothing' (Theodotion), or 'idle and indistinguishable' (Symmachus); that is, as formless pre-matter out of which the world was to be created. The 'earth' of the first day is, to use Philaret of Moscow's expression, an 'astonishing emptiness',[30] a chaotic primary substance containing the pledge of future beauty and cosmic harmony. The 'darkness' and the 'deep' underscore the disorganisation and formlessness of matter, while the water denotes its plasticity. It is said that the Holy Spirit was 'moving', fluttering over the water. Elsewhere in the Bible this same verb is used to signify the hovering of birds over the nest of their young: '[The] eagle . . . stirs up its nest . . . flutters over its young, spreading out its wings, catching them, bearing them on its pinions' (Deut. 32:11). The Holy Spirit in the same way protects and animates the material world, 'fluttering' over it and breathing into it the 'spirit of life'.

'And God said, "Let there be light"; and there was light. And God saw that the light was good' (Gen. I:3–4). The light of the first day is neither sunlight nor moonlight (these appeared on the fourth day), but the light of the Godhead reflected in created being. The words 'said' and 'saw' are anthropomorphisms and both have a profound meaning. 'Said' points to the operation of the Word of God, while 'saw that it was good' indicates the state of perfection to which material creation is brought by the Holy Spirit. These biblical expressions point to the consciousness and the expediency of God's creative activity, and to the Artist's satisfaction that the Cosmos which he has created is truly beautiful.

One cannot but notice the affinity between the cosmology of the Bible and that of other ancient civilisations, such as those of Mesopotamia and Greece. 'From chaos there was born darkness and the dark night', writes Hesiod.[31] The word 'chaos', from a verb meaning 'to express surprise by letting one's jaw drop', corresponds precisely to the 'astonishing emptiness' of primordial matter. Plato calls the 'cosmos' a 'god, which was faced with existence' (though distinct from the 'eternally existing' God).[32] He speaks of the intelligence and the 'animated' nature of the Cosmos:

Desiring that all things should be good and nothing, if possible, should be evil, God cared for all visible things which abided not in repose but in disordered, inharmonious movement. He brought them out of disorder into order ... He arranged the intellect to be in the soul and the soul in the body, and in this manner created the universe with the intention of making the finest and the best creation ... Our cosmos is a living being with soul and intellect, and was truly born with the aid of Divine Providence.[33]

Plato says that the Cosmos is an icon of God: it 'reproduces the Prototype and reveals itself as the likeness of the true Image'.[34]

On the second day God created the 'firmament', an expanse which was firm and stable. On the third day he formed the dry land and the sea, separating one from the other. On the fourth day God created the sun, moon and other lights. From this moment the rhythmic changing cycle of day and night was put into motion. On the fifth day, at God's command, the waters brought forth fish and creeping things, while the air became the habitation of the birds. Finally, on the sixth day, appeared the animals and then human beings.

Christian scholars have noted the geocentric nature of the biblical account: having spoken of the creation of the universe on the first and second day, from the third day onwards the Genesis narrative focuses on the earth and what happens on it. This has profound symbolic meaning:

This is not the residue of a primitive cosmology ... which would keep faith with our post-Copernican universe. For this is not a physical geocentrism, but a spiritual one: the earth is spiritually central because it is the body of man, and because man . . . is the central being of creation, the being who reunites in himself the sensible and the intelligible and thus participates, richer than the angels, in all the orders of 'earth' and 'heaven'. At the centre of the universe beats the heart of man.[35]

There is no need here to compare the biblical story of creation with modern scientific theories of the origin of the universe. The lengthy dialogue between science and theology has not yet come to any definitive conclusions about the relationship between biblical revelation and scientific developments. There have been some notable attempts to reconcile Scripture with modern science, among them the theological-evolutionist theory of Teillhard de Chardin. It is, however, quite clear that the Bible does not aim to present a scientific account of the origin of the universe, and it is rather naive to base one's arguments on a literal understanding of the biblical narrative. Scripture regards all of history from the perspective of the interrelationship between the human and the divine. The authors of biblical stories often use metaphorical and symbolic language and although they inevitably rely on the scientific knowledge of their own time, this does not diminish the significance of the Bible as a book through which God speaks to humanity and reveals himself in all his creative power.

Having created the spiritual world and populated it with angels, God then creates the material world as a reflection, an icon of his beauty which transcends all imagination. Finally, God places human beings at the centre of the universe. The pre-eternal design of the Creator dictates that all things that live are called upon to praise him:

Praise the LORD from the heavens, praise him in the heights! Praise him, all his angels, praise him, all his host! Praise him, sun and moon, praise him, all you shining stars! Praise him, you highest heavens, and you waters above the heavens! Let them praise the name of the LORD! For he commanded and they were created . . . Praise the LORD from the earth, you sea monsters and all deeps, fire and hail, snow and frost, stormy wind fulfilling his command! Mountains and all hills, fruit trees and all cedars! Beasts and all cattle, creeping things and flying birds! Kings of the earth and all peoples, princes and all rulers of the earth! . . . Praise him in his mighty firmament! . . . Let everything that breathes praise the LORD!

(Ps. 148:1–5, 7–11; 150:1, 6)

The universe is a book which reveals the Creator to those who can read it. Those who have no faith, when observing the material world, cannot see in it the reflection of a higher non-material Beauty; for them the world contains nothing miraculous, everything is natural and conventional. But for believers, the beauty and harmony of the universe is a most powerful testimony to the existence of God, the Creator of all. St Anthony, the fourth-century Egyptian hermit, was once visited by a famous philosopher and was asked: 'Father, how can you endure to live here, deprived as you are of all consolation from books?' Anthony answered: 'My book, O philosopher, is the nature of created things, and whenever I wish I can read in it the works of God.'[36]

## 'We are called to see other dawns ...'

The sun had declined beyond the western horizon. Half of the sky glowed like a golden fire. Even the smallest of the lilac clouds had golden edges. Beneath the heavens were the melancholy expanses of the fields. What depths of melancholy are there in Russia's fields! ... They call the soul into a country located far, far away from the earth. The doors to the church were closed. From inside one could hear the singing of the vesperal hymn: 'Bless the Lord, O my soul! Blessed art thou, O Lord! How manifold are thy works' ... From the church windows one could see how the evening goodness and peace lay across the fields, the arable lands and the distant forests ... We are called to see other dawns and daybreaks which are incomparably more beautiful than the earthly ones, we are to go further, to the place where true repose and peace for the heart are to be found.

*'Reminiscences of a Priest'*

## The powerful silence

And then there opened up to our gaze an astonishing view of the mountain ridges and the captivatingly picturesque beauty of the locality in all directions, stretching across to the horizon as far as the eye could reach ... The sun was setting and its golden rays shone across the entire country: on both the mountain tops and the deep ravines, their darkness beckoning with fear, and the tiny glades, covered in green, occasionally seen through the mountains ... In the entire expanse around us there reigned a dead quietness and utter silence: the absence of all earthly vanities. Here nature, far removed from the world, celebrated her repose from vanity and revealed the mystery of the age to come ... This was the temple of God not made by hands where every object spoke of His glory and fulfilled its ministry to

[ 53 ]

God ... proclaiming His great strength, eternally existing power and deity ... Here the book of nature opened up for us one of her most luxuriant pages and we could see and read everywhere the traces of God, and through the contemplation of the created world we came to know the invisible nature of God ... The silence of the mountains and the valleys brought forth a new sensation: first a state of ineffable quietness and peace ... then a gladsome and spiritual joy of *a still small voice, where the Lord is* (I Kings 19:12) ... So it was that we sat in silence, looking in amazement and in holy rapture sustaining our hearts, experiencing those exalted moments of the inner life when one feels the closeness of the invisible world, enters into sweet communion with it and listens to the terrible presence of the Godhead. It is at such moments, replete with sacred feelings, that one forgets all earthly things. The heart is warmed like wax before the fire and becomes receptive to impressions of the celestial world. It burns with the purest of love for God, and one tastes of the bliss of inner enrichment; one hears an inner voice whispering that it is not for earthly vanities but for participation in eternity that the short days of our earthly existence are given.

*'On the Mountains of the Caucasus'*

## 'There is an Eternal One...'

Let us glorify the Greatest of artists Who has created the world in wisdom and refinement, and from the beauty of that which we can see let us recognise the One Who transcends in His beauty all things, and from the majesty of these sensible things let us conclude that there is an Eternal One transcending all majesty and through His power surpassing all knowledge.

*St Basil the Great*

## 'The ability to be amazed'

The person who has lost the ability to be amazed and to revere is dead. To know that there exists a hidden Reality which is revealed to us as the highest Beauty and to feel this – this is the core of true spirituality.

*Albert Einstein*

## God revealed through creation

Consider ... the rich variety, the lavish abundance of fruits, the special beauty of the particularly important kinds ... Their value shines through clearer than gems, since nature has made a sort of open banquet and served you with all you need to live and enjoy life. The purpose of this is to make you recognise God at least from the benefits you receive ... Leave here and range over mother earth's length and breadth ... Traverse her abundant, overflowing fountains of cool drinking-water above ground, besides all those which flow underground. Under caverns they flow, till forced out by the pressure of the wind, their temperature raised in the vehemence of the struggling-match, they burst out ... spontaneously ... Tell me the cause of all this, explain the nature of this spontaneous fabric ... Reason has no explanation of what upholds the world except the will of God ... As for the sea, if I had felt no wonder at its size, I should have felt it for its stillness, at the way it stands free within its proper limits ... What binding force brought the sea together? What causes it to swell yet stay in position, as if in awe of the land its neighbour? How can it take in all rivers and stay the same through sheer excess of quantity? ... Who poured out the air so unstintingly? ... Who has made heaven rotate and set stars in order? ... What makes the Sun a beacon for the whole world to look at, a chorus-leader, as it were, who puts the other stars in the shade by his superior brilliance? ... What do you think? Shall we stop our preaching here at matter and objects of sight? Or ... shall we pass through the first veil, transcending sense, to bend our gaze on holy things, on ideal and heavenly reality? ... You see how we become dizzy with the theme and can get no further than the stage of being aware of angels and archangels, thrones, dominions, princedoms, powers, of glowing lights, ascents, intellectual powers or minds, being of nature pure and unalloyed. Fixed, almost incapable of changing for the worse, they encircle God, the First Cause, in their dance ... Each has under him a different part of the universe, which God alone, Who defined their ranks, knows ... They hymn God's majesty in everlasting contemplation of everlasting glory ...

*St Gregory the Theologian*

## The angelic world

He is the Maker and Creator of the angels. He brought them from nothing into being ... One of these angelic powers was chief of the terrestrial order and had been entrusted by God with the custody of the earth. Although he was not evil by nature, but good, and although he had been made for good and had in himself not the slightest trace of evil from the Creator, he did not keep the brightness and dignity which the Creator has bestowed on him. By his free choice he turned from what was according to nature to

[ 55 ]

what was against it. Having become stirred up against the God Who created him and having willed to rebel against Him, he was the first to abandon good and become evil. For evil is no more than the privation of evil, just as darkness is the absence of light. And good is spiritual light, while in the same way evil is spiritual darkness.

*St John Damascene*

### Divine love revealed through creation

What that invisible Being is like, Who is without any beginning in His nature, unique in Himself, Who is by nature beyond the knowledge, intellect and feel of created beings, Who is beyond time and space, being the Creator of these, who at the beginning of time was learnt about through hints and was made known as if it were through His mark by means of the establishing of the fullness of creation, who made His voice heard in connection with His handiwork and so the Being of His Lordship was made known, the fountainhead of innumerable natures – this Being is hidden, for as He dwelt in His Being for aeons without number or limit or beginning, it pleased His graciousness and He made a beginning of time, bringing the worlds and created beings into existence. Let us consider then, how rich in its wealth is the ocean of His creative act, and how many created things belong to God, and how in His compassion He carries everything, acting providentially as He guides creation, and how with a love that cannot be measured He arrived at the establishment of the world and the beginning of creation; and how compassionate God is, and how patient; and how He loves creation, and how He carries it, gently enduring its importunity, the various sins and wickednesses, the terrible blasphemies of demons and evil men.

*St Isaac the Syrian*

### The creative Light

> Before there were the heavens, before earth was made,
> God existed, the Trinity, the Unique One and He alone.
> Light eternal, uncreated Light, Light absolutely inexpressible . . .
> There was no air as now, nor darkness, absolutely nothing:
> No light, no water, no atmosphere, nothing of such that exist.
> But there was only spirit, God, totally in the form of Light . . .
> Then He created the Angels, the Principalities,

[ 56 ]

And the Powers, the Cherubim and Seraphim, the Dominions and
    the Thrones,
And the nameless hosts that serve Him
And stand around in His presence in fear and trembling.
Later He created the firmament, as a vault,
Material and visible, having a thickness . . .
Likewise He created the earth and the waters . . .
Thus the firmament was made material
And stands separated by nature . . . from the immaterial light.
It indeed remained without any light, a great dwelling place as it
    were.
But the Master of all lighted the sun and the moon,
To shine brightly in a sensible way for all creatures of sense,
And He gave into our hands a light to shine in the night
Born marvellously from iron and stone.
But He is separated from all light,
He is above light, above every radiance,
He completely transcends every creature.
For just as when the sun shines, the stars do not appear,
So likewise if the Master of the sun wishes to shine,
No living being can bear the rising of this Sun.

*St Symeon the New Theologian*

*Chapter Five*

---

# THE HUMAN PERSON

## THE CREATION OF HUMANITY

Human beings are the crown of creation, the peak of the Holy Trinity's creative acts. Before creating Adam, the three Persons took counsel together: 'Let us make man in our own image, after our likeness' (Gen. 1:26). The 'Pre-eternal Counsel' of the Trinity was necessary, first, because humans were a higher creature with reason, will and dominion over the visible world; and second, because, being free and independent, humanity would break the commandment and fall away from the bliss of Paradise. The Son's sacrifice on the Cross would then be the way for humans to return to God. In creating human beings, God knew their subsequent destiny, for nothing is hidden from his gaze.

If God could foresee the fall of Adam, and since everything took place according to the Maker's will, does this not make Adam an innocent victim? St John of Damascus answers this question by pointing out the distinction between 'foreknowledge' and 'predestination': 'One should know that God foreknows all things but that he does not predestine them all. Thus, he fore-knows the things that depend upon us, but he does not predestine them – because neither does he will evil to be done nor does he force virtue.'[1] Thus, it is not God's foreknowledge that determines the fate of humanity. Sin was not built in to Adam's nature: to sin or not depended solely upon his free will. When we sin, God knows beforehand, but this in no way exonerates us from the responsibility for sinning. At the same time, God's mercy is so great that he declares his eternal readiness to sacrifice himself in order to redeem us from the consequences of sin.

God formed Adam 'of dust from the ground', that is, from matter. His flesh was the flesh of the earth from which he was moulded by the hands of God. Yet God also 'breathed into his nostrils the breath of life; and man became a living being' (Gen. 2:7). Although a material or earthly being, Adam received a divine principle, a pledge of his communion with the Godhead. The reference to 'the breath of life' can be taken to mean the Holy Spirit. Human beings partake of the divine nature by the very act of creation and are thereby utterly different from other living beings: humans do not simply assume a higher position in the hierarchy of animals, but are 'demi-gods' set over the animal kingdom. The Church Fathers call the human being a 'mediator' between the visible and invisible worlds, a 'mixture' of them both.

St Basil says that Adam 'had dominion according to the likeness of the angels' and that 'in his life he was like the archangels'.[2] However, as the heart of the created world, combining within themselves both the spiritual and the corporeal, human beings in a sense surpass the angels. It was not angels but human beings who were created by God in his own image. And it was not angelic but human nature that was assumed by God at the Incarnation.

## IMAGE AND LIKENESS

'So God created man in his own image, in the image of God he created him; male and female he created them' (Gen. 1:27). Because a solitary monad cannot love, being alone, God created not a single unit but a couple, with the intention that love should reign among people. Yet the love between the couple is not yet the perfection of love, because the couple is made up of two opposing principles, thesis and antithesis, which must find their fulfilment in a synthesis. This synthesis may be realised in the birth of a child. God commands: 'Be fruitful and multiply' (Gen. 1:28). From two human beings the third, their child, is to be born: the fully realised family – husband, wife and child – which is a reflection of the divine love in three Hypostases. Indeed, one cannot but notice the parallel in the way the Bible moves between singular and plural when it speaks of God ('Let *us* make man in *our* image' and 'God created man in *his* own image') and when it speaks of human beings ('created him' and 'created them'). This interchange emphasises the unity of the nature of the human race even though each individual person is unique. 'God is a Nature and three Persons; man is a nature and "innumerable" persons; God is consubstantial and in three Hypostases, man is consubstantial and in innumerable hypostases.'[3]

The theme of image and likeness is central to a Christian theory of personhood. To a greater or lesser extent it was addressed by nearly all the Early Church writers. The theme has a dual origin, being rooted in both biblical and Hellenistic traditions. Plato spoke of how God 'minted' living beings 'according to the nature of the prototype'.[4] Philo of Alexandria said that humans had been 'created according to the *eikon* of the ideal Prototype'.[5] The Greek word *eikon* means 'image', 'icon', 'portrait' or 'depiction', that is, something created according to a model (*prototypos*) and having an affinity with the model even if it is not identical to it by nature.

The Church Fathers usually equated 'the image of God' with the rational and spiritual nature of humans as 'intelligent beings'. 'What is *after the image* if not our intellect?' asks John of Damascus.[6] 'We are created in the image of the Maker, we possess reason and the faculty of speech, which comprise the perfection of our nature', writes Basil the Great.[7] Elsewhere St Basil states that it is the human heart that was created in God's image.[8]

Is the human body made in the divine image? St John Chrysostom believes not;[9] but according to Photios of Constantinople the body, like all of God's creation, bears the reflection of the Maker: 'The human body, like the soul, is the artistic product of God's philanthropic and beneficent design.'[10]

'The image of God' has been understood by some Fathers as our free will and self-determination. 'When God in his supernal goodness creates each soul in his own image, he brings it into being endowed with self-determination', says Maximus the Confessor.[11] God created us absolutely free: in his love he does not wish to force us into either good or evil. In return, he expects from us not blind obedience but love. It is only in our being free that we can be assimilated to God through love for him.

Other Fathers identified 'the image of God' as our immortality, our dominant position in the world and our striving towards good. Tatian refers to human beings as 'the image of divine immortality'.[12] Macarius the Great says that God created the soul 'according to the image of the virtues of the Spirit', having put into it 'the laws of virtues, discernment, knowledge, prudence, faith, love, and the rest of the virtues according to the image of the Spirit'.[13]

Our ability to create, as a reflection of the creative ability of the Maker himself, is also regarded as being 'in God's image'.[14] God is the 'worker': 'My Father is working still, and I am working', says Christ (John 5:17). Adam was also commanded to 'till' the garden of Eden (Gen. 2:15), that is, to labour in it and work the land. Though we are unable to create out of nothing, we can nevertheless create from materials given to us by God, and this material is the entire earth, over which we are appointed stewards. The world has no need to be improved by us; rather, we ourselves need to apply our creative abilities in order to be assimilated to God.

Some Church Fathers distinguish 'image' from 'likeness' by identifying the image as that which is originally fixed by the Creator, and the likeness as that which is to be attained through a life of virtue: 'The expression *according to the image* indicates that which is reasonable and endowed with free will, while the expression *according to the likeness* denotes assimilation through virtue, in as far as this is possible.'[15] We are called upon to realise all our creative abilities in 'tilling' the world, in creativity, in virtue, in love, so that we can be assimilated to God. For, as Gregory of Nyssa says, 'the limit of a life of virtues is the assimilation of God'.[16]

## SOUL AND BODY

While all ancient religious traditions maintain that humans are composed of both material and spiritual elements, the relationship between the two has been understood in different ways. Dualistic traditions view matter as intrinsically evil and hostile towards humanity: the Manichees even believed that Satan was the maker of the material world. Classical philosophy regards the body as a prison in which the soul is held captive. Indeed, Plato claims the word *soma* (body) comes from *sema* (tombstone, tomb): 'Many people believe that the body is like a tombstone concealing the soul buried beneath it in this life ... The soul endures punishment ... while the flesh does duty as its fortress so that it can be healed, while located in the body as in a torture chamber.'[17]

The ancient Indian philosophies speak of the transmigration of souls from one body to another, even from a human being to an animal (and vice versa): 'As when the person sheds his old clothes and assumes new ones, so does the soul abandon the body for a new, different one.'[18] The doctrine of *metempsychosis* (reincarnation) was rejected by Early Church tradition as incompatible with divine revelation. It was proclaimed false on the basis that a human being, who possesses reason and free will, cannot be transformed into an animal, which does not possess reason, since all intelligent being is immortal and cannot disappear. Moreover, what is the point of being punished for sins committed in an earlier life if one does not know the reason for the punishment (it is, after all, impossible to recollect one's previous 'existence')?

Basing themselves on Scripture, the Church Fathers taught that the soul and the body are not alien elements united temporarily in an individual person, but are given simultaneously and for all time in the very act of creation: the soul is 'betrothed' to the body and is inseparable from it. Only the totality of soul and body together comprises a complete person, a hypostasis. Neither the soul nor the body can exist as such by itself: 'For what is the human person if not an intelligible living being consisting of

[ 61 ]

soul and body?' asks Justin Martyr. 'So, is the soul by itself a human being? No ... And can we call the body a human person? No ... Only a being comprised of both elements can be called a person.'[19] Gregory of Nyssa calls the unbreakable link between soul and body an 'inclination of affection', a 'commixture', 'community', 'attraction' and 'acquaintance', which are preserved even after death.[20] Such a concept is far removed from Platonic and oriental dualism.

In speaking of the body and matter in general, the Church Fathers emphasise their divine origin: 'I declare that matter is the creation of God, and a good thing', says John of Damascus. 'I do not worship matter; I worship the Creator of matter who became matter for me ... and accomplished my salvation through matter.'[21] Christianity is sometimes falsely accused of preaching that the flesh should be despised and the body treated with contempt. These views, held by a number of heretics (the Gnostics, Montanists, Manichees) and by some Greek philosophers, were subjected to rigorous criticism by John Chrysostom:

Many of the Greeks and heretics say that the body was not even created by God. It is not worthy of having been created by God, they say, pointing towards the impurity, sweat, tears, labour, exhaustion and other imperfections of the body ... But do not speak to me of this fallen, condemned and degraded person. If you want to know how God created our body originally, then let us enter Paradise and look at the first-created person.[22]

In Christian ascetic literature, whenever questions of enmity between flesh and spirit arise – beginning with St Paul: 'For the desires of the flesh are against the spirit, and the desires of the spirit are against the flesh' (Gal. 5:17) – they concern fallen flesh as the totality of passions and vices, not the body as such. The expression 'mortification of the flesh', found in monastic sources, refers to putting to death the sinful desires and 'lusts of the flesh', not a contempt for the body itself. The Christian ideal is not to debase the flesh, but to purify it and transfigure it, to liberate it from the consequences of the Fall; to return it to its primordial purity and make it worthy of assimilation to God.

The spiritual principle in humans is most often denoted by the word 'soul' (*psyche* in Greek). In the Bible this word may signify any living being,[23] but in other instances it refers to the principle of life contained within the flesh,[24] the blood of a living creature,[25] or quite often human life.[26] In the Psalms the soul is often mentioned as the inner immaterial principle within a human being: 'O God, thou art my God, I seek thee, my soul thirsts for thee; my flesh faints for thee' (Ps. 63:1).

It is this last meaning that applies to the word 'soul' as it occurs in patristic writings. St Athanasius offered the following definition of the soul: 'The soul is an intelligible essence, incorporeal, dispassionate, immortal.'[27] Gregory of Nyssa states: 'The soul is an essence that has been given birth, a living being, intelligible, communicating the life force to the organ and sensible body.'[28] In both instances the soul is called an essence (*ousia*), meaning that it is not merely a function of the body, its capability, senses or manifestation: it has its own independent being. According to Gregory Nazianzen, the soul is 'a part of God' in the human person,[29] a 'breath of God',[30] 'a piece broken from the invisible Deity'.[31]

Besides the soul, each person has a higher spiritual principle called 'spirit' or 'intellect'. The word 'spirit' (in Hebrew *ruah*, and in Greek *pneuma*) is of biblical origin and its first meaning is 'breath', or 'wind'.[32] The term 'intellect' (*nous*) comes from classical philosophy, and does not occur at all in the Septuagint. St Paul, on the other hand, uses it frequently, while for the Church Fathers it is this word (and not 'spirit') that becomes the fundamental anthropological concept. The intellect differs in kind from all else that is within a person. It has the ability to comprehend the meaning of things, to penetrate their essence. 'The intellect sees all things, even the celestial. Nothing darkens it except sin', claims a saying ascribed to St Anthony the Great.[33] It is precisely through the intellect that we can come into contact with God and pray to him. It is with the intellect, too, that we can hear God's 'answer' to our prayer.

The notion of 'heart' also holds a special position for the Fathers. For them, it is not simply an organ of the body but also the centre of our spiritual and mystical life, the seat of divine presence and inner grace. Hence the term 'heart' is almost synonymous with 'soul' and 'mind'. In the following text from the *Macarian Homilies*, the mind is understood as being located in the heart (rather than in the brain, as one might expect):

... Divine grace writes on the *tables of the heart*[34] the laws of the Spirit and the heavenly mysteries. For the heart directs and governs all the other organs of the body. And when grace pastures the heart, it rules over all the members and the thoughts. For there, in the heart, the mind abides as well as all the thoughts of the soul and its hopes.[35]

The biblical tradition has always held an exceptionally elevated view of the human being as a totality of spirit and matter. What is a human being from the point of view of an atheist? An ape, only with more developed abilities. For a Buddhist or Hindu the soul exists quite independently of the body in which it is incarnated, and may pass through many incarnations, animal as well as human.

The Christian tradition, however, presents an exalted image of the human being. Each one of us is regarded as a person created in the image of God, an icon of the Creator. Humans are not lower than the angels. As the Psalms say: 'What is man that thou art mindful of him, and the son of man that thou dost care for him? Yet thou hast made him little less than God, and dost crown him with honour and glory. Thou hast given him dominion over the works of thy hands' (Ps. 8:4–6).

The ancient Greek philosophers, as well as some Church Fathers, speak of a human being as a microcosm, a small universe which unites within itself the totality of created being.[36] However, as Gregory of Nyssa emphasises, the concept of microcosm does not really dignify the human being: 'What great thing is there in the human person's being accounted a representation and likeness of the world – of the heaven that passes away, of the earth that changes?' According to St Gregory, our true dignity consists in our 'being in the image of the nature of the Creator'.[37] We are commensurable, almost 'identical' to God:

Man is more precious than all the rest of the cosmos. Man, completed and perfected, is wondrous, even as God is wondrous. He is immortal and supra-cosmic. He is more than a microcosm – he is a micro-*theos*. For the eternal Logos of the Father to be made flesh *in the likeness of man*[38] means that, with the gift of his love, man in turn may become God, even to identity. Between God and man there is and must be commensurability in spite of all that is non-commensurable . . . If man by the nature of his spirit is not 'like unto God', then neither could God have been made man.[39]

When God created human nature, he created it not only for us but also for himself, since he knew that one day he would himself become a human being. Thus, he fashioned something adequate to himself, something possessing infinite potential. Gregory Nazianzen calls each person a 'created god'.[40] The notion of humanity's commensurability with God 'does not remove the ontological distance between God the *Creator* and man the *created*'.[41] Yet in spite of this distance every person is called to become 'god'. In his potential, man is a *god-man*.

## HUMANITY BEFORE THE FALL

An atheistic viewpoint claims that in the early developmental stages of the human race people were like animals; they did not know God, nor did they possess concepts of morality. Opposed to this is the Christian belief in the bliss of the first humans in Paradise, their subsequent fall and eventual expulsion from Eden. Accounts of primordial human bliss and a subsequent fall from grace occur in the mythology of many peoples, and these traditions have a striking similarity to one another. Is the biblical story, then, one such myth? Is it possible to treat it as a genuine part of human history, or should it be understood as an allegory?

First, let us define the term 'myth'. In Greek, the word *mythos* denotes a story, or legend, usually concerning gods and heroes, that is, the prehistoric past of the human race. According to a Russian philosopher, A. F. Losev, a myth is neither an invention, nor a fantastic tale, nor an allegory, but 'life itself', 'being itself', 'reality'. In other words, myth is actual history expressed in words and symbols. At the same time, a myth is a miracle, and this is what makes it different from conventional historical narrative, which is based on rational analysis of facts and events. The language of myth is the language of symbols. Actual history arrays itself in symbolic words and images, in this way becoming myth.[42] When a particular people becomes increasingly estranged from belief in the one God, genuine reality, which was originally fixed in its mythology, becomes increasingly distorted and assumes the character of a fairy tale: 'mythical' in the negative sense. Yet an element of truth is always present in any mythology, and this explains why various mythologies have many features in common.

We believe that biblical narrative is different from other ancient myths in that it belongs to a chosen people, the only nation to which the true faith was entrusted. Therefore no distortions would have crept into the text: the tradition remained unsullied. Moreover, the Church accepts everything in the Bible as truth divinely revealed through God's chosen people: teachers, apostles and prophets. In this sense the biblical narrative is genuine history, not an allegory or a parable – but like any ancient myth it is written in symbolic language where each word and image requires explanation. We realise that 'heaven and earth' are symbols of something far more significant than our astronomical heavens and the earthly globe. And the 'serpent' that was 'more subtle than any other wild creature' is not a conventional reptile, but an evil force which entered into it. In Scripture everything to the last letter is the truth, yet not everything ought to be understood literally. The biblical narrative may be defined as *a symbolic story of actual events*.

Thus, having created Adam, God brings him into Paradise – a garden which he had 'planted ... in Eden, in the east' (Gen. 2:8). Paradise was Adam's possession and he lived in harmony with nature. He understood the language of the animals, and they obeyed him; all the elements were subject to him as if to a king. 'The Lord made man the prince of this age and master of all things visible. Neither fire could overcome him, nor water drown him, nor any beast harm him', says Macarius of Egypt. Adam's face emitted 'radiant glory'; he was God's friend, he lived in purity, had dominion over all his thoughts and experienced bliss.[43] The Word dwelt in Adam, and he contained within himself the Spirit of God. 'The Word himself was with him and was everything to him: both knowledge and experience and inheritance and teaching.'[44]

God brings to Adam all the animals, 'to see what he would call them; and whatever the man called every living creature, that was its name' (Gen. 2:19). Adam gives a name to every animal and bird, and by doing so he demonstrates his ability to know the meaning, the hidden *logos*, of every living creature. A name is more than a mere symbol or a conditional identification of a particular being.

The name ... is the foundation, the power, the purpose, the creativity and accomplishment of the whole of life ... A name is the element of intelligible communion of living creatures in the light of meaning and noetic harmony, the revelation of mysterious countenances and the radiant perception of the living energies of being ... Each living creature bears its own name.[45]

By giving Adam the right to name the whole of creation, God brings him into the very heart of his creative process and calls him to participate in creation:

Adam had to contemplate the unnamed construction inherent in every animal. And they all came to Adam, thereby proclaiming their subjection to him ... God says to Adam: be the maker of names, since you cannot be the maker of all living creation ... We share with you the glory of creative wisdom ... Grant names to those whom I have granted being.[46]

Thus God brings primordial man into existence to be a priest of the entire visible creation. He alone of all living creatures is capable of praising God verbally and blessing him. The entire universe is entrusted to him as a gift, for which he is to bring a 'sacrifice of praise' and which he is to offer back to God as 'thine own of thine own'. In this unceasing eucharistic offering lies the meaning and justification of human existence. The heavens, the earth, the sea, the fields and mountains, the birds and the animals, indeed, the whole of creation, assign to humans this high-priestly ministry in order that God may be praised through their lips.

God allows Adam and Eve to eat from all the trees of Paradise, including the tree of life which grants immortality. However, he forbids them to eat

from the tree of the knowledge of good and evil, because 'to know evil' is
to become party to it and to fall away from bliss and immortality. St John
of Damascus explains that God gave this commandment 'as a sort of trial,
test, and exercise of man's obedience and disobedience'.[47] In other words,
Adam is given the right to choose between good and evil, even though
God makes him aware of the correct choice and warns him of the consequences of falling from grace. In choosing evil, Adam falls away from life
and 'dies a death'; in choosing good, he ascends to perfection and attains
the highest goal of his existence.

The Fathers of the Eastern Church teach that the purpose of human
life is 'deification' (*theosis*).[48] Assimilation to God and deification are one
and the same thing:

Now this blessed Deity which transcends everything and which is one and
also triune has resolved, for reasons unclear to us but obvious to itself, to
ensure the salvation of rational beings, both ourselves and those beings who
are our superiors. This can only happen with the deification of the saved.
And deification consists of being as much as possible like and in union
with God.[49]

## THE FALL

'Now the serpent was more subtle than any other wild creature that the
LORD God had made' (Gen. 3:1). Thus begins the biblical narrative of
the Fall of humanity. This is the very same 'great dragon [who] was thrown
down, that ancient serpent, who is called the Devil and Satan, the deceiver
of the whole world' (Rev. 12:9), once the Light-Bearer (*Lucifer*), who fell
away from God's love and became the enemy of all that is good. The devil
beguiled humans with the 'hope of deification'.[50] They could not discern
this lie since the striving for deification had already been placed in them
by the Creator. Yet deification is impossible without God; thus, to attempt
to become his equal without his assistance is a sign of pride and delusion.

The story of the Fall prefigures the entire tragic history of the human
race. It shows us who we were and what we have become. It reveals that
evil entered the world not by the will of God but by the fault of humans
who preferred diabolical deceit over divine commandment. From generation
to generation the human race repeats Adam's mistake in being beguiled by
false values and forgetting those that are true – faith in God and fidelity
towards him.

Sin was not built in to human nature, but the possibility of sin existed from the beginning in the free will given to humans. It was indeed freedom that rendered the human being an image of the Maker; but it was also freedom that contained within itself the possibility of falling away from God. Archimandrite Sophrony states that God, in creating humans free, was in a sense taking a risk:

To produce something new is always a gamble, and God's creation of man in his image and after his likeness involved a certain degree of risk. It was not that He risked introducing an element of instability or shock into his eternal Being but that to give man god-like freedom shut the door against predestination in any form. Man is at full liberty to determine himself negatively in relation to God – even to enter into conflict with him . . . Man is free to disagree, even to resist him.[51]

Out of his love for humanity, God did not want to interfere in human freedom and forcibly prevent sin, but neither could the devil force them to do evil. The sole responsibility for the Fall is borne by humans themselves, for they misused the freedom given to them.

What constituted the sin of the first people? St Augustine believes it to be disobedience:

It is impossible that the will would not have collapsed on man by the great weight of the fall if he preferred it to the higher will. Man has felt this in having disobeyed the Divine commandment and has through this experience come to know the difference between the good of obedience and the evil of disobedience.[52]

On the other hand, the majority of Early Church writers say that Adam fell as a result of pride: 'The devil, and Adam after him, one being an angel and the other a person, fell away from their nature and became proud before God, desiring to be gods themselves.'[53] Pride is the wall that separates humans from God. The root of pride is the state of being turned in on oneself, self-love, lust for oneself. Before the Fall, God was the only object of human love, but then there appeared a value distinct from God: the tree was suddenly seen to be 'good for food', 'a delight to the eyes', and something 'to be desired' (Gen. 3:6). Thus the entire hierarchy of values collapsed: my own 'I' occupied the first place while the second was taken by the object of 'my' lust. No place remained for God: he had been forgotten, driven from my life.

The forbidden fruit failed to bring happiness to the first people. On the contrary, they began to sense their own nakedness: they were ashamed and tried to hide from God. Being aware of nakedness denotes loss of the divine light-bearing garment that cloaked humans and defended them from the knowledge of evil. Adam's first reaction after committing sin was a burning sensation of shame. The second was his desire to hide from the Creator. This shows that he had lost all notion of God's omnipresence and would search for any place where God was 'absent'.

This rupture with God was not total, however. The Fall did not mean complete abandonment: humans could repent and regain their former dignity. God goes out to find the fallen Adam. He seeks him out among the trees of Paradise, asking, 'Where are you?' (Gen. 3:9) God's humble wandering through Paradise prefigures Christ's humility as revealed in the New Testament, the humility with which the Shepherd seeks the lost sheep. God had no need to search Adam out: with a voice of thunder he can call down from the heavens or shake the foundations of the earth. Yet he does not wish to be Adam's judge, or his prosecutor. He still wants to count him as an equal and puts his hope in Adam's repentance. There is, in God's question, a call to repentance, as Origen shows:

God says to Adam 'Where are you?' not because he wanted to know all about him, but rather to remind him. For he reminds he who at first went in bliss but soon broke the commandment and became naked, saying 'Where are you? Come and see the condition in which you were in and where you are now when you have fallen from the sweetness of Paradise.'[54]

Symeon the New Theologian maintains that if Adam had confessed his sinfulness, he would undoubtedly have been forgiven.[55] But rather than repenting, Adam attempts to justify himself, laying the blame for everything on his wife: 'The woman whom thou gavest to be with me, she gave me fruit of the tree, and I ate' (Gen. 3:12). In other words, 'It was you who gave me a wife; it is you who are to blame.' In turn, Eve lays the blame for everything on the serpent.

The consequences of the Fall were catastrophic for the first human beings. Not only were they deprived of the bliss and sweetness of Paradise, but their whole nature was changed and disfigured. They fell away from their natural condition and entered an unnatural state of being.[56] All elements of their spiritual and corporeal make-up were damaged: their spirit, instead of striving for God, became engrossed in the passions; their soul entered the sphere of bodily instincts, while their body lost its original lightness and was transformed into heavy sinful flesh. After the Fall every person 'became deaf, blind, naked, insensitive to the good things from which he had fallen away, and above all became mortal, corruptible and without sense of purpose... Instead of divine and incorruptible knowledge he received fleshly knowledge, for once the eyes of his soul were blinded he began to see with the eyes of the flesh.'[57] Disease, suffering and pain entered human life. Humans became mortal, for they had lost the opportunity of tasting from the tree of life.

Not only humanity but also the entire world changed as a result of the Fall. The original harmony between people and nature had been broken; the elements had become hostile; storms, earthquakes and floods could destroy life. The earth would no longer provide everything of its own accord; it would have to be tilled 'in the sweat of your face', and would produce 'thorns and thistles'. Even the animals would become enemies of human beings: Adam was told that the serpent would 'bruise his heel' and other predators would attack him.[58] All creation would be subject to the 'bondage of decay'. Together with humanity it would now 'wait for freedom' from this bondage, since it did not submit to sin voluntarily but through the fault of mankind.[59]

Finding themselves outside Paradise and surrounded by a hostile world, pitiful and helpless, Adam and Eve began to weep:

They cried and wept, beat themselves about the head, weeping for their former hardness of heart, and they did this not for one or two or ten days, but for the rest of their life. For how could they not weep in remembering the humble Lord, this ineffable sweetness of Paradise, this indescribable beauty of flowers, this carefree and effortless life, this ascending and descending of the angels to them?[60]

On the eve of Great Lent the Church recalls Adam's expulsion from Paradise with these words:

Adam sat before Paradise and, lamenting his nakedness, he wept: 'Woe is me! By evil deceit was I persuaded and led astray, and now I am an exile from glory. Woe is me! In my simplicity I was stripped naked, and now I am in want. O Paradise, no more shall I take pleasure in thy joy; no more shall I look upon the Lord my God and Maker, for I shall return to the earth whence I was taken . . .'[61]

## 'ORIGINAL SIN'

After the Fall, sin became inseparable from human existence. While Adam and Eve were guilty of pride and disobedience, their son Cain killed his brother Abel. Cain's descendants soon forgot about God and set about organising their earthly existence. Cain himself 'built a city'. One of his closest descendants was 'the father of those who dwell in tents and have cattle'; another was 'the father of all those who play the lyre and pipe'; yet another was 'the forger of all instruments of bronze and iron' (Gen. 4:17–22). The establishment of cities, cattle-breeding, music and other arts are passed on to humankind by Cain's descendants as a substitute for the lost happiness of Paradise.

The consequences are described by St Paul: 'Therefore as sin came into the world through one man and death through sin, and so death spread to all men because all men sinned' (Rom. 5:12). This text, which forms the basis of the Church's teaching on 'original sin', may be understood in a number of ways: the Greek words which are translated as 'because all men sinned' can also mean 'in whom [that is, in Adam] all men sinned'.[62] Different readings of the text may produce different understandings of what 'original sin' means.[63]

If we accept the first interpretation, we are each responsible for our own sins, and not for Adam's transgression. Here, Adam is merely the prototype of all future sinners, who, in repeating Adam's sin, bear responsibility only for their own sins. 'When evil thoughts become active within us, we should blame ourselves and not ancestral sin', says St Mark the Ascetic.[64] Adam's sin, therefore, is not the cause of our sinfulness; we do not participate in his sin and his guilt cannot be passed on to us.

If we read the text to mean 'in whom all have sinned',[65] however, this can be understood as the passing on of Adam's sin to all future generations of people, since human nature has been infected by sin in general. A disposition towards sin became hereditary and responsibility for turning away from God is universal. As St Cyril of Alexandria states, human nature itself has 'fallen ill with sin';[66] thus we all share Adam's sin as we all share his nature. St Macarius of Egypt speaks of 'a leaven of evil passions'[67] and of 'secret impurity and the abiding darkness of passions',[68] which have entered into our nature in spite of our original purity. Sin became so deeply rooted in human nature that not a single descendant of Adam has been spared from a hereditary predisposition to it.

The Old Testament writers had a vivid sense of their inherited sinfulness: 'Behold, I was brought forth in iniquity, and in sin did my mother conceive me' (Ps. 51:5). They believed that God 'visits the iniquity of the fathers upon the children to the third and the fourth generation' (Exod. 20:5), which refers not to innocent children but to those whose own sinfulness is rooted in the sins of their ancestors.

Objectively speaking, it would be unjust to punish the entire human race for Adam's sin. Many theologians in recent centuries, labouring under the concept of 'religion solely within the bounds of reason',[69] have rejected this doctrine as being incompatible with deductive logic. No Christian dogma, however, has ever been fully comprehended by reason. Religion within the bounds of reason is not religion but naked rationalism, for faith transcends reason and logic. The doctrine of original sin is disclosed in the light of divine revelation and acquires full meaning when seen against the dogma of humanity's atonement through the New Adam, Christ:

... As one man's trespass led to condemnation for all men, so one man's act of righteousness leads to acquittal and life for all men. For as by one man's disobedience many were made sinners, so by one man's obedience many will be made righteous ... so that, as sin reigned in death, grace also might reign through righteousness to eternal life through Jesus Christ our Lord.

(Rom. 5:18–21)

## ANTICIPATING THE MESSIAH

Despite humanity's falling away from God, the divine plan did not alter. As before, human beings were predestined to deification, but now it was no longer within their power: a Mediator was needed who would reconcile humanity with God. This is made clear by God himself, who, at the moment of Adam's and Eve's expulsion from Paradise, says to the devil: 'I will put enmity between you and the woman, and between your seed and her seed; it shall bruise your head, and you shall bruise his heel' (Gen. 3:15). In the Septuagint we read 'he shall watch against your head'. The male pronoun 'he' does not agree with the word 'seed', which is neuter and usually denotes 'posterity'; but in the present context it has been taken by Christian commentators to mean a concrete person ('seed' can also mean 'son' or 'descendant') who will watch after the devil's head.

The anticipation of the Messiah-Redeemer is a leitmotif throughout the entire Old Testament. We can recall, for example, Jacob's words, as he lay dying and spoke directly of the Reconciler, who would come from the tribe of Judah: 'The sceptre shall not depart from Judah ... until he comes to whom it belongs; and to him shall be the obedience of the peoples' (Gen. 49:10). The whole of the second psalm speaks prophetically of the Messiah, who is referred to as the Son of God and the Christ (the Anointed One): 'The kings of the earth set themselves, and the rulers take counsel together, against the LORD and his anointed ... The LORD ... said to me, "You are my son, today I have begotten you"' (Ps. 2:2, 7).

Some of the most striking prophecies about the Messiah are found in the book of Isaiah. The prophet speaks of the birth of the Messiah from a Virgin: 'Behold, a virgin shall conceive and bear a son, and shall call his name Immanuel, that is, God is with us' (Isa. 7:14). Isaiah foretells the birth of the Child,[70] and the descent of the Holy Spirit upon him.[71] Particularly striking are the prophecies about the sufferings of the Messiah:

As many were astonished at him – his appearance was so marred, beyond human semblance, and his form beyond that of the sons of men – so shall he startle many nations; kings shall shut their mouths because of him; for that which has not been told them they shall see, and that which they have not heard they shall understand. Who has believed what we have heard? And to whom has the arm of the LORD been revealed? For he grew up before him like a young plant, and like a root out of dry ground; he had no form or comeliness that we should look at him, and no beauty that we should desire him ... Surely he has borne our griefs and carried our sorrows; yet we esteemed him stricken, smitten by God and afflicted. But he was wounded for our transgressions, he was bruised for our iniquities ... and with his stripes we are healed. All we like sheep have gone astray; we have turned every one to his own way; and the LORD has laid on him the iniquity of us all. He was oppressed, and he was afflicted, yet he opened not his mouth ... And they made his grave with the wicked and with a rich man in his death, although he had done no violence, and there was no deceit in his mouth.

(Isa. 52:14–53:2; 53:4–7, 9)

Isaiah speaks of Christ with such power and realism as only a person who has seen Christ could. The prophets were witnesses to Christ before his coming – the Holy Spirit revealed the future to them, and they spoke about it as though it were the present. St Peter writes that the Spirit of Christ dwelt within the prophets: 'The prophets who prophesied of the grace that was to be yours searched and inquired about this salvation; they inquired what person or time was indicated by the Spirit of Christ within them when predicting the sufferings of Christ and the subsequent glory' (I Pet. 1:10–11). The spiritual insight of the prophets anticipated what would be revealed in the New Testament and prepared the people of Israel to meet the Messiah. The last of the prophets, John the Baptist, was the first of the apostles: he foretold the coming of Christ and also bore witness to him when he came. John the Baptist stands on the bridge between two eras, completing one and opening another: it was in his person that the Old Testament encountered the New.

In the years leading directly up to the birth of Christ the expectation of a Messiah was universal. 'I know that Messiah is coming (he who is called Christ); when he comes he will show us all things', says the simple Samaritan woman (John 4:25). Not only the people of Israel but also the pagan world dreamed of a 'golden age'. The Roman poet Virgil in the first century BCE spoke of a mysterious Child, whose birth would mark the beginning of a new blessed era of salvation.[72] 'Virgil gazed into the future and unwittingly spoke in the language of Isaiah and truly became a prophet of the classical world', writes Father Alexander Men.[73] Humankind languished in keen expectancy of the coming into the world of the Saviour.

## The crown of creation

The world is beautiful – the creation of a mighty God. But there is nothing more beautiful than man, a true man – the son of God.

*Archimandrite Sophrony*

## The pre-eternal counsel

It is worthy of our attention than when the foundation was put on the specious world and its basic parts thus comprising a whole, creation was completed in seeming haste . . . The formation of the human person was preceded by a counsel, and the future creature was sketched out by the Artist: what it was to be, what type of prototype the likeness was to bear within itself, what it will exist for, what it will do after creation and what it is to have dominion over – all of this was foreseen by the Word so that the human person could assume a dignity higher than his being, acquire power over creatures before he himself would come into existence. For it is said: 'Then God said, "Let us make man in our image, after our likeness" ' (Gen. 1:26) . . . O wonder! The sun is created, and there is no counsel to proceed it, the same with the heavens, yet there is nothing its equal in the created world . . . It is only with the formation of the human person that the Maker approaches with a forethought so that . . . his image could be assimilated to the prototypal beauty . . .

*St Gregory of Nyssa*

## 'Man stands in the heart of God's creation'

According to the Orthodox worldview, God has formed two levels of created things: first the 'noetic', 'spiritual' or 'intellectual' level, and secondly, the material or bodily. On the first level God formed the angels, who have no material body. On the second level he formed the physical universe – the galaxies, stars and planets, with the various types of mineral, vegetable and animal life. Man, and man alone, exists on both levels at once. Through his spirit or spiritual intellect he participates in the noetic realm and is a companion of the angels; through his body and soul, he moves and feels and thinks, he eats and drinks . . . Our human nature is thus more complex than the angelic, and endowed with richer potentialities. Viewed in this context, man is not lower but higher than the angels . . . Man stands at the heart of God's creation. Participating as he does in both the noetic and the material realms, he is an image, or mirror of the whole creation, *imago mundi*, a 'little universe' or microcosm. All created things have their meeting place in him . . . St Irenaeus states the same: 'The glory of God is a living man.' The human person forms the centre and crown of God's creation.

*Bishop Kallistos of Diokleia*

## 'God alone can heal this illness . . .'

In the beginning God created the human person, He placed him in Paradise, as Holy Scripture tells us, embellished him with virtue and gave him the commandment not to taste of the tree in the centre of Paradise. And he found himself in the enjoyment of Paradise, in prayer and contemplation, in all glory and honour, possessing healthy senses and finding himself in his natural (condition) in which he was created. For God created the human person according to His image, that is, immortal, free, made beautiful through virtue. Yet when he transgressed the commandment by tasting of the fruit of the tree which God had forbidden him to taste of, he was then expelled from Paradise, fell away from his natural condition and entered a condition contrary to his nature, that is, sin, vainglory, a thirst for mundane pleasures and other passions which possessed him, for he had become their slave through disobedience. The evil began to grow gradually and death began to reign. Nowhere could there be found veneration for God, and all around there was ignorance of God . . . Thus the good God gave people the law as an aid for conversion and for the correcting of evil, but it was not corrected. He sent the Prophets, yet they were without success. For evil had gained the upper hand, as the Prophet Isaiah says: 'From the sole of the foot even to the head, there is no soundness in it, but bruises and sores and bleeding wounds; they are not pressed out, or bound up, or softened with oil' (Isa. I:6). It is as though he had said that evil does not reside in one place but in the whole body, has embraced the whole soul, possessed all of its powers . . . God alone can heal this illness . . .

*St Dorotheos of Gaza*

[ 75 ]

### *The consequences of the Fall*

Adam was created pure by God for service to Him, and placed at the service of Adam was all of creation, for Adam had been placed as lord and king of all creation. But when the word of evil found access to him and spoke with him, Adam at first perceived it with his external hearing, and then this word penetrated into his heart and embraced his entire being. And thus after the captivity of Adam the whole of creation subject to him also fell into captivity, for through it death began to reign over every soul and, as a result of Adam's disobedience, so distorted his image that people changed and went even as far as worshipping demons. For now the fruits of the earth, created by God, are offered to demons: on their altars are laid bread, wine, oil and animals. Even their [the pagans'] sons and daughters are sacrificed to the demons.

*St Macarius of Egypt*

### *'You bear the very same wounds . . .'*

When Adam fell and died for God, the Maker grieved for him: the angels, all the hosts, the heavens, the earth and all creation mourned his death and fall. For the creatures saw that he who had been given to them as king had become a slave of a contrary and evil power. Thus he cloaked his soul in darkness, bitter and cunning darkness, for now the prince of darkness reigned over him. He was now that same man beaten by robbers and left for dead when he left Jerusalem for Jericho (Luke 10:30). And Lazarus, whom the Lord raised from the dead, the same Lazarus, filled with a great stench so that nobody could approach his tomb, was the image of Adam who had taken into his soul the great stench and who had been filled with blackness and darkness. Yet when you hear of Adam, of the man beaten by the robbers, of Lazarus, do not let your mind wander as though across mountains, rather enclose yourself in your own soul, for you bear the very same wounds, the very same stench, the very same darkness. All of us are children of this darkened generation . . . We have been wounded by such an incurable wound that only the Lord can heal it. For this reason He came, for none of the Old Testament righteous, nor the law, nor the prophets could heal this wound.

*St Macarius of Egypt*

## 'Humankind thirsted for Godmanhood . . .'

It is not only the Holy Writ of the Old Testament that is replete with
prophecies of the coming Redeemer from sin and its consequences – death
and hell: the expectation of the coming God, the conqueror of hell, the
suffering one, the one who dies and is resurrected like lightning cleaved
the darkness of the pagan mind . . . Humankind thirsted for
Godmanhood . . . The prophecy of the suffering god who descends into hell
for proud and wicked Prometheus is one of the most striking images in
Aeschylus. Hermes turns to Prometheus and says: 'Know that your
sufferings will cease only when one of the gods consents to descend instead
of you into the dark kingdom of Hades, into the gloomy depths of the
netherworld.'

*V. Ilyin*

## Adam's lament

Adam . . . in Paradise knew the sweetness of the love of God; and so when
for his sin he was driven forth from the garden of Eden, and was widowed
of the love of God, he suffered grievously and lamented with a mighty
moan . . . He sorrowed less after Paradise and the beauty thereof – he
sorrowed that he was bereft of the love of God, which insatiably, at every
instant, draws the soul to Him . . . Adam pined on earth and wept bitterly,
and the earth was not pleasing to him. He was heartsick for God, and this
was his cry:

> 'My soul wearies for the Lord, and I seek Him in tears.
> How should I not seek Him? . . .
> I cannot forget Him for a single moment,
> and my soul languishes after Him . . .'

Adam knew great grief when he was banished from Paradise,
but when he saw his son Abel slain by Cain his brother,
    Adam's grief was even heavier.
His soul was heavy, and he lamented and thought:
'Peoples and nations will descend from me, and multiply,
and suffering will be their lot, and they will live in enmity and seek
    to slay one another.'
And his sorrow stretched wide as the sea,
and only the soul that has come to know the Lord and the magnitude
    of His love for us can understand . . .
Adam lost the earthly Paradise and sought it in weeping. But the

Lord through His love on
the Cross gave Adam another Paradise, fairer than the old – a
Paradise in heaven where
shines the Light of the Holy Trinity.
      What shall we render unto the Lord for His love to us?
*St Silouan of Mount Athos*

### Chapter Six

# CHRIST

## THE NEW ADAM

At the heart of all the good news of the New Testament is the mystery of the Incarnation of the Son of God.

The first Adam, the progenitor of the human race, was unable to fulfil the vocation laid before him: to achieve deification and bring to God the visible world by means of spiritual and moral perfection. Having broken the commandment and fallen away from the sweetness of Paradise, he had closed the way to deification. Yet everything that the first man left undone was accomplished in his stead by God Incarnate, the Word-become-flesh, the Lord Jesus Christ. He trod that path to us which we were meant to tread towards him. And if this would have been the way of humanity's ascent, for God it was the way of humble condescension, of self-emptying (*kenosis*).

St Paul calls Christ the 'second Adam'. Contrasting him with the first, he says: 'The first man was from the earth, a man of dust; the second man is from heaven' (I Cor. 15:47). This parallelism was developed by St John Chrysostom, who referred to Adam as the prototype of Christ:

Adam is the image of Christ . . . as the man for those who came from him, even though they did not eat of the tree, became the cause of death, then Christ for those who were born of him, although they have done no good, became the bearer of righteousness, which he gave to all of us through the Cross.[1]

Gregory the Theologian makes a detailed comparison between Christ's sufferings and Adam's fall:

For each of our debts we are given to in a special way . . . The tree of the Cross has been given for the tree we tasted of; for our hand stretched out greedily, we have been given arms courageously extended; for our hands following their own inclination, we have been given hands nailed to the Cross; for the hand that has driven out Adam, we have been given arms uniting the ends of the earth into one. For our fall we have been given his raising up on a Cross; for our tasting of the forbidden fruit, we have been given his tasting of bile; for our death, his death; for our return to the earth, his burial.[2]

Few people accepted the second Adam or believed in him when he came to earth. The Incarnate Christ, who suffered and was raised, became 'a stumbling block to Jews and folly (*skandalon*) to Gentiles' (I Cor. 1:23). Declaring himself to be God and making himself equal to God,[3] Jesus scandalised the religious hierarchy and was accused of blasphemy. At the question of Caiaphas, 'Are you the Christ, the Son of the Blessed?', Jesus replied 'I am', at which the high priest tore his garments as though he had heard the most terrible blasphemy.[4] We do not know for certain how Christ's 'I am' sounded in Aramaic, but was this not the very same sacred name of God, *Yahweh* ('I am what I am'), which nobody had the right to utter, apart from the high priest once a year when he went into the Holy of Holies?

So far as the Greeks were concerned, Christianity was folly because their way of thinking sought a logical, rational explanation for everything; it was powerless to comprehend a suffering and dying God. For many centuries Greek religion and philosophy had raised a temple to 'an unknown God' (Acts 17:23). For the Greeks, this unknowable, incomprehensible, all-powerful, omniscient God could never become a mortal, suffering, weak human person. A God, born of a Virgin, nursed in swaddling clothes, who slept and was fed with milk? All of this seemed absurd to the Greeks.

Even among early Christians, the mystery of 'godmanhood' was explained in a number of different ways. In the second century, the Docetists claimed that Christ's human nature was merely transparent: it only *seemed* that he suffered and died on the Cross, while God in fact, being passionless, could not suffer at all.[5] The Docetists considered all that was material to be evil and could not concede that God had put on sinful and evil flesh, that he had united himself with dust. At the other extreme was the teaching of Arianism, which denied Christ's divinity and reduced the Son of God to the level of created being. How were these extremes to be avoided and how was the Church to find an authentic understanding of the mystery of Christ?

## THE CHRIST OF THE GOSPELS: GOD AND MAN

In the gospels Jesus Christ is described as possessing all the attributes of an ordinary human being. He is born and grows, eats and drinks, becomes tired and sleeps, mourns and rejoices. Many, especially in recent times, have attempted to reconstruct an image of the 'historical Christ'. By contrasting him with the 'Christ of faith' or the 'Christ of believers', they have discarded all that is miraculous and 'mystical' in the gospels and have kept only what agrees with 'common sense'. This is the general thrust of *La Vie de Jésus* by Ernest Renan, where Christ's miracles are regarded as 'hocus pocus': he *thought* he was accomplishing miracles, when in reality there were none. Leo Tolstoy went even further: in his *Interpretation of the Gospel* he does his utmost to disprove not only Christ's birth from the Virgin, but also his Transfiguration, Resurrection and Ascension, and all of the healings and miracles. Tolstoy's 'version' of the gospel resembles a caricature:

The sick man waits for twenty years for a miracle. Jesus looked at him and says: in vain have you waited for a miracle here from an angel, there are no miracles. Wake up. Gather up your bed and live according to God. The sick man tried this, arose and went away . . . I knew a young noble girl who lay in bed for twenty years and got up only when she was sprinkled with morphine. Twenty years went by and the doctor who sprinkled her admitted that he had done it with water, and when she learnt of this, the woman took up her bed and left.[6]

In these writings human suffering is cynically mocked, and healing is reduced to charlatanism. The so-called 'historical Christ', who is free from the 'veneer of mysticism and miracles', is transformed at best, as with Renan, into a Christ of human fantasy, a cloying portrait that has little in common with the real Christ. At worst, as with Tolstoy, it all ends with a parody on the gospels, a blasphemy against God and humanity.

We come to know the real, living Christ when we accept the entire gospel, down to the last letter, as the revelation of divine truth. The gospel is not a book to be comprehended by human reason: from beginning to end it is replete with miracles and is in itself a miracle and sacrament. Indeed, the very first chapters are a testimony to the divinity of Christ and the existence of angels and the devil. Matthew begins by telling us about Christ's birth from a Virgin without a husband; Mark speaks of Christ's temptation in the desert and his encounter with the devil; Luke describes the appearance of the archangel at the Annunciation; and John claims that the Word became flesh, and the Son of God a human being. They confront us with a choice: to be humble, submitting ourselves to faith and the revelation of the Divinity, or to close the book since it contradicts 'human reason'.

From the outset the Christ of the gospels is simultaneously revealed as both God and man: all his actions and words are those of a human being which, nonetheless, are marked with the divine imprint. Jesus is born like all other children, but from the Holy Spirit and the Virgin rather than from a husband and a wife. Brought into the Temple like other infants, he is greeted by a prophet and prophetess who recognise him as the Messiah. Jesus grows and becomes strong in spirit while living at his parents' home, yet at the age of twelve he sits in the Temple among the teachers and utters mysterious words about his Father. Like others, he comes to be baptised in the Jordan, but at the moment of immersion the voice of the Father is heard and the Holy Spirit appears in the form of a dove. Tired from a journey, he sits by a well and asks a Samaritan woman to quench his thirst, yet he neither drinks nor eats when offered food by his disciples. He sleeps in the stern of a boat, but subdues a violent storm upon waking. Ascending Mount Tabor, he prays to God as any other person, but is transfigured and reveals the light of his divinity to the apostles. At the tomb of Lazarus he mourns the death of a friend, yet with the words 'Lazarus, arise!' he raises him from the dead. In fear Jesus prays to his Father to remove the cup of suffering, but surrenders himself to the Father's will and agrees to die for the life of the world. Finally, he accepts humiliation and crucifixion, and dies on the Cross like a criminal, yet on the third day he rises from the tomb and appears to his disciples.

The gospels speak uncompromisingly of Christ's godmanhood. We should note that, though inspired by God, the gospels were written by living people, each of whom described events as he saw and understood them, or as he heard about them from witnesses.[7] In the four gospel accounts there are differences in detail, but these differences bear testimony to their unity rather than to contradiction. Had the narratives been absolutely identical, we could presume that their authors conferred among themselves or copied from each other. The gospels are testimonies of eyewitnesses, in which each detail deserves our faith, even though presented from different perspectives. The gospels complement each other, each distinct in its length, its narrative style, and the material used. If the first three unfold events according to their chronological order, the fourth draws attention to isolated occurrences which are provided to serve as illustrations of particular theological themes. Thus, the encounter with the Samaritan woman at the well illustrates Christ as 'the living Water of life'; the feeding of the five thousand is introduced in conjunction with his saying 'I am the Bread of life'; the healing of the blind man is evidence that Christ is the 'Light of the world'; the raising of Lazarus confirms his words, 'I am the Resurrection and the Life.'

## THE CHRIST OF FAITH: TWO NATURES

Holy Scripture is the main source of our knowledge about God in general and about Christ in particular. Yet Scripture can be understood and interpreted in various ways; indeed, all heresies have been underpinned by references to Scripture and quotations from the Bible. It is therefore essential to find some criteria for a correct understanding of the Bible. For the Church the criterion is Holy Tradition, of which Scripture is a part. Tradition comprises the centuries-old experience of the life of the Church, reflected not only in Scripture but also in the acts and definitions of faith of the Ecumenical Councils, in the works of the Church Fathers and in liturgical worship.

Tradition is not merely a supplement to Scripture; it bears testimony to the permanent and living presence of Christ in the Church. The authors of the New Testament books emphasise that they are 'witnesses': 'That which was from the beginning, which we have heard, which we have seen with our eyes, which we have looked upon and touched with our hands, concerning the word of life – the life was made manifest, and we saw it, and testify to it, and proclaim to you the eternal life which was with the Father and was made manifest to us' (I John I:1–2). Yet Christ continues to live in the Church, and the experience of contact with him, of life in him, engenders a new witness which is fixed in Tradition. The gospels speak of Christ as both divine and human, and Church Tradition was faced with the task of formulating a dogma concerning the unity of divinity and humanity in Christ. This dogma was developed in the course of the christological debates of the fourth to the seventh centuries.

### Controversies leading to the christological formula of Chalcedon

In the second half of the fourth century, Apollinarius of Laodicea spoke of the pre-eternal God-Logos who took human flesh; in his opinion, Christ did not possess a human intellect or soul. In the person of Christ divinity merged with human flesh, which together comprised a single nature. Hence Apollinarius's celebrated formula (later employed by St Cyril of Alexandria): 'one nature of God the Word incarnate'. According to the Apollinarian teaching, Christ could not be fully consubstantial with humans as he had no human intellect or soul. He was a 'heavenly man' who had merely assumed a human shell, not a complete earthly human being.

Diodorus of Tarsus and Theodore of Mopsuestia represent another tendency in christological thinking. They taught that within Christ there were two separate, independent natures which related to each other in the following way: God the Logos lived in the man Jesus of Nazareth, whom he had chosen and anointed and with whom he had 'come into contact' and 'cohabited'. The union of humanity with the Divinity was not absolute but relative: the Logos resided in Christ as in a temple. The earthly life of Jesus, Theodore believed, was the life of a human being in contact with the Logos. God foresaw from eternity the highly virtuous life of Jesus and in view of this elected him as his instrument and as the temple of his divinity. At first, at the moment of birth, this contact was incomplete, but as Jesus grew in spiritual and moral perfection it became fully realised.

In the fifth century Theodore's disciple, Nestorius, Patriarch of Constantinople, followed his teacher in separating Christ's two natures, making a distinction between the Lord and the 'form of a servant', the temple and the 'One who lives in it', the Almighty God and the 'man who is worshipped'. Nestorius preferred to refer to the Holy Virgin as *Christotokos* (the Birth Giver, or Mother of Christ) and not *Theotokos* (the Birth Giver, or Mother of God), for, he said, Mary did not give birth to the Divinity. Popular disturbance regarding the term *Theotokos* (the people refused to renounce this attribution of the Virgin Mary which had been sanctified by Tradition), together with St Cyril of Alexandria's powerful attack on Nestorianism, led to the convening in 431 of the Third Ecumenical Council in Ephesus, which formulated (though not definitively) the Church's doctrine on the God-man.

In speaking about the Son of God, the Council of Ephesus chiefly used the terminology of St Cyril, who taught not the 'contact' but the 'union' of the two natures in Christ. At the Incarnation God appropriated human nature to himself, while remaining at the same time who he is: although perfect and complete God, he had become a human being in the fullest sense. In order to counteract Theodore and Nestorius, Cyril constantly asserted that Christ was a single Person, a single Hypostasis. Thus Mary gave birth to the same Person as God the Word. Following this reasoning, St Cyril thought that to renounce the title *Theotokos* would mean to renounce the mystery of the Incarnation of God, for God the Word and Jesus the man are one and the same.

Thus we confess that our Lord Jesus Christ, the only-begotten Son of God, is perfect God and perfect man, consisting of a rational soul and body, that he was begotten from the Father before all ages according to the Divinity, and that in these latter times was begotten for us and for our salvation from the Virgin Mary; that he is consubstantial with the Father in his Divinity and consubstantial with us in his humanity, for in him there was accomplished the unity of two natures. Therefore we acknowledge one Christ, one Son, one Lord. On the basis of this union without confusion we confess the Most Holy Virgin to be the Mother of God because God the Word was incarnate and became man and in the conception itself united with himself the temple received from her . . . God the Word came down from heaven and, taking the form of a servant, emptied himself, and was called the Son of man, remaining that which he is – God.[8]

By the middle of the fifth century, a new wave of christological debates became linked with the names of Eutyches, an archimandrite from Constantinople, and his supporter Dioscorus, St Cyril's successor to the episcopal throne of Alexandria. Eutyches spoke in terms of the complete 'merging' of the Divinity with the humanity into a 'single incarnate nature of God the Word': this formula, which was used by Cyril (but derived from Apollinarius), became his motto. 'I confess that our Lord consisted of two natures before the union, but after the union I confess one nature', said Eutyches.

The Fourth Ecumenical Council, convened in 451 at Chalcedon, condemned Eutychian Monophysitism (insistence on one nature in Christ) and proclaimed the dogma of 'a single hypostasis of God the Word in two natures, divine and human'. The Orthodox doctrine had been articulated by St Leo, Pope of Rome, even before the Council began:

. . . He is one and the same, truly Son of God, and truly Son of Man. He is God, in so far as *In the beginning was the Word, and the Word was with God, and the Word was God.*[9] He is Man, in so far as *The Word became flesh, and dwelt among us* . . . [10] The nativity of the flesh is a manifestation of human nature; the Virgin's child-bearing is an indication of divine power. The infancy of the Baby is exhibited by the humiliation of swaddling clothes: the greatness of the Highest is declared by the voices of angels . . . To hunger, to thirst, to be weary, and to sleep, is evidently human. But to satisfy five thousand men with five loaves, and give to the Samaritan woman that living water to draw which can secure him that drinks of it from ever thirsting again; to walk on the surface of the sea with feet that sink not, and by rebuking the storm to bring down the 'uplifted waves', is unquestionably divine. As then ... it does not belong to the same nature to weep with feelings of pity over a dead friend and ... by a voice of command to raise him up to life again ... so it does not belong to the same nature to say, *I and the Father are one*, and to say, *My Father is greater than I.*[11]

Thus each nature preserves the fullness of its properties, yet Christ is not divided into two persons; he remains the single hypostasis of God the Word. This belief was expressed in the Council's dogmatic definition:

Thus in following the Holy Fathers we all of one accord confess one and the same Son, our Lord Jesus Christ, perfect in Divinity, perfect in humanity, truly God, truly human being, with a rational soul and body, consubstantial with the Father in His Divinity and consubstantial with us in his humanity, in all things like us except sin, begotten before all ages according to the Divinity, and in these latter times for us and for our salvation from the Virgin Mary and the Mother of God according to his humanity, one and the same Christ, the Son, the Only-begotten Lord, discerned in two natures without confusion, without change, without division, without separation, as the difference in the two natures is in no way destroyed by the union; moreover, the attributes of each nature are preserved and united in one Person, one Hypostasis – not into two divided persons, but one and the same Only-begotten Son, God the Word, our Lord Jesus Christ.[12]

These clearly defined formulas demonstrate the refinement and insight of theological thought in the fifth century. At the same time they show the caution with which the Church Fathers used different terms and formulae in trying to 'express the inexpressible'. Four terms, each of which was strictly apophatic, were used to convey the union of the two natures: 'without confusion, without change, without division, without separation'. The union of the divine and human natures in Christ is a mystery which transcends the intellect and no language is capable of describing it. Precise formulations state the ways in which the natures are *not* united: this is to avoid heresies which could confuse, change and divide the natures. However, precisely how the natures *are* united remains concealed from human understanding.

### Energy and will: Maximus and the Monothelites

In the sixth century some theologians, while confessing the two natures of Christ, spoke of him as having a single divine-human 'action', a single energy. Hence the name of the heresy called Monoenergism. Again, at the beginning of the seventh century, a new movement arose, Monothelitism, which recognised only a divine will in Christ, claiming that his human will was completely swallowed up by the divine. Apart from pursuing purely theological goals, the Monothelites hoped to reconcile the Orthodox with the Monophysites (those who held to the belief in one nature in Christ) by means of a compromise.

In the middle of the seventh century there were two main opponents of Monothelitism: Maximus the Confessor, a monk from Constantinople, and St Martin, the Pope of Rome. St Maximus taught that Christ had two energies and two wills: 'Christ, being God by nature, made use of a will which was naturally divine and paternal, for he had but one will with his Father; being himself man by nature, he also made use of a naturally human will which was in no way opposed to the Father's will.'[13] Christ's human will is especially evident in his prayer in the garden of Gethsemane: 'My Father, if it be possible, let this cup pass from me; nevertheless, not as I will, but as thou wilt' (Matt. 26:39). This prayer would have been impossible had the human will of Christ been fully swallowed up by the divine.

For his determination to confess the Christ of the gospels, St Maximus was subjected to cruel punishment: his tongue was cut out and his right hand cut off. Like St Martin, he died in exile. Nonetheless, the Sixth Ecumenical Council of Constantinople, 680–1, twenty years after Maximus's death, upheld his teaching in its entirety: 'We preach that in him [Christ] there are two natural wills and desires, and two natural energies without confusion, without change, without division, without separation. These two natural wills are not opposed to each other ... but his human will submits itself to the divine and omnipotent will.'[14] As a fully human person, Christ possessed free will, but this freedom did not mean the choice between good and evil. The human will of Christ freely chooses only the good: his human will is in total conformity with the divine.

In these ways the mystery of the divine-human person of Christ, the New Adam and Saviour of the world, was made manifest in the theological experience of the Church.


## REDEMPTION

### Redemption as a ransom – paid to whom?

In the New Testament Christ is called the 'ransom', or 'redemption', for the sins of the human race.[15] The original Greek word *lytrosis* means 'ransom', that is, a sum of money paid to give freedom to a slave or to save the life of someone sentenced to death. Having fallen into the slavery of sin,[16] we needed redemption in order to be liberated from this slavery.

Early Church writers posed the question: to whom did Christ pay this ransom? Some suggested that it was paid to the devil, through whom human beings had become enslaved. Origen, for example, asserted that the Son of God surrendered his spirit into the hands of the Father and gave his soul to the devil as a ransom for humanity: 'To whom did the Redeemer give his soul as a ransom for many? Not to God, but to the devil ... The soul of the Son of God was given as a ransom for us, and not his spirit, for he had already surrendered it to his Father with the words *Father, into Thy hands I commit my spirit*,[17] nor his body, as we find no indication of this in Scripture.'[18] Gregory the Theologian, however, rebuked Origen for his interpretation of redemption: 'If the great and most glorious blood of God the high priest and sacrifice is given as the price of redemption to the evil one, then how grievous this is! The brigand receives not only the price of the ransom from God, but God himself!'[19]

According to Gregory of Nyssa, the redemption was a 'deception' and 'bargain with the devil'. In order to ransom the human race, Christ offers the devil his very own flesh, 'concealing' the divinity within it. The devil rushes on this bait, but swallows the 'hook', Christ's divinity, along with it, and perishes. To the question whether 'deception' is an immoral act inappropriate to the Divinity, St Gregory answers that since the devil himself is a deceiver, it is completely just that God should deceive him: 'The devil used deceit for the corruption of nature, while the just, good and most wise God used the fabrication of deception to save that which had been corrupted, thereby bringing good not only to the human race which had perished but to the one who had caused our destruction (the devil) ... Therefore it would not seem wholly unjust to the enemy should he feel this goodness.'[20]

Other Fathers speak of how the devil was 'deceived', but do not go so far as to say that God deceived him. In a work ascribed to John Chrysostom, we hear that hell was 'mocked' by Christ's Resurrection and 'fell' when it did not recognise the invisible God beneath the visible man: 'Hades was embittered when it met thee face to face below ... It was embittered, for it was mocked ... It received a body, and it encountered God. It received earth, and came face to face with Heaven. It received that which it saw, and fell whence it saw not.'[21] In one of the three 'kneeling' prayers read at Pentecost, it is said that Christ 'enticed, by divinely wise allurements, the origin of mischief and the serpent of the abyss'.[22]

A different interpretation, articulated by some Western medieval theologians,[23] maintained that the ransom was not paid to the devil, who has no power over humans, but to God the Father. It was claimed that humanity's Fall aroused God's anger and divine justice necessarily required satisfaction. Since no human sacrifice could be sufficient, the Son of God himself became the ransom in order to satisfy divine justice. By his death, grace was returned to the human race. The acquisition of this grace is nevertheless impossible without certain virtues, such as faith and good works. Since human beings do not of themselves possess these virtues, they can derive them from Christ and the saints, who in their lives accomplished more good works than was necessary for their salvation, and so had them in abundance to share. This theory, which rose at the heart of Latin scholastic theology, is legalistic in character, and reflects the medieval concept of an offended honour that demands satisfaction. According to this understanding, the death of Christ does not abolish sin, but merely liberates us from suffering its full consequences.

The Eastern Orthodox Church reacted against this understanding in the twelfth century.[24] The Local Council of Constantinople, convened in 1157, examined and condemned the teaching of Soterichos Panteugenes, whose understanding of redemption resembled that of his Western contemporaries. The participants at this Council, among whom St Nicholas of Methone was a leading figure, agreed that Christ brought his redemptive sacrifice not to the Father alone, but to the Trinity as a whole:

Christ voluntarily offered himself as a sacrifice, offered himself in his humanity and himself accepted the sacrifice as God with the Father and the Spirit . . . The God-man of the Word offered his redemptive sacrifice to the Father, to himself as God, and to the Spirit, through whom the human person is called from non-being into being, whom he has offended in breaking the commandment and with whom reconciliation has been effected through Christ's sufferings.[25]

The Orthodox Liturgy itself speaks of Christ as the One who both offers and accepts the sacrifice: 'For thou art the Offerer and the Offered, the Receiver and the Received, O Christ our God.'[26] In a homily ascribed to Cyril of Jerusalem, we read:

I see the Child offering a lawful sacrifice on earth, yet I also see him receiving the sacrifice from all in the heavens . . . He is the Gifts, the High Priest, the altar, the purifier, he is the Offerer and he is the Offered as a sacrifice for the world. He is the true fire, he is consummation, he is the Tree of life and knowledge, he is the sword of the Spirit, he is the Pastor and the priest, he is the Law and the One who fulfils the Law.[27]

## Redemption as reconciliation between God and humanity

Many Early Church authors avoid the topic of 'ransom' in the literal sense altogether, taking redemption to mean the reconciliation of the human race with God and our adoption as his children. They speak of redemption as the manifestation of God's love for humanity, a view supported by the words of St John's gospel: 'For God so loved the world that he gave his only Son, that whoever believes in him should not perish but have eternal life' (John 3:16). It is not the anger of God the Father but his love that lies behind the sacrificial death of his Son on the Cross. Symeon the New Theologian believes that Christ himself offers humanity redeemed by him as a gift to God, freeing the human race for all eternity from the power of the devil.[28] Since human beings are enslaved by the devil from birth throughout their lives, the Lord passes through every stage of human development in order that the devil may be vanquished:

[Christ] was made incarnate and was born, sanctifying conception and nativity, and as he gradually grew blessed all ages ... He became a servant, taking the form of a servant and raised us servants of sin to the dignity of masters and made us lord and master over the devil who had before been our tyrant ... In being crucified he became the curse and destroyed all the power and energy of the enemy who had power over us through death and sin.[29]

The Incarnate Christ, in wishing to be like us in all things, not only goes through human development, but also through all types of anguish right up to the most agonising of all: to be abandoned by God. The cry of the Saviour on the Cross, 'My God, my God, why hast thou forsaken me?' (Matt. 27:46), is the culmination of his suffering on Golgotha. Yet the great mystery of this moment lies in the fact that the divinity of Christ is not separated for a single instant from his humanity. God has not left him, although as a human being he feels the human pain of being abandoned by his Father. Even when the body of the dead Christ lay in the tomb, and his soul descended into hell, his divinity is not separated from his humanity: 'In the tomb with the body; in hell with the soul, as God; in Paradise with the thief; and on the throne with the Father and the Spirit wast Thou, O Christ, filling all things, thyself uncircumscribed.'[30] Christ is simultaneously in Paradise and in hell, in heaven and on earth, with the

Father and the Spirit and with people: he fills all things with himself without being 'circumscribed', that is, without being limited by anything.

It is in Christ that the union of God with humans is accomplished:
Do you see the depth of the mysteries? Have you come to know the infinite majesty of the super-abundant glory? . . . Christ will have with us the same union by grace as he has with the Father by nature . . . The glory which the Father gave to the Son, the Son gives to us by grace . . . Once he had become our relative in the flesh and, making us partakers of his divine nature, he thereby made us his relatives . . . We have the same union with Christ as a man has with his wife and the wife with her husband.[31]

### Renewal of the human race

Every human being is recreated and renewed in Christ. The redemptive act of Christ was not accomplished for an abstract 'mass' of people, but for every single individual. As St Symeon says, 'God sent his only-begotten Son to earth for you and for your salvation, for he has seen you and destined you to be his brother and co-heir.'[32]

It is in Christ that the whole history of the human race, including the Fall and expulsion of humans from Paradise, receives justification, perfection and absolute meaning. The Kingdom of heaven, given by Christ to all who believe in him, is something far greater than primordial Eden. It is, in the words of St Peter, 'an inheritance' which is imperishable, undefiled, and unfading' (I Pet. I:4). It is also the 'third heaven' before which St Paul was speechless because the 'things that cannot be told' which were uttered there transcended every human word.[33] The Incarnation of Christ and his redemptive act have even greater meaning for us than the act of our creation. From the moment of God's Incarnation our history begins anew: we find ourselves again face to face with God, even closer to him, perhaps, than the first human beings. Christ brings us into the 'New Paradise', the Church, where he reigns and where we reign together with him.

To whom is Christ's redemptive sacrifice extended? The answer is given in the gospels: to all those who believe in Christ – 'that whoever believes in him should not perish but have eternal life' (John 3:16). Faith in Christ makes us God's children, renders us born of God.[34] Through faith, Baptism and life in the Church we become heirs with Christ of the Kingdom of God, freed from all the consequences of the Fall, and we are raised together with Christ, becoming partakers of eternal life.

It is in Christ that the purpose of human existence is realised:

communion with God, union with God, deification. According to a work ascribed to Maximos the Confessor, God 'yearns for the salvation of all men and hungers after their deification'.[35] In his immeasurable love for us, Christ ascended Golgotha and endured death on the Cross, which reconciled and united the human race with God.

## The mystery of Christ

... It is impossible to put into writing all that belongs to the Saviour's glory. When, therefore, we consider these great and marvellous truths about the nature of the Son of God, we are lost in the deepest amazement that such a being, towering high above all, should have emptied Himself of His majestic condition and become man and dwelt among men ... But of all the marvellous and splendid things about Him there is one that utterly transcends the limits of human wonder and is beyond the capacity of our weak mortal intelligence to think of or understand, namely, how this mighty power of the divine majesty, the very Word of the Father, and the very Wisdom of God, in which were created *all things visible and invisible* (Col. 1:16), can be believed to have existed within the compass of that Man Who appeared in Judaea; yes, and how the Wisdom of God can have entered into a woman's womb and been born as a little child and uttered noises like those of crying children; and further, how it was that He was troubled, as we are told, in the hour of death, as He Himself confesses when He says, *My soul is very sorrowful, even to death* (Matt. 26:38); and how at the last He was led to that death which is considered by men to be the most shameful of all, even though on the third day He rose again. When, therefore, we see in Him some things so human that they appear in no way to differ from the common frailty of mortals, and some things so divine that they are appropriate to nothing else but the primal and ineffable nature of deity, the human understanding with its narrow limits is baffled, and struck with amazement at so mighty a wonder knows not which way to turn, what to hold to, or whither to betake itself. If it thinks of God, it sees a man; if it thinks of a man, it beholds one returning from the dead ... after vanquishing the kingdom of death. For this reason we must pursue our contemplation with all fear and reverence, as we seek to prove how the reality of each nature exists in one and the same person, in such a way that nothing unworthy or unfitting may be thought to reside in that divine and ineffable existence, nor on the other hand may the events of His life be supposed to be the illusions caused by deceptive fantasies. But to utter these things in human ears and to explain them by words far exceeds the powers we possess either in our moral worth or in mind and speech. I think indeed that it transcends the capacity even of the holy apostles; nay more, perhaps the explanation of this mystery lies beyond the reach of the whole creation of heavenly beings.

*Origen*

### 'If anyone does not worship Him Who is crucified . . .'

If anyone says that Christ passed through the Virgin as though through a tube and was not formed within her as both divine and human . . . If anyone says that within the Virgin there first of all was formed a man who then conceded his place to God . . . If anyone believes in two sons – one from God the Father, the other from the Mother, and not one and the same son . . . If anyone says that the Divinity acted graciously within Christ as it did within the prophets and is not conjoined in essence . . . If anyone does not worship Him Who is crucified, then let there be an anathema upon him and may he be counted among the murderers of God.

*St Gregory the Theologian*

### 'Two natures, two natural wills and two natural energies . . .'

We maintain that in one and the same Lord and Saviour Jesus Christ everything is dual, that is, we confess in Him two natures . . . We confess also that each of His natures has natural attributes: the divine has all that which pertains to God, the human all that which pertains to the human being, apart from sin . . . In confessing two natures, two natural wills and two natural energies in our one Lord Jesus Christ, we do not teach that they are opposed and hostile to each other . . . we do not teach that they are divided as though into two persons or hypostases.

*St Agatho of Rome*

### The two wills and two operations

Since, then, Christ has two natures, we say that He has two natural wills and two natural operations. On the other hand, since these two natures have one Person, we say that He is one and the same who wills and acts naturally according to both natures, of which and in which is Christ our God, and which are Christ our God . . . *Coming to the place He said: 'I thirst.' And they offered Him wine to drink, mingled with gall; but when He had tasted it, He would not drink it* (Matt. 27:33–4; John 19:28–9). Now, if it was as God that He thirsted and having tasted did not want to drink, then as God He was subject to passion, for thirst is a passion and so is taste. If, however, it was not as God, then it was entirely as man that He thirsted, and as man also He was volitive . . . Now, we also say that in our Lord Jesus Christ there are two operations . . . While the power of working miracles was an operation of His divinity, the work of His hands, His willing, and His saying, *I will; be clean* (Matt. 8:3) were operations belonging to His humanity. And as to the effect, the breaking of the loaves, the healing of the leper, and the 'I will' belongs to His human nature, whereas to His divine nature belongs the multiplication of the loaves and the cleansing of the leper.

*St John Damascene*

## The hypostatic union

Even after the union the natures remained unmingled and their properties unimpaired. Moreover, by reason of its most unalloyed union with the Word, that is to say, the hypostatic union, the Lord's flesh was enriched with the divine operations but in no way suffered any impairment of its natural properties. For not by its own operation does the flesh do divine works, but by the Word united to it, and through it the Word shows His own operation. Thus the steel which has been heated burns, not because it has a naturally acquired power of burning, but because it has acquired it from its union with the fire. And so the same flesh was mortal by itself and life-giving by its hypostatic union with the Word. Likewise, we say that the deification of the will was not by a transformation of its natural motion, but by its being united with His divine and almighty will and being the will of God made man.

*St John Damascene*

## 'Can these things be performed without great love?'

When the entire extent of creation had abandoned and forgotten God and had perfected themselves in every kind of wickedness, of His own will and without any supplication or request from elsewhere He came down to their abode and lived among them in their body just as one of them, and with a love exalted beyond knowledge or description by any created being, He begged them to turn back to Himself, showing them concerning the glorious establishment of the world to come, having intended before all worlds to introduce felicity such as this for creation: He informed them of its existence and forgave them all the sins which they had previously committed, and confirmed this goodwill by means of authoritative signs and wonders, and the revelation to them of His Mysteries; and finally He has stooped down to such an extent that He is willing to be called 'Father' of sinful human nature, dust from the earth, despicable human beings, flesh and blood: can these things be performed without great love?

*St Isaac the Syrian*

## 'He became equal to us in all things except sin'

He is God of God, the Son Who has no beginning, of the Father Who has no beginning, the incorporeal of the incorporeal, the incomprehensible of the incomprehensible, the eternal of the eternal, the unapproachable of the unapproachable, the infinite of the infinite, the immortal of the immortal, the invisible of the invisible, the word of God and God, through Whom all things are brought into being, all that is in heaven and all that is on earth . . . In being such and abiding in the Father and the Father abiding in Him, without being separated from Him and without abandoning Him, He came down to earth and was incarnate of the Holy Spirit and the Virgin Mary, became man and became equal to us in all things except sin so that in experiencing all that which is ours He could restore and renew the first human being and through him restore and renew all those who have been born and are born like their forefather Adam.

*St Symeon the New Theologian*

## 'That which He was not He hath assumed'

O come, let us rejoice in the Lord, as we declare this present mystery: The partition wall of disunion hath been destroyed, the flaming sword is turned back, and the Cherubim withdraw from the Tree of Life, and I partake of the food of Paradise, whence, because of disobedience, I was expelled.
For the Image Immutable of the Father, the Imprint of his Eternity, taketh the form of a servant, having come forth from an unwedded Mother, yet having suffered no change: for that which He was that He remaineth, being very God; and that which He was not He hath assumed, becoming very man because of His love toward mankind. Unto Him let us cry aloud: O God, Who wast born of a Virgin, have mercy upon us.

*Hymn from the Feast of the Nativity of Christ*

### Chapter Seven

# THE CHURCH

## THE KINGDOM OF CHRIST

'There is no Christianity without the Church.' These words were written in the early twentieth century by a Russian Orthodox bishop who became a martyr.[1] The Church is Christ's Kingdom, purchased by the price of his blood. Christ leads into it those he has chosen as his children and who have chosen him as their Saviour.

The first reference to the Church was made by Christ in conversation with his disciples at Caesarea Philippi. When Peter recognised him as the Son of God, Jesus replied: 'Blessed are you, Simon Bar-Jona! For flesh and blood has not revealed this to you, but my Father who is in heaven. And I tell you, you are Peter, and on this rock I will build my church, and the powers of death shall not prevail against it' (Matt. 16:17–18).

Peter's confession, then, became the foundation stone of the Church of Christ. The true foundation of the Church, however, is Christ himself. Indeed, St Peter refers to Christ as the cornerstone: 'Come to him, to that living stone, rejected by men but in God's sight chosen and precious; and like living stones be yourselves built into a spiritual house, to be a holy priesthood, to offer spiritual sacrifices acceptable to God through Jesus Christ' (1 Pet. 2:4–5). St Paul also refers to Christ as the cornerstone: 'You are fellow citizens with the saints and members of the household of God, built upon the foundation of the apostles and prophets, Christ Jesus himself being the cornerstone, in whom the whole structure is joined together and grows into a holy temple in the Lord; in whom you also are built into it for a dwelling place of God in the Spirit' (Eph. 2:19–22). St Paul calls the community of Corinth 'God's building', himself the 'master builder' and Christ the 'foundation': 'For no other foundation can any one lay than that which is laid, which is Jesus Christ' (1 Cor. 2:9, 10, 11).

The Greek word *ekklesia*, meaning 'church', or literally, 'an assembly of people', comes from the verb *ekkaleo*, 'to call'. The Christian Church is an assembly of those called by Christ, who believe in him and live by him. Yet the Church is more than a fellowship of people united by a common faith. Gathered together, the members of the Church comprise a single body, an indivisible organism:

The Church is humanity united with its divine principle in Christ – the living body of the Incarnate Divine Logos. It is the body of Christ, at first appearing as a tiny seed in the form of the small community of the first Christians, it gradually grows and develops in order to embrace the whole of the human race and all nature in a single divine-human organism.[2]

The first to refer to the Church as the body of Christ was St Paul: 'For by one Spirit we were all baptised into one body – Jews or Greeks, slaves or free – and all were made to drink of one Spirit . . . Now you are the body of Christ and individually members of it' (1 Cor. 12:13, 27). Through the sacraments, especially Holy Communion, we are united with him and we become one body in him: 'Because there is one bread, we who are many are one body, for we all partake of the one bread' (1 Cor. 10:17). The Church is the eucharistic body of Christ, and the Eucharist unites us to him and to each other. Moreover, the closer we are to God, the closer we are to each other; the more we are filled with love for Christ, the stronger our love for our neighbour. In being united to God through a life in the sacraments, we are united to each other, we overcome our usual lack of communication and alienation, we become members of an undivided organism bound together in a union of love.

The mystery of the Church was prefigured in the people of Israel, who were chosen and set apart from the other peoples. The Christian Church sees itself as the only legitimate heir to the biblical religion of revelation,[3] preserving and continuing that revelation in her Tradition. The latter includes both the Old and the New Testaments, the memory of Jesus Christ's earthly life, his miracles and teaching, his death and resurrection. It is also comprised of the experience of the primitive Church, the teachings of Early Fathers and Ecumenical Councils, the lives of saints and martyrs, the Liturgy, the sacraments, and the entirety of spiritual and mystical experience, transmitted from generation to generation. In other words, Tradition in Orthodox understanding means the continuity of theological teaching and spiritual experience within the Church from Old Testament times up to the present. As Father Georges Florovsky writes:

Revelation is preserved in the Church. It was given by God to the Church, not to separate individuals, just as in the Old Testament *the words of God*[4] were entrusted not to individuals but to the People of God. Revelation is given, and is accessible only in the Church . . . This means that genuine knowledge is only possible in the element of *Tradition*. Tradition is a very important concept, one which is usually understood too narrowly: as oral tradition in contrast to Scripture. This understanding not only narrows, but also distorts the meaning of Tradition. Sacred Tradition as the 'tradition of truth' – *traditio veritatis*, as St Irenaeus stated – is not only historical memory, not simply an appeal to antiquity and to empirical unchangingness. Tradition is the inner, mystical memory of the Church. It is above all the 'unity of the Spirit', the unity and continuity of the spiritual experience and the life of grace . . . The faithfulness to Tradition is not a loyalty to antiquity but rather the living relationship with the fullness of the Christian life.[5]

It is absolutely essential for a Christian to be a member of the Church, connected with the revelation of God which is preserved in its living memory. The experience of God is given to individuals, but the revelation of God belongs to the whole body of the Church. The personal experience of each individual believer is to be incorporated into the collective memory of the Church. Every person is called to share his experience with others, and to examine it against the revelation which is given to the people as a community. In this way the Christian becomes united with other Christians and the house of the Church is formed from individual stones.

## HEAVEN ON EARTH

'The Church is an earthly heaven, where the heavenly God lives and moves', says St Germanus, Patriarch of Constantinople.[6] God's presence in the Church is real and tangible. We believe that at his Ascension into heaven after the Resurrection, Christ did not abandon his disciples, but remained among them in a mysterious way, 'in no way parted from those that love thee, but abiding always with them'.[7] His promise that 'I am with you always, to the close of the age' (Matt. 28:20) is fulfilled in the Church which he founded as the place where he encounters and speaks with people. Along with Christ, the Mother of God and the multitude of angels and saints are invisibly present, all of whom participate in the Liturgy with the people. The heavenly Church – the angels and the departed, and the Church on earth – the living people, are united into the one body of Christ, single and indivisible.

Occasionally, people visiting an Orthodox service for the first time, or even finding themselves by chance in an empty church, feel an invisible presence. Bishop Kallistos of Diokleia describes his first visit to a Russian church in London at the age of seventeen:

As I entered St Philip's – for that was the name of the church – at first I thought it was entirely empty ... The first thing that caught my attention was an absence. There were no pews, no chairs in neat rows; in front of me stretched a wide and vacant expanse of polished floor. Then I realised that the church was not altogether empty. Scattered in the nave and aisles there were a few worshippers ... Somewhere out of sight a choir was singing. After a while a deacon came out from the sanctuary and went round the church censing the icons and the people ... My initial impression of an absence was now replaced, with a sudden rush, by an overwhelming sense of presence. I felt that the Church ... was full – full of countless unseen worshippers, surrounding me on every side. Intuitively I realised that we, the visible congregation, were part of a much larger whole, and that as we prayed we were being taken up into an action far greater than ourselves, into an undivided, all-embracing celebration that united time and eternity, things below with things above. Years later, with a strange shock of recognition, I came across the story of St Vladimir's conversion, recorded in the *Russian Primary Chronicle*. Returning to Kiev, the Russian envoys told the Prince about the Divine Liturgy which they had attended in Constantinople. 'We did not know whether we were in heaven or on earth', they said. 'We cannot describe it to you: of this alone we are sure, that God dwells there among humankind. For we cannot forget that beauty.' I started with amazement as I read those words, for such exactly had been my own experience at the Russian Vigil Service in St Philip's ... The outward setting lacked the splendour of tenth-century Byzantium, but like St Vladimir's emissaries I too had encountered 'heaven on earth'. I too had felt the immediacy of the celestial Liturgy, the closeness of the angels and the saints, the uncreated beauty of God's Kingdom.[8]

There are many examples in Holy Tradition which bear testimony to the presence of the Mother of God and the angels in the church. For example, St Andrew the Fool in Christ, who lived in tenth-century Constantinople, once saw the Mother of God covering the people with her veil during the service. It is also recorded that St Sergius of Radonezh was attended by an angel when he served the Divine Liturgy. Again there is the ancient legend of a bishop, travelling with his deacon, who stumbled upon an almost completely ruined church far from any inhabited place and wanted to serve the Liturgy there. When they began the service in the empty church and the deacon chanted, 'In peace let us pray to the Lord', they suddenly heard an invisible choir responding 'Lord, have mercy'. The singing of the angels remained with them for the whole service.

## THE ATTRIBUTES OF THE CHURCH

The words of the Nicene-Constantinople Creed, 'I believe in One, Holy, Catholic and Apostolic Church', define the Church as a divine-human organism.

The Church is one, for it is constituted in the image of the Holy Trinity and reveals the mystery of unity in essence, while being differentiated in hypostases. It consists of many separate people welded together by unity in the faith and in the sacraments. As St Paul says, 'There is one body and one Spirit . . . one Lord, one faith, one baptism, one God and Father of us all, who is above all and through all and in all' (Eph. 4:4–6). It was for the same unity among Christians that Jesus Christ prayed at the Last Supper: 'Holy Father, keep them in thy name, which thou hast given me, that they may be one . . . I do not pray for these only, but also for those who believe in me through their word, that they may all be one; even as thou, Father, art in me, and I in thee, that they also may be in us' (John 17:11, 20–1). The love among the three Persons of the Trinity is reflected in the unity of the Church.

There is no unity on earth that can be compared with Church unity; such unity can be found only in heaven. In heaven the incomparable love of the Father, the Son and the Holy Spirit unites the three Persons into a single Essence, so that there are not three Gods, but a single God living a triune life . . . People who have become part of the Church and who have come to love each other are like the three Persons of the Most Holy Trinity.[9]

St Paul speaks of the holiness of the Church by comparing Christ with a bridegroom and the Church with his bride: 'Christ loved the church and gave himself up for her, that he might sanctify her . . . that he might present the church to himself in splendour, without spot or wrinkle or any such thing, that she might be holy and without blemish' (Eph. 5:25, 27). The sanctity of the Church is not conditioned by Christ's holiness as her head, but by the holiness to which all her members are called. The epistles refer to Christians as 'the saints', thereby suggesting that holiness is not an

[ 100 ]

unattainable ideal, but the norm for members of the Church. Every Christian is called to holiness, and throughout the Church's history there have been true saints. Those who have managed to transcend sin and the passions, however, are very few. The majority of Christians are sinners who are members of the Church not by virtue of having attained holiness, but by virtue of their striving for this holiness and their repentance. The Church's task is to sanctify them and lead them to God. In this sense it is said of Christians that they are *in patria et in via* – in the homeland and on the way, that is, simultaneously within the Church and yet on the way towards her.

The Greek word *katholike* (Catholic) means 'universal', uniting Christians dispersed around the world, and including the saints and the departed. St Cyril of Jerusalem says that 'the Church is called Catholic because she universally and unremittingly teaches all that ought to be a part of human knowledge – the dogma of the visible and the invisible, the heavenly and the earthly'.[10] The Russian religious philosopher A. Khomiakov emphasises that not only the living and the dead, but also those who have not yet been born are included in the universal body of the Church:

Those who are alive on earth, those who have finished their earthly course, those who, like the angels, were not created for a life on earth, those in future generations who have not yet begun their earthly course, are all united together in one Church, in one and the same grace of God; for the creation of God which has not yet been manifested is manifest to him; and God hears the prayers and knows the faith of those whom he has not yet called out of non-existence into existence.[11]

At first, the Church was a tiny community consisting of the disciples in Jerusalem. By the end of the first century, however, the preaching of the apostles meant that communities had been formed in Rome, Corinth, Ephesus and in other towns of Europe, Asia and Africa. All these communities, each headed by its own bishop, comprised a single 'universal' Church with Christ as the head.

In the era of the Ecumenical Councils the primacy of honour in the Christian Church (but not the primacy of jurisdiction) was enjoyed by the Bishop of Rome. He was the primate of the apostolic see, 'occupying the place of Peter and the grade of the sacred throne', to use the expression of St Cyprian of Carthage.[12] After the schism between West and East in 1054, the Bishop of Rome remained the sole head of all the Churches in the West, while in the East each local Church was governed by a Patriarch (or Metropolitan, or Archbishop). In the Eastern Church, Christ himself is considered to be the supreme authority, the only 'Head of the Church' in the proper sense. Decisions binding for the whole Orthodox world are taken solely by an Ecumenical Council.[13] The catholicity of the Church is considered primarily as conciliarity which is expressed in practice by the absence of a single visible head. According to Orthodox doctrine it is the Church as the Church that possesses 'infallibility' in questions of faith: the guardians of the truth are the people.[14]

The apostolicity of the Church is derived from the fact that it was founded by the apostles, preserves the truth of their teaching, receives succession from them and continues their mission on earth. The Church is 'built upon the foundation of the apostles and prophets', states St Paul (Eph. 2:20). By apostolic succession we mean the unbroken chain of ordinations (episcopal consecrations) going back to the apostles and coming down to present-day bishops: the apostles ordained the first generation of bishops, who in turn ordained the second generation, and so on down to our times. Christian communities whose succession has been broken are considered to have fallen away from the Church until their apostolic succession is restored. The bishops continue the apostles' mission on earth – a mission of ministry, preaching, the guidance of existing church communities and the creation of new ones. This idea was expressed in the second century by St Clement of Rome:

The apostles have preached the Gospel to us from the Lord Jesus Christ; Jesus Christ was sent from God . . . Having therefore received their orders, and being fully assured by the resurrection of our Lord Jesus Christ, and established in the word of God, with full assurance of the Holy Spirit, the apostles went forth proclaiming that the kingdom of God was at hand. And thus preaching through countries and cities, they appointed the first-fruits of their labours, having first proved them by the Spirit, to be bishops and deacons of those who should afterwards believe . . . Our apostles . . . appointed those (ministers) already mentioned, and afterwards gave instructions, that when these should fall asleep, other approved men should succeed them in their ministry.[15]

Not only the bishops and priests, but every member of the Church is called to an apostolic, missionary service, to preach Christ in word and deed: 'Go therefore and make disciples of all nations, baptising them in the name of the Father and of the Son and of the Holy Spirit' (Matt. 28:19). This mission, which was laid by Christ on the apostles and their successors, is far from complete. There are whole nations on earth which have barely been touched by the preaching of Christ. Many countries that were once Christian are now in spiritual crisis and are in need of new apostles.

The community of the apostles became fully aware of itself as the Church at Pentecost, when the Holy Spirit descended upon the apostles in the form of tongues of fire and they received the power to preach the Gospel 'to all nations'. A liturgical hymn reveals the inner meaning of this event: 'When the Most High confounded the tongues, he dispersed the nations: but when he distributed the tongues of fire, he called all men into unity. Wherefore, with one accord, we glorify the All-Holy Spirit.'[16] Here we are reminded of the tower of Babel when God, seeing the folly of people who tried to erect a tower to the heavens, descended and confused their languages. No longer understanding one another, they stopped building the tower, which collapsed and buried them under the rubble.[17] The unity of the human race once destroyed by people is now restored in the Church, where neither national nor linguistic distinctions are made. Rather, each person is granted a 'new tongue': the language of faith and prayer, of unity of mind and love. Every time the tower of Babel collapses (and it has fallen repeatedly throughout the course of history), there is a new 'confusion of tongues': conflicts among nations arise, misunderstandings and distrust grow. Only the Holy Spirit, who is the 'spirit of wisdom and understanding, the spirit of counsel and might, the spirit of knowledge and the fear of the LORD' (Isa. 11:2), who lives and acts within the Church, can reconcile all people, calling them to unity and accord.

## CHURCH HIERARCHY

In ancient Israel only men who belonged by birth to the tribe of Levi could become priests; the priesthood was not open to others. The Levites were consecrated and chosen to serve God – they alone had the right to make sacrifices, burn incense, say prayers and sing in the Temple. The participation of the people in the service was reduced to a passive presence. Yet even the Old Testament sacrifices could not redeem humanity from the slavery of sin: 'For it is impossible that the blood of bulls and goats should take away sins ... And every priest stands daily at his service, offering repeatedly the same sacrifices, which can never take away sins' (Heb. 10:4, 11). Christ therefore sacrificed himself in order to save the human race: 'We have been sanctified through the offering of the body of Jesus Christ once and for all ... But when Christ had offered for all time a single sacrifice for sins, he sat down at the right hand of God ... For by a single offering he has perfected for all time those who are sanctified' (Heb. 10:10, 12, 14).

Christ was both Priest and Sacrifice, the Offerer and the Offered. Not himself a member of the tribe of Levi, he became the sole true 'priest for ever after the order of Melchizedek' (Ps. 10:4). Genesis tells us that Melchizedek met Abraham, brought him bread and wine, and blessed him. A priest 'without father or mother or genealogy, [having] neither beginning of days nor end of life' (Heb. 7:3), Melchizedek was the Old Testament prototype of Christ. By surrendering his Body to death and shedding his Blood for the people, and by offering this Body and Blood to the faithful in the sacrament of the Eucharist, Christ established his Church which became the New Israel, abolishing the Old Testament Church with its sacrifices and Levitical priesthood. At the same time, he removed the curtain that separated the Holy of Holies from the people and destroyed the impenetrable wall between the sacred Levitical priesthood and the secular laity. In the Church of Christ all people are 'kings and priests' (Rev. 1:6), and all are led into the Holy of Holies in order to offer spiritual sacrifices. All become the 'chosen people':

And like living stones be yourselves built into a spiritual house, to be a holy priesthood, to offer spiritual sacrifices . . . But you are a chosen race, a royal priesthood, a holy nation, God's own people, that you may declare the wonderful deeds of him who called you out of darkness into his marvellous light. Once you were no people . . . once you had not received mercy but now you have received mercy.

(1 Pet. 2:5, 9–10)

The teaching on the royal priesthood of all Christians is very clearly expressed in the New Testament. Yet even from apostolic times a hierarchical priesthood existed in the Church: men chosen to celebrate the Eucharist and lead the people. The book of Acts speaks of the election of seven deacons (in Greek *diakonos* means 'servant', or 'minister') who were set apart to serve.[18] The apostles founded Christian communities in the various cities of the Roman Empire, where they preached and ordained bishops (in Greek *episkopos*: 'overseer', 'visitor' or 'guardian') and presbyters (elders) to lead these communities. The ministry of bishops, presbyters and deacons involved leading in prayer, teaching and spiritual guidance. It was conditioned by the different duties of all church members, who together comprised a single organism. As in the human body each member fulfils its function, so the members of the Church have a variety of services. According to St Paul, 'Now there are varieties of gifts, but the same Spirit;

and there are varieties of service, but the same Lord; and there are varieties of working, but it is the same God who inspires them all in every one . . . And God has appointed in the church first apostles, second prophets, third teachers' (1 Cor. 12:4–6, 28).

The hierarchical priesthood exists within the Church by virtue of the universal royal priesthood of all Christians. An ordained cleric who falls away from the Church for whatever reason, and finds himself beyond the Church's limits, abandons the royal priesthood of the people of God and loses his priestly rights. The hierarchical priesthood cannot be separated from the people of God; one cannot exist without the other. As a community cannot be the Church without a priest, so a priest cannot be a priest without the community. The priest is by no means the sole celebrant of the sacraments. They are all celebrated together with the people. The Liturgy clearly demonstrates how the priest celebrates in the name of the people, who participate actively in the service. Each priestly exclamation is sealed by the people with the word 'Amen' (meaning in Hebrew, 'so be it');[19] each blessing of the priest is reciprocated by one from the people. 'Peace to you all', says the priest. 'And to thy spirit', reply the people. Sometimes, as in the office of Compline, the priest asks for the people's blessing: 'Bless me, holy fathers and brethren and sisters, and forgive me, a sinner', to which the people reply, 'May God forgive you'. In the Early Church the ordination of a priest or bishop was carried out by the consent and election of the people. To this day the ordination service retains the people's exclamation 'Axios' ('he is worthy'), which expresses their approval of the ordination of this particular person.

There are three ranks of ordination in the Church: bishop, priest and deacon. Bishops are in charge of Church provinces, or dioceses, which are made up of a number of parishes. Priests care for individual parishes and their churches. Deacons assist the priests and the bishops at the Liturgy. Dionysius the Areopagite sees in this threefold gradation a reflection of the threefold structure of the celestial hierarchy, a direct continuation of which is the ecclesiastical hierarchy.[20] According to Dionysius, the light and energy of the Divinity are conveyed by delegation from the higher order of angels to the lower, and from them to the ecclesiastical hierarchy and to the laity.

This threefold hierarchy of bishops, presbyters and deacons has existed in the Church from earliest times, though probably not from the first century. In the letters of the apostles we do not see any clear distinction between bishop and presbyter – the words are often interchangeable: 'This is why I left you in Crete, that you might amend what was defective, and appoint elders (presbyters) in every town as I directed you, if any man is blameless, the husband of one wife, and his children are believers ... For a bishop, as God's steward, must be blameless' (Titus 1:5–6, 7). In apostolic times there was still no distinction between diocese and parish: the Church community, whether it was in Crete, Ephesus or Rome, incorporated all the faithful of that city or country and was a 'local' Church (that is, a Church of that locality).

As the Church expanded, however, a need arose for senior presbyters in charge of the communities in a single province and possessing the right to ordain presbyters for them. As early as the second century, Ignatius of Antioch clearly refers to the bishop as the head of the Church and the presbyters as his concelebrants, of one mind with him and obedient to him: 'The presbyters are in harmony with the bishop as the strings of a lyre.'[21] By submitting themselves to the bishop, the presbyters submit to Christ himself. For St Ignatius, the bishop embodies the plenitude of the Church, so that to be out of harmony with him constitutes a break away from the Church. The threefold hierarchy is to be treated with the greatest respect on the part of the faithful: 'All must respect the deacons as Christ's commandments and the bishops as Jesus Christ himself ... the presbyters are to be respected as the assembly of God, as the host of angels. Without them there is no Church.'[22]

The Church teaches that the moral imperfection of the celebrant in no way affects the validity of the sacraments, for when the priest celebrates the services he is simply an instrument of God. It is Christ himself who baptises; it is he who offers the Eucharist and gives Communion to the people; it is he who absolves sins in the sacrament of Confession. In Confession the priest says to the penitent, 'Behold, Christ stands here invisibly and receives your confession ... and I am but a witness, bearing testimony before him of all things which you have said to me.' However, if Christ in his infinite mercy tolerates sinful servants of the Church as he tolerated Judas among the apostles, this in no way justifies ministers of the Church who are unworthy of their vocation. The sins and vices of the clergy have always been a sickness within the Church. They undermine her authority in the eyes of the people and destroy their faith in God, even though they do not affect the validity of the sacraments. God is judged above all by the actions of his servants, for they are the image of Christ in the Church. It is indeed demoralising to see in a priest indifference instead of compassion, disdain instead of love, depravity instead of moral purity, hypocrisy instead of sincerity. A priest wears on his breast a cross bearing an image of Christ crucified for humanity. He is therefore expected to show the same compassion and love as Christ himself showed. 'Set the believers an example in speech and conduct, in love, in faith, in purity', says St Paul to the newly ordained Timothy (1 Tim. 4:12).

## THE PLACE OF WOMEN IN THE CHURCH

Throughout the entire history of the Church, the office of priest or bishop has been fulfilled only by men. This is not merely a tradition that stems from the inequality between men and women in the ancient world. From the very beginning priesthood has been a service of spiritual fatherhood. A woman can be a mother, wife or daughter, but she cannot be a father. So, while motherhood is in no way inferior to fatherhood, its mission, service and vocation are different. Only a child knows what distinguishes fatherhood from motherhood, even though he cannot express it in words. The difference between spiritual fatherhood and any other form of service is known to every Christian who has a spiritual father. The Orthodox Church rejects the ordination of women to the priesthood which has been introduced in some Protestant Churches. This is not simply because Orthodoxy is traditional and conservative, nor is it that Orthodoxy denigrates women or considers them inferior to men. It is because Orthodoxy, taking fatherhood in the Church very seriously, does not want to entrust to women a service which is alien to them. Within the organism of the Church, every member carries out particular functions and each person is irreplaceable. There is no substitute for fatherhood, and if the Church were to lose it she would be deprived of her integrity by becoming a family without a father or an organism without all its necessary members.

It is in this sense that we can understand the Christian attitude towards marriage and the role of the woman in the family. The Christian family is a 'small church' created in the image of Christ's Church. According to apostolic teaching, it is the husband, not the wife, who is the head of the family. The headship of the man does not entail inequality, however. The power of the man is the same power of love as Christ's power in the Church: 'As the church is subject to Christ, so let wives also be subject in everything to their husbands. Husbands, love your wives, as Christ loved the church and gave himself up for her ... let each one of you love his wife as himself, and let the wife see that she respects her husband' (Eph. 5:24–5, 33). The headship of the husband is his readiness to sacrifice himself in the same way as Christ does for the Church. As head of the family, the husband must love and respect his wife: 'Likewise you husbands, live considerately with your wives, bestowing honour on the woman as the weaker sex, since you are joint heirs of the grace of life' (1 Pet. 3:7). It is not inequality, but a harmonious unity that retains a diversity of functions which should exist in both family and the Church. For if the family is a domestic church, then the Church is a large family.

The fatherhood of the priest is not limited to his function as leader and guide of the community. In practice, leadership of the community is sometimes entrusted to a woman. For example, Orthodox convents are always under the guidance of an abbess, who directs not only the nuns but also the priests who serve the convent. In the convents of the Byzantine era there were female elders who had the right to hear the nuns' confessions, and this practice continues in some places today. Even the sacrament of Baptism can be carried out validly and legally by a woman in special circumstances, for example, if the candidate is on the verge of death and there is no priest at hand.

There are, however, no instances in Orthodox Church history when women served the Liturgy or were ordained priests. The priest celebrating the Eucharist symbolises Christ, God who has become man. The Church attaches great importance to liturgical symbolism: in the Orthodox understanding there is a direct interdependence between a symbol and reality so that, should the symbol be changed, there is a change in the reality which stands behind it. Father Thomas Hopko articulates the Orthodox view of the relationship between symbol and reality in the following terms:

The body of believers is headed by a bishop or presbyter who images Jesus, who himself images God the Father. The sacramental service of the presbyter/bishop in and for the Church is essentially masculine, paternal and husbandly . . . Christ's Church is a monarchical, patriarchal and hierarchical community . . . in imitation of the Trinity . . . There is no doubt that the pastoral office was everywhere and always in Orthodox tradition sacramentally joined to the Persons of God the Father and His Son Jesus Christ – and not, we must note, to God-in-general, or to the Divinity as such, or to the Godhead . . . In the life of the Church . . . the presbyter/ bishop manifests the presence and power of Christ, the head of the Church, Whose own 'head' is the Father . . . It is also necessary to note that when Orthodox Christians use the terms symbol, image and icon . . . we normally do so in the sense that these realities make actual and present the realities which they embody because of their natural competence and capacity to do so . . . A sacramental image – and the presbyter/bishop is certainly such an image in Orthodox church life – is the living and active presence of that reality of which it is the sacrament.[23]

In the Early Church there were, however, deaconesses who had a wide range of obligations. For example, they helped the bishop perform Baptisms and took part in the celebration of the Eucharist. The question of whether to restore the order of deaconesses is now open for discussion in the entire Orthodox Church. It could be answered positively by a Pan-Orthodox Council, if such a Council were ever convened. In fact, many important and irreplaceable services within the Church akin to those of deaconesses in the Early Church are carried out by women today: they bake the bread for the Eucharist, read and sing in church, and often direct the choir.

## THE MOTHER OF GOD AND THE SAINTS

We can judge the Church's attitude towards women by the high position accorded to the Most Holy Mother of God. The Church glorifies her more than all the saints and even more than the angels. She is praised in hymns as 'more honourable than the Cherubim and beyond compare more glorious than the Seraphim'. The Holy Virgin is the Mother of Christ and Mother of the Church – it is in her person that the Church glorifies motherhood, the inalienable inheritance and privilege of women. It is interesting that some Protestant Churches that have entrusted the celebration of the Eucharist and other priestly functions to women neither venerate the Mother of God nor pray to her. Yet without the Mother of God the Church community loses its fullness in the same way that it is incomplete without the priesthood. If fatherhood is realised in the Church in the episcopate and the priesthood, motherhood is personified in the Most Holy Mother of God.

The Orthodox Church glorifies the Mother of God as ever-Virgin. This term was upheld by the Fifth Ecumenical Council in 533 and emphasises the virginity of the Mother of God before, during and after Christ's birth. Christ's 'brothers', mentioned in Matthew 3:3, are regarded by Church Tradition to be the sons of Joseph from his first marriage. She is also called Most Holy, Most Pure and Immaculate.[24] The Orthodox Church follows Early Church tradition in believing that at her death the Holy Virgin was assumed bodily into heaven like Christ and the Old Testament saints Enoch and Elijah.

Very little is said about Mary in Scripture: her place in the New Testament is very modest compared with the place she occupies in the life of the Church. The veneration of the Mother of God is based not so much on Scripture as on the centuries-old experience of many people to whom, in one way or another, the mystery of the Holy Virgin was revealed.

One of those people was St Silouan of Mount Athos, who dedicated these lines to her:

Many are the marvels and mercies that I have witnessed at the hands of the Lord and of the Mother of God ... Once ... in church ... I reflected, 'Maybe the Mother of God sinned at one time or another, if only in thought.' And, marvellous to relate, in unison with my prayer a voice sounded in my heart, saying clearly, 'The Mother of God never sinned even in thought.' Thus did the Holy Spirit bear witness in my heart to her purity. But during her earthly life even She was not quite perfect and complete – She did make some mistakes that did not involve sin. We can see this from the Gospel when on the return from Jerusalem She did not know where her Son was, and together with Joseph sought him for three days.[25] My soul trembles and is afraid when I consider the glory of the Mother of God. Small and of no account is my mind, poor and sickly my heart, but my soul rejoices and would fain set down if but a little concerning her ... The Mother of God committed to writing neither her thoughts nor her love for God and her Son, nor her soul's suffering at the Crucifixion, because in any case we could not have understood, for her love for God is stronger and more ardent than the love of the Seraphim and Cherubim, and all the hosts of angels and archangels marvel at her. And though the life of the Mother of God is hidden, as it were in a holy silence, our Lord allows our Orthodox Church to know that She embraces the whole world in this love of hers, and in the Holy Spirit sees all the peoples of the earth, and like her Son pities all men and has compassion on them ... She is our joy and our expectation. She is our Mother in the spirit, and kin to us by nature, as a human being, and every Christian soul leaps to Her in love.[26]

The Mother of God stands at the head of the host of saints glorified by the Church. In accordance with ancient tradition, the Church venerates the saints and addresses prayers to them. Accusations that the Church worships mere human beings in the same way as God are unfounded. Greek theology makes a clear distinction between the worship (*latreia*) of God and veneration (*proskynesis*) of the saints. The latter are not venerated as gods, but as people who have attained a great spiritual height and who have become united with God. The saints are closely connected with each other and with Christ. In venerating the saints we venerate Christ, who lives in them:

Christ is the beginning, the middle and the end. He is in all people – the first, the middle and the last. Those who have become saints from one generation to the next through fulfilling the commandments, replace the previous saints and are united to them, they are illumined and become like them through communion with the grace of God, and they all become a golden chain, each individual link being connected with the previous through faith, deeds and love.[27]

The golden chain of Christian holiness stretches from apostolic times to our own age: even now there are no few saints – secret and known – who will one day be glorified by the Church.

Official numbering among the saints, or canonisation, is a comparatively late phenomenon: there were no acts of canonisation or glorification in the Early Christian Church. Martyrs who suffered for Christ would become the object of reverential veneration by believers soon after their death; they would pray to them and would celebrate the Liturgy on their tomb. In the Russian Orthodox Church it has always been the rule to celebrate the Liturgy on an 'antimension', a cloth into which the relics of a saint or martyr have been sewn, and which is placed on the altar. Alternatively, there may be relics placed under the holy table. In this way the link is made between the Church on earth today, made up of living people, and the Church triumphant in heaven, made up of saints glorified by God. It also shows how the martyrs are the basis and foundation of the Church. 'The blood of the martyrs is the seed of Christianity', said Tertullian.[28]

Solemn canonisation of saints and martyrs is not always possible. Throughout the history of the Church they have often been venerated in secret. The Greek Church, which was under the dominion of the Ottoman Empire for several centuries, could not openly proclaim as saints her new martyrs who had suffered at the hands of the Turks. Yet they were still universally venerated among Greek Orthodox Christians. In the same way, also, the Russian Church, under the power of the Bolsheviks, was unable to glorify openly the thousands of new martyrs who perished after 1917 during one of the most savage persecutions of the Church that history has ever known. However, the faithful and individual priests celebrated services to them in secret without waiting for their formal canonisation, this being impossible under the prevailing conditions.

The veneration of a particular saint does not follow from the act of canonisation. In fact the reverse is true: canonisation of a saint comes about as a result of popular veneration. There are saints about whose lives almost nothing is known, and yet they are universally venerated. One such is St Nicholas, Archbishop of Myra in Lycia in the fourth century. He is glorified by Christians of both East and West and is loved by children and adults (Christmas holidays in the West would be unthinkable without

Santa Claus visiting the home and bringing presents). Even non-Christians who pray to St Nicholas receive help from him. This universal veneration of the saint is rooted in the experience of many generations of people: he has become the 'personal friend' of thousands of individuals whom he has helped and even saved from death.

God himself sometimes gives visible confirmation of the sanctity of a particular person. There are many saints whose bodies have been free from decay. The relics of St Nicholas, located in Bari, Italy, exude a healing and sweet-smelling myrrh. Those of the holy martyrs Anthony, John and Eustathius in the Monastery of the Holy Spirit in Vilnius, Lithuania, who died in 1346, remained intact for six hundred and fifty years, even though they lay beneath the earth for many years.[29] Many people have testified to the healing power of their relics.

Some people find it difficult to understand why it is necessary to pray to the saints when we can pray to Christ. Yet the saints are not mediators between us and Christ: rather, they are our heavenly friends, able to hear us and help us through their prayers. Without friends in heaven it is difficult to understand the reverential veneration which surrounds the saints. It has to be said, therefore, that where there is no direct and living communion with the saints, the completeness of the Church as the mystical Body of Christ uniting the living and the dead, saints and sinners, cannot be fully experienced.

## THE HOLY ICONS

In the Orthodox tradition the icon is not merely an adornment or an object to be used in worship: people pray before it, kiss it and treat it as a sacred object.

Tradition has it that the first icon of Christ appeared in his lifetime. King Abgar of Edessa was ill with leprosy and sent his servant to the Saviour with a request that he should come and heal him. Should Christ be unable to come, Abgar asked the servant, an artist, to paint his portrait and bring it to him. Upon receiving the king's letter, Christ washed his face and wiped it on a clean white cloth, upon which the image of his face appeared. This image of Christ 'not-created-by-hands' was kept for many centuries in Edessa. When Constantinople was sacked by the Crusaders in 1204 the image was in all probability lost, as there is no mention of its location after this.[30]

Apart from the Edessa image, there were other ancient images of Christ. Eusebius of Caesarea, a fourth-century Church historian, mentions a statue of Christ erected by the woman with the issue of blood whom he had healed.[31] Eusebius also maintains that he saw portraits of Christ and the apostles Peter and Paul drawn in their lifetime.[32] According to the Tradition of the Church, the first icon of the Mother of God was painted by the evangelist Luke.

Although icons have existed since ancient times, various movements have been opposed to their veneration. These culminated in the seventh and eighth centuries in the iconoclast heresy that was condemned at the Seventh Ecumenical Council. The accusation made by the iconoclasts against the venerators of icons was that of idolatry. They based their arguments on the Old Testament prohibition against depicting God: 'You shall not make for yourself a graven image, or any likeness of anything that is in heaven above, or that is in the earth beneath or that is in the water under the earth; you shall not bow down to them or serve them; for I the LORD your God am a jealous God' (Exod. 20:4–5). It is clear, however, that these words are directed at the idols worshipped by pagan peoples. The author of the book of Deuteronomy makes clear which idols are meant:

Beware lest you act corruptly by making a graven image for yourselves, in the form of any figure, the likeness of male or female, the likeness of any beast that is on the earth, the likeness of any winged bird that flies in the air, the likeness of anything that creeps on the ground, the likeness of any fish that is in the water under the earth. And beware lest you lift up your eyes to heaven, and when you see the sun and the moon and the stars, all the host of heaven, you be drawn away and worship them.

(Deut. 4:16–19)

The author emphasises that the true God is invisible and cannot be depicted. When Moses spoke with God on Mount Sinai, he was told he could not see God face to face:

And you came near and stood at the foot of the mountain, while the mountain burned with fire to the heart of heaven, wrapped in darkness, cloud, and gloom. Then the LORD spoke to you out of the midst of the fire; you heard the sound of words, but saw no form; there was only a voice . . . you saw no form on the day that the LORD spoke to you . . . out of the midst of the fire.

(Exod. 25:18–20)

Any image of the invisible God would have been the product of human fantasy and a lie against God; worship of this image would have been worship of the creature rather than the Creator. This does not mean, however, that there were no images whatsoever in Old Testament worship: God tells Moses to build a tabernacle and decorate it with golden Cherubim.[33]

The New Testament is the revelation of God who became man and who could be seen by people. With the same insistence as Moses, who said that the people on Sinai *did not see God*, the apostles emphasise that they *did indeed see him*: 'We have beheld his glory, the glory as of the only Son from the Father' (John 1:14); 'That which was from the beginning, which we have heard, which we have seen with our eyes, which we have looked upon and touched with our hands, concerning the Word of life' (I John 1:1). Christ revealed the invisible God to the world, that is, he made him visible: 'No one has ever seen God; the only Son, who is in the bosom of the Father, he has made him known' (John 1:18). That which is invisible cannot be depicted in images, while that which is visible can be depicted, as it is no longer the product of fantasy, but a reality. St John of Damascus suggests that the Old Testament prohibition against depicting the invisible God points towards the possibility of depicting him when he becomes visible: 'It is obvious that when you contemplate God becoming man, then you may depict him clothed in human form. When the invisible One becomes visible to flesh, you may then draw his likeness ... Use every kind of drawing, word, or colour.'[34]

The iconoclast heresy of the eighth century continued, under a new guise, the christological heresies that were condemned at earlier Ecumenical Councils. Unlike the earlier controversies, however, iconoclasm did not arise among theologians, but was imposed on the people by the Byzantine emperor Leo Isaurus, who issued a decree in 726 forbidding the veneration of icons. Leo ordered an imperial official to destroy the miraculous image of the Saviour that hung over the entrance to the royal palace. The people resisted this desecration and the official was killed. Many notable Church leaders of the time, as well as monks and laypeople, came to the defence of icons and their veneration. But the emperor declared himself 'Caesar and High Priest' and chose to ignore the opinions of the bishops. St John of Damascus, speaking out against imperial claims of authority over the Church, said: 'We will obey you, O emperor, in those matters which pertain to our daily lives: payments, taxes, tributes ... But as far as the government of the Church is concerned, we have our pastors, and they have preached the word to us; we have those who interpret the ordinances of the Church.'[35]

The defence of icons became a defence of belief in the Incarnation of Christ, for iconoclasm was one of the ways of denying the reality of this Incarnation. For the Orthodox, the icon is not an idol taking the place of the invisible God, but a symbol and sign of his presence in the Church. The Fathers of the Seventh Ecumenical Council concurred with St Basil the Great in saying that 'the honour rendered to the image passes on to the Prototype'.[36] The Council's decree summarised the centuries-old tradition of the veneration of icons and gave it theological justification:

We keep unchanged all the ecclesiastical traditions handed down to us, whether in writing or verbally, one of which is the making of pictorial representations, agreeable to the history of the preaching of the Gospel, a tradition useful in many respects, but especially in this, that so the incarnation of the Word of God is shown forth as real and not merely phantastic, for these have mutual indications and without doubt have also mutual significations. We, therefore, following the royal pathway and the divinely inspired authority of our Holy Fathers and the traditions of the Catholic Church . . . define with all certitude and accuracy that just as the figure of the precious and life-giving Cross, so also the venerable and holy images, as well in painting and mosaic as of other fit materials, should be set forth in the holy churches of God, and on the sacred vessels and on the vestments and on hangings and in pictures both in houses and by the wayside, to wit, the figure of our Lord God and Saviour Jesus Christ, of our spotless Lady, the Mother of God, of the honourable angels, of all saints and of all pious people. For by so much more frequently as they are seen in artistic representation, by so much more readily are people lifted up to the memory of their prototypes, and to a longing after them; and to these should be given due salutation and honourable reverence (*proskynesin*), not indeed that true worship of faith (*latreian*) which pertains alone to the divine nature; but to these, as to the figure of the precious and life-giving Cross and to the book of the gospels and to the other holy objects, incense and lights may be offered according to ancient pious custom. For the honour which is paid to the image passes on to that which the image represents, and he who reveres the image reveres in it the subject represented . . . Those, therefore who dare to think or teach otherwise . . . if they be Bishops or clerics, we command that they be deposed; if religious or laics, that they be excommunicated.[37]

The Fathers of the Seventh Ecumenical Council insisted that, in bowing down to the icon, Christians do not worship wood and paint, but the person depicted: Christ, the Holy Virgin, the saints. There is therefore nothing in common between idolatry and the veneration of icons. The icon does not stand before us as a self-sufficient object of worship. It is not even placed between us and God. To use the expression of Father Paul

Florensky, the icon is a window onto the other world: through the icon we come into direct contact with the spiritual world and those who live there.

## THE CROSS

The Holy Cross has central significance for the Church. An instrument of death, it has become the instrument of salvation. Basil the Great identifies the 'sign of the Son of man' mentioned by Christ in connection with his Second Coming[38] with the arms of the Cross pointing towards the four ends of the universe.[39] The Cross is a symbol of Christ himself and is infused with miraculous power. The Orthodox Church believes that Christ's energy is present in the Cross. Therefore Christians not only make crosses and place them on the same level as icons in churches, they also wear crosses hung around their necks, make the sign of the Cross over themselves and bless each other with the sign of the Cross. They even address the Cross as something capable of hearing them: 'Rejoice, life-bearing Cross', 'O most honourable and life-creating Cross of the Lord'.

The Church knows about the salvific and healing power of the Cross and of the sign of the Cross from her experience. The Cross protects a person travelling, working, sleeping, praying. Indeed, in all places, through the sign of the Cross, Christ's blessing comes upon every good deed which we undertake: 'The Cross is the protector of the whole world, the Cross is the beauty of the Church, the Cross is the power of kings, the Cross is the foundation of the faithful, the Cross is the glory of the angels and the sore of the demons', sings the Church at festivals of the Cross.[40]

The teaching on the Holy Cross as a symbol of divine dispensation and as an object of religious veneration is expounded by Isaac the Syrian in one of his newly discovered works from the fourth century. According to St Isaac, the power in the Cross is no different from that through which the universe came into being and which governs the whole creation in accordance with the will of God. In the Cross lives the very same power that existed in the Ark of the Covenant, which was the object of fearful veneration by the people of Israel:

The limitless power of God dwells in the Cross, just as it resided in an incomprehensible way in the Ark which was venerated amidst great honour and awe by the Jewish People, performing by it miracles and awesome signs in the midst of those who were not ashamed to call it 'God',[41] that is, they would gaze upon it in awe as though upon God, because of the glory of

God's honoured name which was upon it. This Ark was not only honoured with this name by the Jewish People, but by foreign peoples, their enemies: *Woe to us, for the God of the People has come to the camp today.*[42] That power which existed in the Ark is believed by us to exist in this revered form of the Cross, which is held in honour by us in great awareness concerning God.[43]

What, then, was in the Ark, asks Isaac, that made it so awesome and filled with powers and signs? The Ark was venerated, he answers, because in it the invisible *Shekhina* (presence) of God dwelt: 'Did not Moses and the People prostrate before the Ark in great awe and trembling? Did not Joshua son of Nun lie stretched out on his face before it from morning until evening?[44] Were not God's fearful revelations manifested there as if to provide honour for this object, seeing that the Shekhina of God was residing in it?' The very same Shekhina is now residing in the Cross: it has departed from the Old Testament Ark and entered the New Testament Cross.[45]

Why was it, St Isaac asks, that before the wooden construction of the Ark, built by the hands of carpenters, 'adoration filled with awe was offered up continuously', in spite of the Law's prohibition against worshipping the work of human hands or any image or likeness?[46] Because in the Ark, he says, in contrast to the pagan idols, the power of God was openly manifest and the name of God was set upon it.[47] Thus, in speaking of the veneration of the Cross, Isaac sweeps aside the accusation of idolatry, the very same accusation that was brought against the eighth-century iconodules in Byzantium.

The Cross is venerated primarily because of our love of Christ, who accomplished our salvation through it. When contemplating the Cross, Christians enter the vision of *the mystery of faith*, they see the face of Christ himself. St Isaac explains:

For true believers the sign of the Cross is no small thing, for all symbols are understood to be contained in it. But whenever they raise their eyes and gaze on it, it is as though they were contemplating the face of Christ, and accordingly they are full of reverence for it: the sight of it is precious and fearful to them, and at the same time, beloved . . . And whenever we approach the Cross, it is as though we are brought close to the body of Christ: this is what it seems to us in our faith in him. And through our drawing near to him, and at our gaze towards him, straightway we travel in our intellects to heaven, mystically. As though at some sight that cannot be seen or sensed, and out of honour for our Lord's humanity, our hidden vision is swallowed up through a certain contemplation of the mystery of faith.[48]

The material Cross, whose type was the Ark of the Covenant, is, in turn, the type of the eschatological Kingdom of Christ. The Cross links the Old Covenant with the New, and the New Covenant with the age to come, where all material symbols and types will be abolished. The whole economy of Christ, which began in Old Testament times and continues until the end of the world, is encircled in the symbol of the Cross.[49] St Isaac ends with a hymn of thanksgiving to God, who intended from eternity to give true knowledge to humanity by means of the Cross, the material symbol of his economy:

Blessed is God who uses corporeal objects continually to draw us close in a symbolic way to a knowledge of his invisible nature . . . Let our hearts rejoice in the mysteries of the faith which we hold; let us exult in God who is so concerned with us . . . How much to be worshipped is the God who, for our salvation, has done everything in the world to bring us close to him, before the time when what has been prepared will be revealed . . . How much to be worshipped is the symbol of the Cross, seeing that it has given to us all these things, and through it we have been deemed worthy of the knowledge of angels – that is, through the power by which all created things, both visible and invisible, were created.[50]

## CHURCH TIME

The Church exists on earth, yet at the same time she is turned towards heaven; the Church lives in time, yet breathes eternity. This experience of communion with eternity forms the basis of the Church calendar and the cycle of worship throughout the year, week by week and day by day. In the liturgical year the Church recollects and experiences the whole history of the world and humankind, the entire 'economy' or work of the salvation of the human race. In the annual cycle there passes before us the life of Christ from his birth to his Crucifixion and Resurrection; the life of the Mother of God from her Conception to her Dormition; and the lives of the saints glorified by the Church. Within the scope of a week and, indeed, of a single day, we renew and recollect the entire history of the salvation of the human race. Each cycle has a centre towards which it is directed: that of the daily cycle is the Eucharist; of the weekly cycle, Sunday; and of the annual cycle, Christ's Resurrection, Easter.

The Resurrection of Christ is the main, defining event in the history of the Christian faith: 'If Christ has not been raised, then our preaching is in vain and your faith is in vain' (I Cor. 15:14). If Christ had not risen, Christianity would have remained just one of many moral teachings and religious faiths. Christ's Resurrection instituted the Church as a new life, a new divine-human existence in which the person becomes god because God has become a person. From the very beginning of the Church's existence the feast of Christ's Resurrection has been the foundation stone of the Christian calendar.

The feast days of the Church are not mere recollections of events happening in the distant past: they grant access to the spiritual reality behind them, which has a timeless and unchanging significance for all of us. Each one of us receives Christ as our personal Saviour, and so we each make our own all the events of Christ's life through personal experience, to whatever extent we can. The feast day is a realisation here and now of an event that occurred once in time but is always happening outside time. At the feast of the Nativity we sing, '*Today* Christ is born in Bethlehem'; at Epiphany, '*Today* the nature of the waters is sanctified'; and at Easter, '*Today* Christ has trampled down death and risen from the tomb'. If those outside the Church live with reminiscences of an already irretrievable past or hope in an unknown future, those in the Church are called upon to live by the ever-present 'today', which is the reality of everyday communion with God.

This is why the feast of Christ's Resurrection, although it is celebrated only once a year, penetrates the entire Church calendar. The radiance of Easter is reflected in the whole cycle of worship, and is always present as communion with the risen Christ. Throughout the year, Seraphim of Sarov would greet everyone with the Paschal greeting, 'Christ is risen!' It is said of a hermit of old, who lived in unceasing prayer and was famed for his sanctity, that when a disciple came to him and said, 'Elder, today is Easter!' he replied, 'Is it really?'[51] Of course, neither St Seraphim, for whom every day was Easter, nor the hermit, who did not know its precise date, rejected the Church calendar. They lived, however, by their experience of eternity and knew that Easter was not a single day of the year, but an eternal reality in which they participated daily.

In the light of this, the heated arguments that have taken place concerning the problem of the Church calendar may seem unjustified; the more so as they lead to occasional ruptures of Church unity. Until the 1920s all the local Orthodox Churches used the Julian calendar, which now lags behind the Gregorian calendar (used by all other Christians) by thirteen days. In

1923 a number of Orthodox Churches (Greece, Constantinople, Cyprus, Romania) changed to the so-called 'revised Julian' calendar ('new style'), which now coincides with the Gregorian calendar. However, the old method of calculating Easter was retained. At present all of the autocephalous local Orthodox Churches, with the exception of the Churches of Russia, Serbia, Jerusalem and Georgia, follow the new style. As a result, the former celebrate Christmas on 25 December along with Western Christians, while the latter celebrate the same feast on 7 January (or 25 December according to the Julian reckoning). There are some local variations: the monasteries of Mount Athos use the old Julian calendar, while being subject to the Patriarchate of Constantinople, which follows the new style; the diocese of Alaska uses the Julian calendar, though the remaining parishes of the Orthodox Church in America use the new calendar; the Russian Church uses the old calendar, while a number of its foreign parishes use the new calendar. All the Orthodox Churches celebrate Easter on the same day, with the exception of the Orthodox Church of Finland, which uses the Western Christian reckoning for Pascha. This means that there are in fact three calendars in use at present throughout Orthodox Christendom. It is important to add that the calendar question is one of custom, not dogma. It may be hoped that a future Pan-Orthodox Council will introduce some uniformity into this idiosyncratic situation.

A situation where there are two different calendars, one for the world and one for the Church, contradicts the initial purpose of the Church calendar. The yearly cycle of feast days is, as it were, an icon of eternity. As in an icon a timeless spiritual reality is reflected in material colours, so in the Church calendar the realities of eternal life are reflected in the dates of the secular calendar. As an icon encompasses the energy and presence of the one depicted on it, so Church time is full of eternal energy and of the presence of Christ, the Mother of God, the angels and saints, whose memories are commemorated throughout the year.

## THE CHURCH AND CHURCHES: DIVISIONS AND RECONCILIATION

The Nicene-Constantinople Creed speaks of one Church, yet there are many different Christian denominations which call themselves churches. It is not uncommon for them to refuse each other Communion and even to be mutually hostile. Do these things destroy the unity of the Church? Is it not the case that a formerly single Church has disintegrated into various denominations and lost its unity?

To begin with, it should be pointed out that, according to Orthodox ecclesiology, the Church by its very nature is indivisible and will remain so until the end of the age. The schisms that resulted from heresy did not entail the dismembering of the Church, but rather the falling away of heretics from the single organism of the Church. As mentioned above, heresy is characterised by its conscious opposition to universal Church doctrine.

Orthodoxy does not concur with the 'branch theory', according to which all existing Christian denominations constitute branches of the one tree. The unity of the Church is conditioned by its unity around the Eucharist: outside eucharistic Communion there can be no unity. At the Liturgy of St Basil the Great, we pray, 'And unite all of us to one another who become partakers of the one Bread and Cup in the communion of the Holy Spirit.'[52] Belonging to the Church is expressed not only in dogmatic unity but also in the Eucharist. As Archbishop Hilarion (Troitsky) wrote,

Adherence to the Church is conditioned by unity with the Church. There can be no other way, as the Church is not a philosophical school. It is a new humanity, the new gracious organism of love. Christ likened the unity of his disciples with the unity of the body with the branches. Two trees standing next to each other cannot be organically tied to each other. What the soul is to the body, the Holy Spirit is to the Church ... The soul cannot animate a member of the body that has been cut off from it in the same way as the vital sap of a tree cannot be transferred to a branch that has been cut off ... The severed branch will wither.[53]

Those Christian groups who have opposed the common faith of the Church through heresy are the branches which have become separated.

Does this necessarily mean that the Orthodox should regard all non-Orthodox Christian confessions as withered branches? For some Orthodox theologians this is certainly the case. A position of exclusion is taken by some ecclesiastical groups which, being separated from the canonical Orthodox Churches, regard themselves as the only true heirs of authentic Orthodoxy. For many theologians belonging to these groups, all Western confessions, having fallen away from the Church, are deprived of salvation. Some go even further and declare that not only non-Orthodox confessions but also the majority of local Orthodox Churches have fallen away from the unity of the Body of Christ:

Christ did not create all this abundance and variety of 'churches' which now exist on earth ... Christ created only one Church — the Orthodox

Church . . . Yet far from all those who call themselves an 'Orthodox Church' are really the Orthodox Church, but are merely a cunning forgery, a gloss designed to lead the naive and the trusting astray, who are unable to see for themselves the contemporary wicked devices of people . . . Are we not now witnessing an ever widening apostasy from Christ? And not only among the 'heterodox', but also within Orthodoxy itself, of which only a sham remains.[54]

This type of ecclesiology led to a schism within the Orthodox Church. The passage cited above reveals an almost sectarian psychology characterised by hatred for other Christian Churches through a sense of one's own exclusiveness and infallibility.

Extremist views can also be found among certain theologians belonging to the canonical local Orthodox Churches, even though the official position of these Churches is, as a rule, much more open towards other Christian confessions. At present, most local Orthodox Churches take some part in the movement for Christian unity and maintain contacts with Christians of other confessions, especially those whose ecclesiology is identical or close to that of the Orthodox: the Roman Catholic Church and the Oriental Orthodox (pre-Chalcedonian) Churches. Leading Orthodox theologians of this century, such as Fathers Serge Bulgakov, Georges Florovsky, Alexander Schmemann, John Meyendorff, Metropolitan Anthony of Sourozh, Bishop Kallistos of Diokleia and many others, have been able to articulate the Orthodox Church's participation in the ecumenical movement from a firm theological position. We shall limit ourselves to a single citation from Metropolitan Anthony who, objecting to the opinion that outside the Orthodox Church there can be neither grace from God, nor sacraments nor priesthood, says the following:

I believe that the history of the Church and her theology are incompatible with this simple and comforting conclusion, for it does away with all hesitation, all problems in need of a solution that would be worthy of God . . . What are we to do with those who have joined a wrong faith, accepted a mistaken theology, yet who live and die for Christ? And what about his witnesses – those martyrs for faith in the Lord, those Catholics, Protestants and others who live only to pass on their faith in the Saviour to those who do not know of this faith, and who have lived a life of great spiritual deeds and accepted a martyr's death? Can they really be recognised by Christ alone, in eternity, and should they be rejected by his disciples on earth?[55]

Metropolitan Anthony's position in this regard is far from unique. In the nineteenth century St Philaret of Moscow said: 'I dare not call false any Church which confesses Jesus to be the Christ.'[56] Another Russian hierarch, Metropolitan Platon (Gorodetsky) of Kiev, was believed to have said that 'our earthly barriers do not reach up to heaven'.[57] Barriers between the various confessions have often come about for political rather than dogmatic reasons. Over time the political reasons recede into the background, but the enmity remains.

The Early Church took a strict line with heretics. Not only were they excluded from the Eucharist, but they were also forbidden to pray with other people. We must remember, however, that the heresies of the first Christian centuries (Arianism, Sabellianism and Eutychian Monophysitism) contradicted the very foundations of the Christian faith: the divinity of Christ, the equality of the Persons of the Trinity, the fullness of the divine and human natures of Christ. This cannot be said of the majority of today's Christian confessions, for they accept the basic dogmas of the Church. Orthodox Christians, therefore, ought to make a distinction between non-Orthodoxy and heresy. It is counterproductive to apply what was said by the Ecumenical Councils on the excommunication of heretics to contemporary non-Orthodox Christians.

Orthodox rigorists frequently claim that the Church Fathers were strict and rigid theologians who never allowed any contact with heretics. If we read the Fathers carefully, however, we see that some of them took a much broader view on reconciliation between the Church and those who separated themselves on theological grounds. Some great theologians of the Early Church advanced the principle of a 'dogmatic minimum' for reconciliation, a minimum which would not presuppose full agreement on every dogmatic formulation. St Basil the Great was in his own time a defender of the Nicene faith and a promulgator of the divinity of the Holy Spirit. However, because of his Arian surroundings (most of the bishops which belonged to his diocese were Arians), he never proclaimed the divinity of the Holy Spirit directly. He reasoned that, for reconciliation between the Arians and the Orthodox, the common basis of the Nicene faith and a confession that the Spirit is not a creature would be enough:

We demand nothing more: we only offer the Nicene faith to those brethren who want to be reconciled with us, and if they agree on that, we demand that the Holy Spirit should not be named 'creature' . . . Apart from this, I agree not to demand anything. For I am sure that after a long time of their communion with us and after their unequivocal instruction in the dogmas of faith, if anything would be necessary to be added for more clarity, the Lord will give this.[58]

St Basil clearly understood that Churches and theological groups may be in different stages of development: what is perfectly acceptable for some may seem quite unacceptable for others. In due course, the Churches may come to receive those dogmatic formulae which were once seen as alien to their tradition. For St Basil, the unity of the Church was more important than unity in dogmatic language, which might be achieved if the principle of *oikonomia* (economy, dispensation) is applied: 'Most beneficial would be the reconciliation of what was so far separated; this reconciliation will take place if we agree to condescend to the weak in what will not do any damage to our souls.'[59]

Another Church Father of the same period, St Gregory the Theologian, was no less open minded. In his discourse dedicated to Athanasius the Great, Gregory speaks of the latter's efforts to reconcile different theological parties and to bring to agreement the Greek East and the Latin West on trinitarian matters. Speaking of this, Gregory advances several important notions concerning dogmatic disagreements and schisms among different parts of the Universal Church:

As, in the case of one and the same quantity of water, there is separated from it, not only the residue which is left behind by the hand when drawing it, but also those drops, once contained in the hand, which trickle out through the fingers; so not only those who hold aloof in their impiety, but also those who are most pious separate themselves from us, and this is both in regard to dogmas of small importance (*peri dogmaton mikron*), which can be disregarded (*parorasthai axion*), and also in regard to expressions intended to bear the same meaning. We use in an orthodox sense the terms 'one Essence and three Hypostases'; the Italians (Latins) mean the same, but, owing to the scantiness of their vocabulary, and its poverty of terms, they are unable to distinguish between Essence and Hypostases, and therefore introduce the term Persons, to avoid being understood to assert three Essences. The result would be laughable, were it not lamentable. This slight difference of sound was taken to indicate a difference of faith ... And then, from the gradual but constant growth of irritation – the unfailing result of contentiousness – there was a danger of the whole world being torn asunder in the strife about syllables. Seeing and hearing this, our blessed one,[60] true man of God and great minister of souls as he was, felt it inconsistent with his duty to overlook so absurd and unreasonable a rending of the word, and applied his medicine to the disease. In what manner? He conferred in his gentle and sympathetic way with both parties, having carefully weighed the meaning of their expressions, and found that they had the same sense, and were in no way different in doctrine; by permitting each party to use its own terms, he bound them together in unity of action.[61]

This text concerns differences in dogmatic language between the Latin and the Greek theologians. In the Greek-speaking East, there was still great uncertainty as to what the term 'hypostasis' meant: some used it as a generic term, synonymous with 'essence' (*ousia*); others, including the Cappadocians, preferred to apply to it the meaning of 'personal existence', synonymous with 'person' (*prosopon*). In Latin, both *hypostasis* and *prosopon* were translated as *persona*; therefore, the whole point of the Eastern trinitarian arguments was missed by the Latins. Moreover, there were already different approaches to the mystery of the Trinity in East and West. This difference is clear in the trinitarian doctrines of the two third-century theologians Origen and Tertullian. It becomes even more obvious at the end of the fourth century, with St Augustine's *De Trinitate*, where the starting point of all trinitarian theology is not a 'monarchy' of the Father, as it was in the East, but the unity of the divine Nature: the three Persons (*personae*) of the Trinity have one action and one will, and act as one principle (*unum principium*).[62] According to Augustine, the Father and the Son are one principle in regard to the Holy Spirit, which is their 'common gift' and is the love they pour out into our hearts.[63] It was St Augustine's trinitarian doctrine that influenced the whole subsequent development of the Latin doctrine of the Trinity and contributed to the teaching on the double procession of the Holy Spirit, that is, from the Father and from the Son. This doctrine (the *Filioque*) was inserted into the Nicene Creed and was one of the reasons for the schism between East and West in the mid-eleventh century. Though the actual schism occurred then, the differences in trinitarian theology and terminology between East and West were clear to subtle theologians such as Athanasius even from the fourth century.

In the text quoted above, St Gregory advances several important ideas. First, differences in dogmatic terminology do not necessarily presuppose disagreement in understanding the dogmas themselves. Not all arguments about dogmatic questions reflect differences in faith: many are simply 'strife about syllables'. The history of the Church sees many cases where the confession of faith of a certain local Church, translated into a different language or understood in the context of a different theological tradition, was misconstrued, considered heretical, and was rejected by another Church.

In this way, many schisms and divisions arose: some of them were later remedied, but some have remained unhealed to the present.

St Gregory's second thesis is no less significant: there are 'dogmas (teachings) of small importance' about which disagreements are to be tolerated. These are the dogmas that can simply be 'disregarded' for the sake of the unity of the Church.[64]

The third point is that not only the 'impious' but also the 'most pious' separate themselves from the Church for various reasons; for example, in their different understanding of a dogma 'of small significance'. These people, one may consider, somehow remain within the Church while being formally separated from it. Thus, not all Christians who are separated from the Church are to be treated as heretics: a schism can often be the result of a mere misunderstanding. Any contemporary theologian who compares the dogmatic traditions of two Churches which are separated from each other must be able to distinguish between what is a heresy, incompatible with the Church's teaching, what is a disagreement on a 'dogma of small significance' that can be 'disregarded', and what is simply 'strife about syllables' resulting from misinterpretation or misconception.

If we apply to our present situation what St Gregory and St Basil have said about their own age, we will see that they were in fact much more 'liberal' than the most advanced 'ecumenists' of today. Neither Gregory nor Basil regarded the disagreement on the question of the divinity of the Holy Spirit as an obstacle for reconciliation among the Churches; nor did they claim that those who did not confess the Spirit as God were outside the Church. Moreover, it was a common practice in the fourth century – indeed, approved by St Basil – to accept Arians into the Church through repentance, not requiring Baptism or Chrismation. In our own times some Orthodox say that Roman Catholics, being 'heretics', are outside the Church, and should be rebaptised when received into Orthodoxy. Yet neither Catholics nor Protestants would deny the divinity of the Son of God, as did the Arians, nor would they deny the divinity of the Holy Spirit, as did most fourth-century theologians and bishops. And surely the question of the procession of the Holy Spirit is less significant than the question of his divinity. To regard today's Catholics and Protestants as 'pseudo-churches' is totally alien to the spirit of the ancient Church Fathers, such as Basil the Great and Gregory the Theologian. Their understanding of the divisions among the Churches was much more dynamic and multi-dimensional, and much less rigid. Many divisions between the Churches could be healed if contemporary theologians used the methodology advanced by St Gregory.

When dealing with the difficult question of Christian divisions, we must also bear in mind that God alone knows where the limits of the Church are. As St Augustine said, 'Many of those who on earth considered themselves to be alien to the Church will find on the day of Judgement that they are her citizens; and many of those who thought themselves to be members of the Church will, alas, be found to be alien to her.'[65] To declare that outside the Orthodox Church there is not and cannot be the grace of God would be to limit God's omnipotence and to confine him to a framework outside which he has no right to act. Hence faithfulness to the Orthodox Church and her dogmatic teaching should never become naked triumphalism by which other Christian Churches are regarded as created by the 'cunning devices' of people, while the whole world and ninety-nine per cent of humankind is doomed to destruction.

## The eucharistic unity of the Universal Church

And unite us all one with another, as many as are partakers of the one Bread and Cup in the communion of the one Holy Spirit . . . Remember, O Lord, Thy Holy, Catholic, and Apostolic Church that stretcheth unto the ends of the earth, and extend Thy peace to her, which Thou hast purchased with the precious Blood of Thy Christ . . . Cause divisions to cease in the Churches. Quench the raging of the heathen. By the power of Thy Holy Spirit destroy the uprisings of heresy. Receive us all into Thy Kingdom, having made us children of light, children of the day. Thy peace and Thy love grant unto us, O Lord our God.

*Liturgy of St Basil the Great*

## The unity of Christians

You all make up together a single temple of God, one altar, one Jesus.

*St Ignatius of Antioch*

## Christians within the world

Christians do not differ from other people through either their country, language or daily customs. They do not inhabit any peculiar cities . . . and they lead a life no different from others. Only their teaching is not the product of thought or the invention of people seeking novelties; they are not tied to any human doctrine as others are. Yet in living in those Greek and barbarian cities where they chanced to be and observing the customs of the inhabitants in clothing, food and all the rest, they lead an astonishing and truly incredible way of life. They live in their homeland, yet as strangers . . . For them every strange country is a homeland, and every homeland a strange country . . . They are in the flesh, but do not live according to the flesh. They are located on earth, yet are citizens of heaven . . . They are deprived of everything, yet have an abundance of all things . . . In short, what the soul is to the body, the Christians are to the world.

*'Letter to Diognetus'*

## 'Christ cannot be divided'

It was in order that we strive for unity with God and among ourselves that we are merged together, although we have different souls and bodies, that the Only-Begotten Son used the means revealed to Him in His own wisdom and through the Council of the Father. Truly, through mystical Communion He has consecrated believers into Himself as one Body and has made us of one body with Himself and each other. Who then can divide or cut off from this bodily union those who are tied to Christ before he has become united with Him through this one holy Body? For if we are all partakers of the one Bread, then we comprise one Body. Truly, Christ cannot be divided . . . The one and undivided Spirit Himself unites the souls of all . . . and reveals them as making up a single being in Himself.

*St Cyril of Alexandria*

## The Church as the spiritual mother of the faithful

The Universal Church is made of all the local Churches in communion with each other. The Fathers tell us that she is the one ark of salvation given by God to people . . . the one Bride of Christ. She is a spiritual mother who alone through Baptism can give birth to children for a new life and make them sons of God. As the Body of Christ she is the only place where people can truly be united with God and each other through the sanctifying power of the Spirit. Does this mean that no person can be saved and sanctified outside of allegiance to the visible Church? There are hints in the Fathers that they know the freedom of the Holy Spirit in His gifts, and that He can bring them to people beyond the usual ways of salvation, in the place where He finds the corresponding disposition of the heart: 'Many of those who are outside of us belong to us – those whose virtues anticipate faith and who do not possess the name of believer as they already possess the reality', says St Gregory the Theologian . . . Of his sister he says: 'All her life was a purification and perfecting . . . I dare to say that Baptism brought her not grace, but perfection.'

*Archimandrite Placide Deseille*

## 'Not one of the Christian confessions has ever said where the limits of the Church are'

The Early Church Councils . . . defined with striking clarity and precision our faith in our Lord God and the Holy Virgin; they defined what our salvation consists of and the last promises of God; yet in laying out what the profound nature of the Church consists of, they did not define her limits . . . Father Georges Florovsky, someone who for many of us was the very voice of Orthodoxy, in a long article on the Church shows that not one of the Christian confessions has ever said for good where the limits of the Church are. It is up to our century to think through and articulate with humility, rigour and Christian love the historical reality which is the Christian world today . . . It is impossible on the one hand to speak about the Church and on the other of the Christian world simply in order not to entice non-Orthodox into an illusion . . . Yet we ourselves should not forget that God mysteriously makes an inroad into souls and communities separated from the One Who is and always shall be – in spite of the temptations brought about by our conflicts – not an isolated column in the desert, but a Pillar bearing the heaviness of the world, the Pillar of truth.

*Metropolitan Anthony of Sourozh*

*Chapter Eight*

# THE SACRAMENTS

## LIFE IN THE SACRAMENTS

Orthodox theology regards the sacraments as sacred actions through which an encounter takes place between us and God. In them our union with God is realised as far as it is possible in this earthly life. The grace of God comes down upon us and sanctifies our entire nature, both soul and body. The sacraments bring us into communion with the divine nature, animating and deifying us, and restoring us to eternal life. In the sacraments we experience a foretaste of the Kingdom of God, that Kingdom which we can only fully enter into after our death.

The Greek word for sacrament, or 'mystery' as it is sometimes translated, is *mysterion*. It comes from the verb *myo*: to cover or conceal. This word was used more broadly than it is today by the Church Fathers. *Mysterion* is used to refer to the incarnation of Christ, his salvific ministry, his death, Resurrection and events of his life, as well as the Christian faith itself, dogma, worship, Church feast days, the sacred symbols, and so on. Of the sacred actions, Baptism and the Eucharist were pre-eminently named sacraments. Dionysius the Areopagite spoke of three sacraments: Baptism, Chrismation (anointing with chrism) and the Eucharist; while the rites of clerical consecration, tonsuring a monk and burial were also listed among the sacraments.[1] Following the same order, Theodore the Studite in the ninth century referred to six sacraments: Illumination (Baptism), the Synaxis (Eucharist), Chrismation, Priesthood, monastic tonsuring and the burial rite.[2] In the fourteenth century Gregory Palamas emphasised the central place of Baptism and the Eucharist, while the fifteenth-century writer Nicholas Cabasilas, in his book *The Life in Christ*, provides commentaries on three sacraments: Baptism, Chrismation and the Eucharist.[3]

At present the Orthodox Church regards Baptism, the Eucharist, Chrismation, Confession, Anointing with Oil, Marriage and Priesthood as sacraments; all the other sacred actions are listed as rituals. It ought to be borne in mind, however, that the practice of numbering the sacraments and distinguishing between sacraments and rituals has been borrowed from Latin scholasticism. Eastern patristic thought in the first millennium was unconcerned about the number of sacraments and never felt the need to enumerate them. Teaching on the seven sacraments was first formulated in the East by Emperor Michael VIII Paleologos in his *Confession of Faith*, presented to Pope Clement IV in 1267.[4] St Symeon of Thessalonica in the fifteenth century also speaks of seven sacraments.[5] His contemporary, Metropolitan Joasaph of Ephesus, writes: 'I believe that there are not seven sacraments of the Church, but more', and gives a list of ten sacraments, including monastic tonsuring, the burial rite and the rite for the consecration of a church.[6]

Each of the sacraments involves both visible and invisible aspects. The former consists of the rite, that is, the words and actions of the participants, and the 'material substance' of the sacrament (water in Baptism, bread and wine in the Eucharist). The latter is the spiritual transfiguration and rebirth of the person for whose sake the rite is accomplished. It is primarily this invisible aspect, hidden from sight and hearing, beyond the mind and beyond sensible perception, that is the 'mystery'. In the sacrament, however, the body is transfigured and revived along with the soul. There is not only a spiritual but also a bodily communion with the gifts of the Holy Spirit. We enter the divine mystery with our whole being, soul and body becoming immersed in God, for the body too is destined for salvation and deification. It is in this sense that we understand immersion in water and anointing with holy oil and myrrh in Baptism, and the eating of bread and wine in the Eucharist. In the age to come the 'material substance' of the sacrament will no longer be necessary, and we will not partake of the Body and Blood of Christ in the form of bread and wine. Rather, we will communicate with Christ direct. 'Grant that we may more truly have communion with thee in the day of thy Kingdom which knows no eventide',[7] prays the Church, believing that it is in the heavenly homeland that we look for a fuller, closer union with Christ. At present we are only on the way, on earth, and we need the visible signs of God's presence. Hence we communicate with the divine nature through water saturated by God and through bread and wine suffused with him.

The author of all the sacraments is God himself. Before the beginning of the Liturgy the deacon says to the priest, 'It is time for the Lord to act.'[8] This means that the time has come, the moment has arrived, when it is God who will act, while the priest and the deacon are merely his instruments. At the consecration of the Holy Gifts, the priest does not act by himself, but prays: 'Make this Bread the precious Body of thy Christ, and that which is in this Cup, the precious Blood of thy Christ.' In the rite of Baptism the priest says, 'The servant of God . . . is baptised.' Again, it is not the priest, but God himself who performs the sacrament. As St Ambrose of Milan says, 'It is not Damasius, or Peter, or Ambrose or Gregory who baptises. We are fulfilling our ministry as servants, but the validity of the sacraments depends upon you. It is not within human power to communicate the divine benefits – it is your gift, O Lord.'[9]

## BAPTISM

The sacrament of Baptism is the door into the Church, the Kingdom of grace, and the beginning of the Christian life. Baptism is the frontier that separates the members of Christ's Body from those who are outside it. In Baptism we are arrayed in Christ, following the words of St Paul which are sung as the newly baptised person is led around the baptismal font: 'For as many of you who were baptised into Christ have put on Christ' (Gal. 3:27). In Baptism we die to our sinful life and rise again to new spiritual life. This is the meaning of the epistle read during the sacramental rite:

Do you not know that all of us who have been baptised into Christ Jesus were baptised into his death? We were buried therefore with him by baptism into death, so that as Christ was raised from the dead by the glory of the Father, we too might walk in newness of life . . . But if we have died with Christ, we believe that we shall also live with him. For we know that Christ being raised from the dead will never die again; death no longer has dominion over him . . . So you also must consider yourselves dead to sin and alive to God in Christ Jesus.

(Rom. 6:3–4, 8–9, 11)

The prototype of New Testament Baptism was John's 'baptism of repentance for the forgiveness of sins' (Mark 1:4) which he performed in the waters of the Jordan. Water is one of the most ancient of religious symbols. In the Bible it signifies life,[10] the grace of God[11] and a person's spiritual and moral purity.[12] The ancient Jews had a tradition of regular ablutions: these, however, could not wash away original sin or free anyone from the power of the devil. In its outward form John's baptism was similar to this ritual ablution, but its inner meaning already prepared people to encounter Christ: 'Prepare the way of the Lord, make his paths straight' (Mark

1:3). Christ came to John to be baptised not in order to be cleansed, for he was already without sin. Rather, through his immersion he sanctified the waters of the river, infusing them with his energy and power, and rendering them life-giving and life-bearing. In the same manner, in the sacrament of Baptism the water is sanctified by the grace of the Holy Spirit.

The sacrament of Baptism was instituted by Christ himself: 'Go therefore and make disciples of all nations, baptising them in the name of the Father and of the Son and of the Holy Spirit' (Matt: 28:19). Christ's commandment contains the essential elements of the baptismal rite: preliminary teaching, without which the adoption of faith cannot be conscious; immersion in water (the Greek *baptismos* literally means 'immersion'); and the trinitarian formula 'in the name of the Father and of the Son and of the Holy Spirit'. In the Early Church, Baptism was accomplished through complete immersion in water,[13] more precisely, in 'living water',[14] that is, in the running water of a river, not the still water of a lake. However, at an early date special pools (baptisteries) were built and candidates for Baptism were immersed in these. The practice of pouring water over the candidates or sprinkling them with water came later.[15] Nevertheless, even in the Early Church, Baptism by sprinkling was allowed, for example if the candidate were ill. In *The Spiritual Meadow* by John Moschus, there is a case of Baptism not with water but with sand. Some travellers were in the desert, death approached, and there was no water.

During the fourth century, in the time of Constantine and after, adult Baptism was more common than the Baptism of infants, the emphasis being on conscious acceptance of the sacrament. Some, knowing that sins were forgiven in Baptism, waited until the end of their lives. The Emperor Constantine himself was baptised just before his death. Gregory the Theologian, a son of a bishop, was baptised only when he reached maturity, and Basil the Great and John Chrysostom only after completing their higher education.

The practice of baptising infants is no less ancient, however – the apostles baptised whole families which might well have included children.[16] Irenaeus of Lyons, in the second century, says: 'Christ came to save those who through him are reborn into God: infants, children, adolescents and the elderly.'[17] In the third century, the local Council of Carthage pronounced an anathema upon those who rejected the necessity of baptising infants and newly born children.[18]

The sacrament of Baptism, like all other sacraments, must be received consciously. Christian faith is the prerequisite for the validity of the sacrament.[19] If an infant is baptised, the confession of faith is solemnly pronounced by his godparents, who are thereby obliged to bring up the child in the faith and make his Baptism conscious. An infant who receives the sacrament cannot rationally understand what is happening to him, yet his soul is fully capable of receiving the grace of the Holy Spirit. 'I believe', writes St Symeon the New Theologian, 'that baptised infants are sanctified and are preserved under the wing of the All-Holy Spirit and that they are lambs of the spiritual flock of Christ and chosen lambs, for they have been imprinted with the sign of the life-giving Cross and freed completely from the tyranny of the devil.'[20] The grace of God is given to infants as a pledge of their future belief, as a seed cast into the earth. For the seed to grow into a tree and bring forth fruit requires the efforts both of the godparents and of the person who has been baptised as he or she grows up.

In the Early Church, Baptism was not carried out on any day that suited the candidates, but only on special feast days, notably at Christmas, Epiphany and Easter. It was preceded by a long period (several months or years) of teaching. During this period those preparing for the sacrament would come to church and be instructed by a bishop or priest. The catechumens (those preparing for Baptism) were set apart in the Early Church: they were allowed to be present at services, yet they had to leave during the Liturgy after the gospel reading and sermon. Even today, the exclamation 'Depart catechumens!' remains. Only the faithful could remain in the church after the gospel reading, and not even all of them, but only those who were to receive Holy Communion.

To this day, ancient links with Baptism are found in the Paschal office of the Orthodox Church. The nocturnal procession around the church building recalls the journey made by the newly baptised. All in white and holding lighted candles, they would enter the church to be greeted with the hymn 'Christ is risen!'

Although extensive instruction in the faith prior to Baptism is not generally given today, there is an obvious need for it, especially for adult candidates. In practice, the Orthodox rite of Baptism has some elements of catechisation preserved within it. There are prayers for the catechumens, and exorcism (expulsion of the devil); and the candidate makes a solemn renunciation of Satan and all his powers and all his works, and a confession of faith in Christ. There follows the blessing of the water, anointing with holy oil and threefold immersion with the words, 'The servant of God (name) is baptised in the Name of the Father, amen; and of the Son, amen; and of the Holy Spirit, amen.' The sacrament of Chrismation (Confirmation) follows the immersion, after which there is a procession around the baptismal font while the people sing: 'As many of you who

[ 134 ]

were baptised into Christ have put on Christ.' The service is completed with readings from the epistle and the gospel, symbolic cutting of hair and churching.

Immediately after Baptism or within a few days, the newly baptised, irrespective of age, receive Holy Communion. This is in contrast to the Roman Catholic Church where Confirmation and first Communion take place after the child has reached the age of seven. The Orthodox Church, however, admits children to Communion as early as possible, even from infancy, in order not to deprive them of a living, if not fully conscious, contact with Christ.

The sacrament of Baptism occurs only once in a person's life. In Baptism we are granted freedom from original sin, and forgiveness of all our personal transgressions. This, however, is only the first step in the journey towards God. If it is not accompanied by a renewal of one's entire life, a spiritual regeneration and renunciation of the words of the 'old man', it will not bear fruit. The grace of God, received in Baptism as a pledge or as a seed, will grow within us and be made manifest throughout our life, so long as we strive towards Christ, live in the Church and fulfil God's commandments. If Baptism is no more than a formality, for the sake of tradition or fashion, its benefits are lost: we separate ourselves from Christ, and exclude ourselves from the Church.

## CHRISMATION

The sacrament of Chrismation was established in apostolic times. In the Early Church every newly baptised Christian received a blessing and the gift of the Holy Spirit through the laying on of hands by an apostle or a bishop. The book of Acts relates how Peter and John laid hands on women from Samaria so that they could receive the Holy Spirit, 'for it had not yet fallen on any of them, but they had only been baptised in the name of the Lord Jesus' (Acts 8:16). In apostolic times, the descent of the Holy Spirit was occasionally accompanied by visible and tangible manifestations of grace: like the apostles at Pentecost, people would begin to speak in unfamiliar tongues, to prophesy and to work miracles.

In passing on the gift of the Holy Spirit, laying on of hands was a continuation of Pentecost. In later times, because of the increased number of Christians, it was impossible for everyone to meet a bishop personally, so the laying on of hands was replaced by Chrismation. In the Orthodox Church, Chrismation is administered by a priest, but the holy chrism itself, a scented oil, is prepared by a bishop. It contains about sixty-four ingredients, including oil, balsam, herbs and aromatic plants. In contemporary practice only the head of an autocephalous Church (the Patriarch, Metropolitan or Archbishop) has the right to prepare chrism, thus conveying the episcopal blessing to all those who become members of the Church.

In the New Testament epistles the gift of the Holy Spirit is sometimes called 'anointing',[21] and this was also the means by which Old Testament kings were appointed to their realm: 'Then Samuel took a vial of oil and poured it on his head, and kissed him and said, "Has not the Lord anointed you to be prince over his people Israel?" ' (I Sam. 10:1). Ordination to the priestly ministry was also performed through Chrismation: 'Take the finest spices: of liquid myrrh ... sweet-smelling cinnamon ... aromatic cane ... cassia ... and of olive oil ... and you shall make of these a sacred anointing oil ... And you shall anoint Aaron and his sons ... It shall not be poured on the bodies of ordinary men, and you shall make no other like it in composition; it is holy' (Exod. 30:23–6, 32).

In the New Testament, however, there is no distinction between the 'consecrated' and the 'others': in Christ's Kingdom all are 'kings and priests' (Rev. 1:6); a 'chosen race', 'God's own people' (I Pet. 2:9). Every Christian, therefore, receives anointing. According to Cyril of Jerusalem, Chrismation is the final stage in one's way towards becoming Christian:

Beware of supposing this to be plain ointment. For as the bread of the Eucharist, after the invocation of the Holy Spirit is no longer mere bread, but the Body of Christ, so also this holy ointment is no more simple ointment ... after invocation, but it is Christ's gift of grace. By the coming of the Holy Spirit it is made fit to impart Christ's divine nature. This ointment is symbolically applied to your forehead and to your other members. And while your body is anointed with the visible ointment, your soul is sanctified by the Holy and life-giving Spirit ... Having been counted worthy of this Holy Chrism, you are called Christians, verifying the name also by your new birth. For before you were deemed worthy of this grace, you had properly no right to this title, but were advancing on your way towards being Christians.[22]

Through anointing we receive the 'seal of the gift of the Holy Spirit'. As Father Alexander Schmemann explains, this is not the same as the various 'gifts' of the Holy Spirit, but the Holy Spirit himself, who is communicated to us as a gift.[23] Christ spoke of this gift to the disciples at the Last Supper: 'And I will pray the Father, and he will give you another Counsellor, to be with you for ever, even the Spirit of truth' (John 14:16–17). He also said about the Spirit: 'It is to your advantage that I go away, for if

I do not go away, the Counsellor will not come to you; but if I go, I will send him to you' (John 16:7). Christ's death on the Cross made possible the gift to us of the Holy Spirit. And it is in Christ that we become kings, priests and 'christs' (anointed ones), receiving neither the Old Testament priesthood of Aaron, nor the kingdom of Saul, nor the anointing of David, but the New Testament priesthood and the kingdom of Christ. Through Chrismation we become sons of God, for the Holy Spirit is the 'grace of adoption as sons'.[24]

As with the grace of Baptism, the gift of the Holy Spirit received in Chrismation is not to be passively accepted, but actively assimilated. It was in this sense that St Seraphim of Sarov, who lived in Russia in the nineteenth century, said that the goal of a Christian's life is the 'acquisition of the Holy Spirit'. The Divine Spirit is given to us a pledge, yet we still have to acquire him, to make him our own. The Holy Spirit is to bring forth fruit in us. 'But the fruit of the Spirit is love, joy, peace, patience, kindness, goodness, faithfulness, gentleness, self-control . . . If we live by the Spirit, let us also walk by the Spirit' (Gal. 5:22, 25). There is a deeper meaning to all the sacraments, and they are for our salvation only when our life as Christians is in harmony with the gift we have received.

## THE EUCHARIST

The Eucharist (from the Greek *eucharistia*, 'thanksgiving'), or the sacrament of Holy Communion, is 'the sacrament of sacraments', 'the mystery of mysteries';[25] it is 'the perfection of every sacrament and the seal of every mystery'.[26] The Eucharist has a central significance in the life of the Church and of every Christian. It is not merely one of a number of sacred actions or 'a means of receiving grace': it is the very heart of the Church, her foundation, without which the Church cannot be imagined.

The sacrament of the Eucharist was instituted by Christ at the Last Supper as related by all four evangelists, as well as by St Paul, who says:

For I received from the Lord what I also delivered to you, that the Lord Jesus on the night when he was betrayed took bread, and when he had given thanks, he broke it and said, 'This is my body which is for you. Do this in remembrance of me.' In the same way also the cup, after supper, saying, 'This cup is the new covenant in my blood. Do this, as often as you drink it, in remembrance of me.' For as often as you eat this bread and drink the cup, you proclaim the Lord's death until he comes.

(I Cor. 11:23–6)

This supper Christ took with the disciples was, in its outward form, the traditional Jewish Paschal meal when the members of every family in Israel gathered to eat the sacrificial lamb. It was attended by Christ's closest followers: not his blood relatives, but that family which would later grow into the Church. Instead of the lamb, Jesus offered himself as a sacrifice 'like that of a lamb without blemish or spot. He was destined before the foundation of the world' for our salvation (I Pet. 1:19–20). At the Mystical Supper Christ transformed the bread and wine into his body and blood, gave Communion to the apostles and commanded them to celebrate this sacrament in remembrance of him. After his death on the Cross and his Resurrection, the disciples would gather on the first day of the week (the so-called 'day of the sun', or Sunday, when Christ rose from the dead) for the 'breaking of bread'.

Originally the Eucharist was a meal accompanied by readings from Scripture, a sermon and a prayer. It would sometimes continue through the night. The book of Acts relates how Paul brought back to life the youth Eutychus at one such supper. Paul's conversation continued for such a long time that the young man 'sank into a deep sleep' and fell out of the window. Paul went down, bent over him and raised him from the dead. After that Paul went back upstairs. 'When Paul had ... broken bread and eaten, he conversed with them a long while, until daybreak' (Acts 20:9–11).

Gradually, as the Christian communities grew, the Eucharist was transformed from an evening supper into a divine service. There is a second-century description of a baptismal Liturgy by Justin Martyr:

After the believer has been cleansed in this fashion [i.e. after baptism], we lead him to the so-called brethren gathered in a general assembly in order to pray both for ourselves and the newly illumined and all those present ... After the prayers we greet each other with a kiss. Then bread and a cup of water and wine is brought to the presiding brother: he takes it and in the name of the Son and the Holy Spirit offers up praise to the Father and likewise completes the thanksgiving ... All of the people present reply: 'Amen' ... After the thanksgiving of the president and the exclamation of all people ... the deacons give to each of those present to partake of the bread over which thanks have been given and the wine and water, and then take them away to those who are absent. This food we call the Eucharist and nobody else is allowed to participate in it apart from those who believe in the truth of our teaching and have been cleansed for the remission of sins ... For we receive this not as ordinary bread or ordinary food; but as Christ was incarnate and took Flesh and Blood for our salvation, then in the same way this food over which thanks are given is, as we have been taught, the Flesh and Blood of the incarnate Christ.[27]

The most ancient elements that constitute the eucharistic rite are mentioned by St Paul and St Justin: these are the reading from Holy Scripture, prayers for all the people, the kiss of peace, thanksgiving to the Father (to which the people reply 'Amen'), the breaking of bread and Communion. In the Early Church, each community had its own Eucharist, but all these elements were present in every eucharistic rite. The bishop's prayer was originally improvised and only later were eucharistic prayers written down. Thus many different eucharistic rites were in use. They were called 'Liturgies' (from the Greek *leitourgia*, which means 'common action', 'work', or 'service'). Each Liturgy that was celebrated bore the name of a particular apostle or holy hierarch as its author.[28]

The Eucharist is a sacrifice in which Christ himself is 'the Offerer and the Offered, the Receiver and the Received'.[29] Christ is the one true celebrant. He is invisibly present in church and acts through the priest. Orthodox Christians believe that the Eucharist is not merely a symbolic action performed in remembrance of the Mystical Supper. Rather, it is the Mystical Supper itself, renewed daily by Christ and continuing without interruption in the Church from that Paschal night when Christ reclined at the table with his disciples to the present day. 'Of Thy Mystical Supper, O Son of God, accept me this day as a partaker',[30] say the believers as they approach Holy Communion. Not only the Mystical Supper but also Christ's sacrifice on Golgotha is renewed at every Liturgy: 'For the King of kings and the Lord of lords cometh to be slain and to give himself for food to the faithful.'[31]

According to the Council of Constantinople of 1156, the Orthodox Church holds that the sacrifice of Christ is offered not only to the Father, but to the Holy Trinity in its entirety. The eucharistic celebration is trinitarian by nature. Prayers are addressed to God the Father, but it is through the action of the Holy Spirit that the bread and wine are transformed into the Body and Blood of Christ: 'Send down thy Holy Spirit . . . and make this Bread the precious Body of thy Christ . . . and that which is in this Cup the precious Blood of thy Christ . . . changing them by thy Holy Spirit.'[32] In an ancient liturgical rite ascribed to Gregory the Theologian,[33] all the prayers are addressed to Christ, and the words of the transformation are expressed somewhat differently:

O Master, change that which is here set forth, for thou art the author of this mystical service . . . Send down thine All-Holy Spirit so that he may

sanctify and change these precious Gifts here set forth into the very Body
and Blood of our Redeemer ... and make this Bread to be thy holy Body,
of our Lord and God and Saviour and Almighty King Jesus Christ ... and
this Cup to be thy precious Blood of thy New Covenant.[34]

The Orthodox Church believes that in the Eucharist the bread and wine
become not only a symbol of Christ's presence, but his Body and Blood
in actuality. This belief has been held in the Christian Church from the
very beginning. Christ himself says: 'For my flesh is food indeed, and my
blood is drink indeed. He who eats my flesh and drinks my blood abides
in me, and I in him' (John 6:55–6). At the end of the first century, Ignatius
of Antioch spoke of the Eucharist as 'the flesh of our Saviour Jesus Christ,
which suffered for our sins',[35] and Justin Martyr also states that 'this food
is the flesh and blood of the incarnate Christ'. All the ancient liturgical
rites emphasise that the eucharistic bread and wine are the 'precious Body
and Blood' of our Lord Jesus Christ (Liturgy of St Basil the Great),
'the very Body and Blood of our Redeemer' (Liturgy of St Gregory the
Theologian), 'the holy Body and precious Blood of Christ' (Liturgy of St
James), 'the true Body and the true Blood of Christ' (Liturgy of the
Armenian Church), 'the most holy Body and Blood of the Son of God'
(the Roman Catholic Mass). St Cyril of Jerusalem follows this tradition
when he emphasises the reality of the Body and Blood of Christ under the
'symbols' of bread and wine:

With full assurance let us partake of the Body and Blood of Christ: for in
the symbol of bread is given to you his Body, and in the figure of wine his
Blood, so that you, by partaking of the Body and Blood of Christ, may be
made of the same body (*syssomos*) and the same blood (*synaimos*) with him.
For thus we come to bear Christ in us, because his Body and Blood are
distributed through our members. This is how, according to the blessed
Peter, we became partakers of the divine nature ... Do not therefore consider
the bread and the wine as bare elements, for they are, according to the Lord's
declaration, the Body and Blood of Christ. For even though sense suggests
this to you, yet let faith support you. Judge not the matter from the taste,
but from faith be fully assured without misgiving, that the Body and Blood
of Christ have been vouchsafed to you ... Learn these things and be fully
assured that what seems to be bread is not bread, though sensible to taste,
but the Body of Christ; and that what seems to be wine is not wine, though
the taste will have it so, but the Blood of Christ.[36]

Thus the union of the believer with Christ in the Eucharist is not symbolic and figurative, but genuine and integral. As Christ suffuses the bread and wine with himself, filling them with his divine presence, so he enters into the communicant, filling our flesh and blood with his own life-giving presence and divine energy. In the Eucharist we become 'of the same body' with Christ, who enters us as he entered the womb of Mary. Symeon the New Theologian writes of how Christ, in uniting himself with us, renders divine all the members of our body:

You are kin of us in the flesh, and we are your kin in your divinity ... You abide with us now and forever, and make of everyone an abode and reside in all ... Each of us is separately with you, O Saviour, all with the All, and you are in everyone separately, the One with the many ... And thus all of the members of each of us shall become members of Christ ... and we together shall all be rendered gods, co-abiding with God.[37]

St Symeon points here to the connection between communion and deification, which is the aim of the Christian life, as well as to the tangible and corporeal nature of union with Christ. In the Eucharist our flesh receives a leaven of incorruption, it becomes deified, and when it dies and becomes subject to corruption, this leaven becomes the pledge of its future resurrection.

Owing to the unique character of the Eucharist, the Church attaches a special significance to it in the work of salvation. Outside the Eucharist there can be no salvation, no deification, no true life, no resurrection in eternity: 'Unless you eat the flesh of the Son of man and drink his blood, you have no life in you; he who eats my flesh and drinks my blood has eternal life, and I will raise him up at the last day' (John 6:53–4). Hence the Church Fathers advise Christians never to decline the Eucharist and to take Communion as often as possible. 'Endeavour to gather more often for the Eucharist and the glorification of God', says Ignatius of Antioch.[38] The words from the Lord's Prayer, 'Give us this day our daily bread',[39] are sometimes interpreted as a call to daily reception of the Eucharist.[40] 'It is good and extremely beneficial to partake and receive every day the Body and Blood of Christ ...' wrote Basil the Great. 'However, we take communion four times a week: on the Lord's day, on Wednesday, Friday and Saturday, as well as on other days when we remember one of the saints.'[41] According to ancient canonical regulations, those who had not received Communion over a long period without a just cause were to be excommunicated: 'The faithful who do not abide in Holy Communion, are to be excommunicated as bringing disorder into the Church.'[42]

Not only in the Early Church, but at later periods also, many saintly hierarchs, priests and monks called upon people to receive Communion frequently. In the eleventh century, for example, Symeon the New Theologian spoke of the need to take Communion every day with tears. Nicodemus of the Holy Mountain promoted the eighteenth-century 'eucharistic renaissance' and published a book entitled *On Frequent Communion*. More recently, at the beginning of the twentieth century, St John of Kronstadt celebrated the Liturgy every day and gave Communion to thousands.

A practice of receiving Communion infrequently, for example only at great feasts or during fasts, or even just once a year, arose in Russia from a progressive weakening of eucharistic piety. Some avoided Communion out of a sense of their own unworthiness (as if by refraining from Communion they might become more worthy); while for others Communion became a mere formality, a religious duty to be observed.

In our own time, the Orthodox Church is gradually returning to the early Christian practice of taking Communion every Sunday. While it is understood that no one is ever worthy of this great sacrament, the Eucharist exists so that in receiving Communion and becoming united with Christ we are gradually purified and become more worthy of an encounter with God. John Cassian spoke of this as early as the fifth century:

We should not decline the Lord's Communion because we feel ourselves to be sinners. We must more and more hurriedly rush to him for the healing of soul and purification of spirit, yet with such a humility of spirit and faith that, in seeing ourselves as unworthy of receiving such grace, we should desire more and more the healing of our wounds. Otherwise, we cannot take Communion worthily just once a year, as some do . . . because of their high respect to the dignity, sanctity and beneficence of the Heavenly Mysteries; they therefore believe that only the saints and the pure should receive the Mysteries. Yet it would be better to think that these Sacraments render us pure and holy through the communication of grace. Those people really do betray more pride than humility . . . because, in receiving the Mysteries, they believe themselves worthy of receiving them. If we – with humility of heart, by which we believe and confess that we can never be worthy communicants of the Holy Mysteries – received them every Sunday for the healing of our infirmities, this would be far more correct than if we would . . . think that after a year has lapsed we are worthy of receiving them.[43]

The Church reminds us that all those who approach Holy Communion must be ready to encounter Christ. Proper preparation is necessary, and should not be limited to the reading of a certain number of prayers and abstinence from particular types of food. Readiness for Communion is conditioned by a pure conscience, the absence of enmity towards our neighbours or a grievance against anyone, and by peace in all our relationships: 'So if you are offering your gift at the altar, and there remember that your brother has something against you, leave your gift there before the altar and go; first be reconciled to your brother, and then come and offer your gift' (Matt. 5:23–4). Obstacles to Communion are particularly grave sins; a person who has committed such sins should first repent of them in Confession.

In the Orthodox Church it is the rule to take Communion on an empty stomach, as the human body must be cleansed by fasting beforehand. This is an ancient tradition going back to the time when the Liturgy ceased to be a continuation of the *agape* ('love feast', 'meal of love') and was transformed into a solemn divine service celebrated in the morning.

Certain ascetical rules of preparation for Communion, such as fasting for several days and the reading of special preparatory prayers, came into being at a time when Communion was infrequent and irregular. Modern-day practice in some local Orthodox Churches, particularly the Russian Church, prescribes a one-, two-, or three-day fast. Communion must also be preceded by Confession. In some other local Churches, for example, in the Greek East, a eucharistic fast is usually observed from midnight and people are admitted to Communion without necessarily having been to Confession. The Russian practice was evidently imposed on those who received Communion infrequently. For those who receive Communion every Sunday or more often, less strict rules are usually applied.

All prescriptions regarding preparation for Communion are made with the intention that people approaching the sacrament should be aware of their state of sinfulness and approach with a deep sense of repentance. At the prayer before Communion the priest and people recite the words of St Paul, each calling themselves 'the first among sinners': 'I believe, O Lord, and I confess that Thou art truly the Christ, the Son of the living God, who camest into the world to save sinners, of whom I am first.' It is only by being aware of our complete unworthiness that we can be worthy of approaching the Eucharist.

The contrition that comes from a sense of our own sinfulness does not, however, prevent us from receiving the Eucharist as a celebration of joy and thanksgiving. By its very nature the Eucharist is a solemn thanksgiving, fundamental to which is praise of God. It is not by mere chance that on weekdays during Great Lent the full Liturgy is not celebrated. The exultant tone of the eucharistic prayers does not correspond with the penitential character of this period. Herein lies the paradox and mystery of the Eucharist: it has to be approached with both repentance and joy. With repentance from a sense of our unworthiness, and with joy at the fact that in the Eucharist the Lord cleanses, sanctifies and deifies us, rendering us worthy in spite of our unworthiness. Not only are the bread and wine transformed into the Body and Blood of Christ, but also each communicant is transformed from an old into a new person. We are freed from the burden of sin and illumined by divine light.

## THE SACRAMENT OF REPENTANCE

'Repent, for the kingdom of heaven is at hand' (Matt. 3:2). With these words, first uttered by John the Baptist, Jesus Christ began his own mission.[44] From the very beginning Christianity was a call to repentance, to conversion, to *metanoia*, which in Greek means a change of mind. Radical transformation of one's entire way of life and thought, renovation of the mind and senses, rejection of sinful deeds and thoughts, and transfiguration of the person: these are the main elements of Christ's message.

Synonymous with repentance is 'return': 'Return, every one from his evil way, and amend your ways and your doings' (Jer. 18:11). Repentance is a turn: it is a turning away from sinful life and returning to God. The pattern for repentance is set by Jesus himself in the parable of the prodigal son.[45] Having lived a sinful life 'in a far country', that is, far away from God, the prodigal son, after many tribulations, comes to himself and decides to return to his father. Repentance begins with his conversion ('he came to himself'), which is then transformed into determination to return ('I will arise and go'), and finishes with his return to God ('he arose and came'). This is followed by confession ('Father, I have sinned against heaven and before you'), which results in forgiveness ('Bring quickly the best robe'), adoption ('this my son'), and spiritual resurrection ('who was dead, and is alive again'). Repentance is therefore a dynamic process, a movement towards God, rather than the mere act of recognising one's sins.

All Christians have all their sins forgiven in the sacrament of Baptism. However, 'There is no man who shall live and sin not.'[46] Sins committed after Baptism deprive us of the fullness of life in God. Hence the necessity of the 'second Baptism', an expression used by the Church Fathers for repentance, emphasising its purifying, renovating and sanctifying energy. 'Repentance is the renewal of Baptism', says St John Climacus. 'Repentance is a contract with God for a second life ... Repentance is reconciliation with the Lord by the practice of good deeds contrary to the sins. Repentance is purification of conscience.'[47]

The sacrament of repentance is spiritual healing for the soul. Every sin, depending on its gravity, inflicts on the soul a small injury, a deep wound, a serious disease, or even a fatal illness. In order to be spiritually healthy, we each need to visit our father-confessor regularly, as a spiritual doctor: 'Have you sinned? Go to church and repent in your sin... Here is a physician, not a judge. Here nobody is condemned, but everybody receives forgiveness of sins', says St John Chrysostom.[48]

From the very beginning of Christianity, it was the duty of the apostles, and then of bishops and presbyters, to hear confessions and to give absolution. Christ said to his apostles: 'Whatever you bind on earth shall be bound in heaven, and whatever you loose on earth shall be loosed in heaven' (Matt. 18:18). The power of 'binding and loosing', which was given to the apostles and through them to bishops and priests, is manifested in the absolution which the priest gives on behalf of God to the penitent. The book of Acts tells us that many people who believed in Christ came to the apostles, 'confessing and divulging their practices' (Acts 19:18). Therefore, the Christian life of former pagans began with confession. In the Early Church there was a practice of public confession as well as an individual's confession before several priests. This had virtually disappeared by the fifth century, and nowadays only one-to-one confession is practised in the Orthodox Church.

Why is it necessary to confess sins to a priest, a fellow human being? Is it not enough to tell God everything and receive absolution from him? In order to answer this question, one should be reminded that in the Christian Church a priest is only a 'witness' to God's presence and action: it is not the priest who acts in liturgical celebrations and in the sacraments, but God himself. The confession of sins is always addressed to God, and forgiveness is also received from him. In promoting the idea of confession before a priest, the Church has always taken into account a psychological factor: it is always embarrassing to reveal one's sins before a fellow human being. Moreover, the priest is also a spiritual director, a counsellor who can offer advice on how to avoid particular sins in the future. The sacrament of Confession is not limited to a mere acknowledgement of sins. It also involves recommendations, or sometimes *epitimia* (penalties) on the part of the priest. It is primarily in the sacrament of Confession that the priest acts in his capacity of spiritual father.

If a penitent deliberately conceals any of his or her sins, whether out of shame or for any other reason, the sacrament would not be considered valid. Thus, before beginning the rite, the priest warns that the confession must be sincere and complete: 'Be not ashamed, neither be afraid, and conceal thou nothing from me . . . But if thou shalt conceal anything from me, thou shalt have the greater sin.'[49] At the same time, the forgiveness of sins that is granted after confession is full and all-inclusive: 'May our Lord and God Jesus Christ, through the grace and bounties of his love towards mankind, forgive thee, my child (name), *all* thy transgressions. And I, the unworthy priest . . . do forgive and absolve thee from *all* thy sins, in the name of the Father, and of the Son, and of the Holy Spirit.'[50] It is a mistake to believe that only the sins enumerated during confession are forgiven. There are sins which we do not see in ourselves, and there are some, or many, that we simply forget. All these sins are also cleansed by God so long as our confession is sincere. Otherwise total forgiveness would never be possible for anyone, as it is not possible for us to know *all* our sins or to be perfect judges of ourselves.

The importance of frequent confession may be indicated by the fact that those who come very rarely are sometimes unable to see their sins and transgressions clearly. They may say things such as: 'I live like everybody else'; 'I haven't done anything special'; 'I did not kill anyone'; 'There are those who are worse than I am'; and even 'I have no sins'. On the contrary, those who come regularly for confession always find many faults in themselves. They recognise their sins and try to be liberated from them. There is a very simple explanation for this. As dust and dirt are seen only where there is light but not in darkness, so we perceive our sins only when we approach God, the unapproachable Light. The closer we are to God, the more clearly we see our own sin. As long as our soul continues to be a *camera obscura*, our sins remain unrecognised and consequently unhealed.

## ANOINTING WITH OIL

The first human was created with an incorruptible and immortal body. After the Fall it lost these qualities and became corruptible and mortal. According to St Gregory the Theologian, we 'put on the garment of sin, which is our coarse flesh, and became a body-bearer'.[51] Illness and disease became a part of human life. The root of all infirmity, according to the Church's teaching, is human sinfulness: sin entered us in such a way that it polluted not only our soul and intellect, but also our body. If death is a consequence of sin,[52] an illness may be seen as a situation between sin and death: it follows sin and precedes death. It is not, of course, that every particular sin results in a particular illness. The real issue concerns the root of all illness, namely, human corruptibility. As Symeon the New Theologian remarks, 'Doctors cure human bodies . . . but they can never cure the basic illness of human nature, its corruptibility. For this reason, when they try different means to cure one particular illness, the body then falls prey to another disease.'[53] Human nature, according to Symeon, needs a physician who can heal it from its corruptibility, and this physician is Jesus Christ himself.

During his earthly life Christ healed many people. Before healing someone, he often asked them about their faith: 'Do you believe that I am able to do this?' (Matt. 9:28). As well as healing the body, Christ also healed the human soul from its most severe disease, unbelief. He also pointed to the devil as the origin of all illness: of the woman who could not stand upright he said that she was 'bound by Satan'.[54]

The Church has always considered its own mission as the continuation in all aspects of Christ's ministry, including healing. Thus, from apostolic times, a sacramental action existed which would later receive the name of Holy Unction, or Anointing with Oil. It is found in the New Testament:

Is any among you sick? Let him call for the elders[55] of the church, and let them pray over him, anointing him with oil in the name of the Lord; and the prayer of faith will save the sick man, and the Lord will raise him up; and if he has committed sins, he will be forgiven.

(Jas. 5:14–15)

It is clear that this is not a question of an ordinary anointing, which in ancient times was used for medical purposes, but of a special sacramental action. Healing qualities are ascribed here not to the oil, but to the 'prayer of faith'; and the physician is not a presbyter, but 'the Lord'.

In the contemporary practice of the Orthodox Church, the sacrament of Anointing has preserved all the original elements described by St James. It is conducted by seven priests (though in practice, often only two or three), prayers and New Testament passages are read, and the sick person is anointed seven times with blessed oil. The prayer of absolution is read by one of the priests at the end of the sacrament. The Church believes that, in accordance with St James's words, the sins of the one who receives Anointing are forgiven. This in no way implies, however, that Anointing can be regarded as a substitute for Confession. The opinion of some Orthodox believers that in Anointing all *forgotten* sins, that is, those not mentioned at Confession, are forgiven, is also unfounded. The sacrament of Confession, as we said above, results in the forgiveness of *all* sins. The intention behind the sacrament of Holy Unction is not to supplement

[ 147 ]

Confession, but rather to give new strength to the sick with prayers for the healing of body and soul.

Even more misleading is the interpretation of Holy Unction as the 'last anointing' before death. This was the understanding of the sacrament in the Roman Catholic Church before Vatican II, and it still finds its place among Orthodox believers. This is a misinterpretation simply because Anointing does not *guarantee* that a person who receives it will necessarily be healed. Father Alexander Schmemann writes:

A sacrament . . . is always a *passage* and *transformation* . . . It is the transformation not of 'nature' into 'supernature', but of the *old* into the *new* . . . And healing is a sacrament because its purpose or end is not *health* as such, the restoration of physical health, but the entrance of man into the life of the Kingdom, into the 'joy and peace' of the Holy Spirit . . . In this world suffering and disease are indeed normal, but their very 'normalcy' is abnormal. They reveal the ultimate and permanent defeat of man and of life, a defeat which no partial victories of medicine, however wonderful and truly miraculous, can ultimately overcome. But in Christ suffering is not 'removed'; it is transformed into victory. The defeat *itself* becomes victory, a way, an entrance into the Kingdom, and this is the only true *healing*.[56]

In this sense it can be said that Anointing makes those who receive it able to participate in Christ's sufferings, renders their bodily illness salvific and healing, and liberates them from spiritual illness and death. Many saints have received illness with gratitude as a means of liberation from eternal damnation. In *The Spiritual Meadow* by St John Moschos in the sixth century, we read of one old monk who suffered from dropsy and was offered help by his fellow monastics. 'You would do better to pray', he said to them, 'that my inner self would not suffer from dropsy. As far as I am concerned, I pray that God prolongs this illness.' The Archbishop of Jerusalem sent the elder something 'for bodily needs', but he did not accept any of what was sent to him. 'You would do better to pray for me', he said to the Archbishop, 'that I be liberated from eternal damnation.'[57]

According to the teaching of the Church, God is able to transform everything evil into something good. In the particular case of illness, which of itself is evil and a consequence of corruption, it can become a source of spiritual benefit. It can be a means by which a person participates in Christ's sufferings and is risen with Christ to a new life. There are many cases when illness compels people to change their life and to embark upon the path of repentance that leads to God.

## MARRIAGE

The love that exists between a man and a woman is an important theme in many books of Scripture. The book of Genesis, in particular, tells us of couples such as Abraham and Sarah, Isaac and Rebecca, Jacob and Rachel. A special blessing bestowed on these couples by the Lord was the multiplication of their descendants. Love is praised in the Song of Songs, a book which, in spite of all the allegorical and mystical interpretations in the patristic tradition, does not lose its literal meaning.

The very attitude of God to the people of Israel is compared in the Old Testament with that of a husband to his wife. This imagery is developed to such an extent that unfaithfulness to God and idolatry are compared with adultery and prostitution. When St Paul speaks about marital love as the reflection of the love which exists between Christ and the Church,[58] he develops the same theme.

The mystery of marriage was established by God in Paradise. Having created Adam and Eve, God said to them: 'Be fruitful and multiply' (Gen. 1:28). This multiplication of the human race was to be achieved through marriage: 'Therefore a man leaves his father and his mother and cleaves to his wife, and they become one flesh' (Gen. 2:24). Marital union is therefore not a consequence of the Fall but something inherent in the primordial nature of human beings. The mystery of marriage was further blessed by the incarnate Lord when he changed water into wine at the wedding in Cana of Galilee. 'We state', St Cyril of Alexandria writes, 'that he (Christ) blessed marriage in accordance with the economy (*oikonomia*) by which he became man and went . . . to the wedding in Cana of Galilee.'[59]

If we are to speak of a development of dogmatic theology along the lines given in the Introduction, it could be argued that the theology of marriage is a field which most urgently calls for further investigation. Until very recently, marriage has never been a primary focus for theological reflection. During the first Christian centuries, it was regarded as belonging to the realm of civil rather than ecclesiastical law: there was no special rite of marriage in the Christian Church. Marriage was an institution inherited by Christians from their pre-Christian forefathers. Notions of virginity and celibacy were virtually unknown in the pagan world. This is why the Church Fathers considered it necessary to defend virginity and to write special treatises on this subject. In later centuries, the entire field of theology in the East was dominated by monastic writers. In the West, beginning with Tertullian, Ambrose and Augustine, marriage was regarded as having no value of its own but to be justified only by childbirth. This attitude to marriage is still the norm in much Western theology.

There are two misunderstandings about marriage which should be rejected according to Orthodox dogmatic theology. One is that marriage exists for the sole purpose of procreation. What, then, is the meaning of marriage for those couples who have no children? Are they advised to divorce and remarry? Even in the case of those who have children, are they actually supposed to limit sexual relations to once a year for the sole purpose of 'procreation'? This has never been a teaching of the Church. On the contrary, according to John Chrysostom, of the two reasons for which marriage was instituted, namely 'to bring man to be content with one woman and to have children', it is the first which is the most important: 'as for procreation, it is not required absolutely by marriage . . .'[60] In fact, in an Orthodox understanding, the goal of marriage is that man and woman should become one, in the image of the Holy Trinity, whose three Persons are essentially united in love. To quote John Chrysostom again, 'When husband and wife are united in marriage, they are no longer seen as something earthly, but as the image of God himself.'[61] The mutual love of the two partners in marriage becomes life-giving and creative when a child is born. Every human being is therefore to be a fruit of love, and everyone's birth a result of love between his or her parents.

Another misunderstanding about marriage is that it should be regarded as a 'concession' to human 'infirmity', the assumption being that it is better to be married than to commit adultery.[62] Some early Christian sectarian movements (such as Montanism and Manicheanism) held the view that sexuality in general was something unclean and evil, while virginity was the only proper state for Christians. The Orthodox tradition opposed this very strongly as a distortion of Christian asceticism and morality. This can be seen in the following quotation from St Methodius of Patara, who, in his third-century treatise on virginity, *Symposium*, speaks of the mystery of marriage:

God's declaration and ordinance with regard to the begetting of children is still being carried out accordingly up to the present day: the Creator is still fashioning men. For it is clear to everyone that God, like an artist, is still working on his universe, as indeed the Lord also taught when he said, *my Father is working still* [John 5:17] . . . Now man must co-operate in the production of God's image, so long as the universe still exists and continues to be formed. *Be fruitful and multiply* [Gen. 1:28] was the command, and we may not spurn the command of our Creator from whom we too, of course, have ourselves come into being. Man's coming into existence begins with the sowing of the seed in the furrows of the maternal field: and thus bone from bone and flesh from flesh, taken in an invisible act of power and always by the same divine Craftsman, are fashioned into a new human being. In this way, we must believe, is fulfilled the saying, *This at last is bone of my bones, and flesh of my flesh* [Gen. 2:23]. Moreover, this was perhaps the symbolism of that ecstatic sleep into which God put the first man, that it was a type of man's enchantment in love, when in his thirst for children he falls into a trance [in Greek *ekstasis*, literally meaning 'ecstasy'], lulled to sleep by the pleasures of procreation, in order that a new person . . . might be formed in turn from the material that is drawn from his flesh and bone. For under the stimulation of intercourse, the body's harmony . . . is greatly disturbed, and all the marrow-like generative part of the blood, which is liquid bone, gathers from all parts of the body, curdled and worked into a foam, and then rushes through the generative organs into the living soil of the woman. Hence rigidly it is said that *therefore a man leaves his father and his mother* [Gen. 2:24] for man made one with woman in the embrace of love is overcome by a desire for children and completely forgets everything else; he offers his rib to his divine Creator, to be removed that he himself the father may appear once again in the son. If then God is still fashioning human beings, would it not be insolent for us to loathe procreation, which the Almighty himself is not ashamed to accomplish with his undefiled hands?[63]

Although St Methodius uses the expressions 'procreation' and 'desire for children', it is very clear that he is speaking about the positive meaning of sexual love in itself rather than about it being necessary for procreation. God the Creator is in fact regarded as participating in the sexual intercourse between man and woman. When men 'are brought to deposit their seed in the woman's channels', St Methodius continues, 'the seed shares, so to say, the divine creative function'.[64] All elements of sexual life, such as 'enchantment', 'pleasures', 'embrace of love', 'desire' and 'ecstasy', receive a positive and poetic interpretation in St Methodius. There is no suggestion that sexual union is something unclean or unholy. On the contrary, the whole story of the creation of Eve from Adam's rib is taken as symbolising sexual intercourse.

This interpretation is fully consistent with the understanding of sexual love found in the Orthodox marriage service, where we pray: 'Bless their marriage, and vouchsafe unto these thy servants . . . chastity, mutual love in the bond of peace . . . Preserve their bed unassailed . . . Cause their marriage to be honourable. Preserve their bed blameless. Mercifully grant that they may live together in purity . . .'[65] Sexual love is, therefore, seen as compatible with purity and chastity, the latter being, of course, not abstinence from intercourse but rather a fully sexual love that is liberated from all that encumbered it after the Fall of Adam. As Paul Evdokimov says in his challenging book on marriage, 'In harmonious unions . . . sexuality undergoes a progressive spiritualisation in order to reach conjugal chastity.'[66] The mutual love of man and woman in marriage becomes less and less dependent on the sexual aspect and develops into a deep union which integrates the whole of the person. The two become not only 'one flesh', but also one soul and one spirit. In Christian marriage, selfish pleasure or the search for fun are not the main driving force. Rather it is a quest for mutual sacrifice, for readiness to take the partner's cross as one's own, and to share one's whole life with the other. The ultimate goal of marriage is the same as that of every other sacrament, deification of human nature and union with Christ. This becomes possible when marriage itself is transfigured and deified.

If we compare the understanding of marriage in the Byzantine East with the Latin West of the Middle Ages, the most striking differences are, as Father John Meyendorff argues, that 'the Byzantines strongly emphasised the *unicity* of Christian marriage and the *eternity* of the marriage bond; they never considered that Christian marriage was a legal contract, automatically dissolved by the death of one of the partners'.[67] In the Christian East, the words of Christ that the people in the age to come 'neither marry nor are given in marriage' but 'are equal to angels' (Luke 20:35–6) have not been taken to mean that marriage comes to an end after death. They show that people's mode of existence in the future age will differ from that of this transient world. What constitutes the precise nature of this difference remains a mystery. We know that we shall partake of Christ in the future world, even though there will no longer be the eucharistic bread and wine. Our participation will indeed be more integral and more direct than is possible for us here. In the same way, the mystery of marriage will reveal itself even more fully in the future life, in spite of the fact that sexual intercourse will no longer be possible and our entire bodily condition will change. As long as marriage is a sacrament, it has absolute value, like all other sacraments. Its significance will in no way be diminished in the age to come, and can only increase.

Father John Meyendorff also points to the central place of Christ in every Christian marriage, and speaks of marriage as an experience of participation in the life of the age to come:

A Christian is called – already in this world – to experience new life, to become a citizen of the Kingdom; and he can do so in marriage. But then marriage ceases to be either a simple satisfaction of temporary natural urges, or a means for securing an illusory survival through posterity. It is a unique union of two beings in love, two beings who can transcend their own humanity and thus be united not only 'with each other', but also 'in Christ'.[68]

In marriage, then, we are transfigured. Loneliness and egocentricity are overcome and the personality is completed and perfected. In this light Father Alexander Elchaninov, a notable contemporary Orthodox priest and theologian, describes marriage in terms of 'initiation' and 'mystery', in which 'a full transformation of the human person' takes place, 'the enlargement of his personality, new eyes, new perception of life, birth into the world, by means of it, in new fullness'. In the marital union of two individuals there is both the completion of their personalities and the birth of the fruit of their love, a child, whereby two become three:

An integral knowledge of another person is possible in marriage, a miracle of sensation, intimacy, of the vision of another person . . . Before marriage, the human person glides above life, seeing it from outside. Only in marriage is he fully immersed into it, and enters it through another person. This enjoyment of true knowledge and true life gives us that feeling of complete fullness and satisfaction which renders us richer and wiser. And this fullness is even deepened when out of the two of us, united and reconciled, a third appears, our child.[69]

With such a high regard for the mystery of marriage, the Church generally takes a negative view of divorce and remarriage, unless they stem from exceptional circumstances. The attitude of the Orthodox Church is not, however, formulaic. While remaining faithful to the original Christian moral standards as expressed by Christ himself,[70] the Church always acknowledges the possibility of human error. Divorce and remarriage are regarded as exceptions, yet in some cases they are allowed and even recommended. In particular, an Orthodox priest may recommend a 'temporary divorce' to a couple whose marriage has been sufficiently damaged by the misbehaviour of either husband or wife.[71] The Church may approve a full divorce on grounds of infidelity.[72] In this case, as also in the case of the death of one of the partners, a second or even a third marriage may be blessed by the Church.

In the Early Church, there was no special sacrament of marriage. A bridegroom and a bride would come to their bishop for a blessing, after which they attended the Liturgy and received Communion. Eventually the sacrament developed, but it was still linked with Communion.[73] This link can be seen clearly in the existing marriage rite, which begins with the liturgical exclamation 'Blessed is the Kingdom of the Father, and of the Son, and of the Holy Spirit', and includes many prayers from the eucharistic Liturgy, as well as epistle and gospel readings. The bridegroom and bride partake together of a cup of wine which symbolises their union in Christ.

The sacrament of marriage also includes the symbolic crowning of the bride and bridegroom. A crown is first of all a symbol of kingship; each Christian family is a part of the Kingdom of heaven, a 'small church' where the encounter of people with God takes place. But a crown also symbolises martyrdom, and thus the couple is reminded that marriage involves not only the joy of the first months after the wedding ceremony, but also the readiness of both partners to bear together their common cross of pain and suffering. In an era when the dissolution of families, divorce and remarriage are everyday occurrences, when partners in marriage all too often betray each other at the first encounter with difficulty, this symbolic coronation reminds the bridal couple of the responsibility they take for the rest of their lives. It points to the fact that a lasting marriage is not based on fleeting passions, but upon each partner's readiness to sacrifice his or her life for the other. Only the family that has Christ as its cornerstone can become a house founded on the rock and not on the sand.[74]

Christ is the One who is present at every Christian marriage and who conducts the marriage ceremony in the Church. The priest's role is not so much to *represent*, as to *present* Christ and to reveal his presence, as it is in the other sacraments. The story of the wedding in Cana of Galilee is read at the Christian wedding ceremony in order to show that marriage is the miracle of the transformation of water into wine, that is, of everyday routine into an unceasing and daily feast, a perpetual celebration of the love of one person for the other.

## PRIESTHOOD

The sacrament of priesthood includes three liturgical rites of ordination: to the episcopate, to the priesthood and to the diaconate.[75]

According to the present tradition of the Orthodox Church, bishops are chosen from among monks.[76] In the Early Church there were married bishops. St Paul says a bishop must be 'the husband of one wife' (I Tim.

3:2). Even in the early centuries, however, preference was given to monastic or celibate clergy. Thus, among the well-known bishops of the fourth century, only St Gregory of Nyssa was married, while St Athanasius, St Basil the Great, St Gregory the Theologian and St John Chrysostom were celibate. Priests and deacons in the Orthodox Church may be either monastic or married. Clergy may only marry before ordination, however, and only once. It is not usual to ordain a man who has been married a second time as a priest or deacon.

Since apostolic times, ordination into the hierarchical ranks has been accomplished through the laying on of hands. Priests and deacons are ordained by a bishop, and a bishop by several bishops (no less than two, and often more). Ordinations take place during the Liturgy. A bishop is ordained after the singing of 'Holy God' (during the Liturgy of the catechumens), a priest after the Cherubic Hymn, and a deacon after the consecration of the Holy Gifts.

Episcopal ordinations are especially solemn. The priest who is to be ordained enters the altar through the 'royal doors' and goes three times round the altar, kissing its four corners. The clergy and choir sing hymns from the marriage service. The man to be ordained then kneels in front of the altar, and the hierarchs lay their hands on his head, with the presiding celebrant reading the prayer of ordination: 'The grace divine, which always heals that which is infirm and completes that which is wanting, through the laying on of hands elevates thee, the most God-loving Archimandrite, (name), duly elected, to be the Bishop of the God-saved cities, (names). Wherefore let us pray for him, that the grace of the All-holy Spirit may come upon him.'[77] Following this, while *Kyrie eleison* ('Lord, have mercy') is sung by the clergy and the choir, the senior bishop reads other prayers. The newly ordained bishop is then clothed in episcopal vestments, while the people (or the choir) exclaim *Axios!* ('He is worthy!') This exclamation is the only trace of the ancient practice of the election of bishops by all the faithful.[78]

Ordinations to the priesthood and to the diaconate follow a similar order. The one who is to be ordained enters the sanctuary, goes round the altar, kissing its corners, and kneels at its corner (a deacon on one knee, and a priest on both). The bishop lays his hands on him and reads the prayers of consecration. The newly ordained deacon or priest is then clothed in the vestments of his office, while the *Axios* is sung by the people.

The singing of hymns from the marriage rite has a particular meaning in ordination to the hierarchical ranks: it shows that the bishop, priest or deacon is betrothed to his diocese or parish. In the Early Church it was very unusual for a bishop to change his diocese, or a priest his parish.[79] As a rule, an ecclesiastical appointment was for life. Even the Patriarch was chosen not from the bishops of a particular patriarchate, but from the lower clergy, in some cases even from the laity.

The sacrament of priesthood is deeply significant, for with it the Church community receives its new pastor. Despite the Orthodox emphasis on the 'royal priesthood' of all believers, the Church also recognises a difference between laypeople and ordained clergy, the latter being entrusted with the celebration of the Eucharist, and having the power of 'binding and loosing'. Ordination into a hierarchical rank, be it of bishop, priest or deacon, is not only a change of status but a transition to another level of existence. As Archimandrite Cyprian (Kern) wrote, a person who has been ordained 'is no longer a simple layman, but a *theourgos*, an "initiator into mysteries" and a celebrant of sacraments. He is not just Mister X, but Father X. From this moment life begins in its proper sense: no longer activity, but ministry, no longer talks, but sermons, no longer the infirmity of the paralysed man, but the courage of Christ's friend.'[80]

St Silouan, who was a monk of Mount Athos until his death in 1938, and not himself ordained, wrote the following about the high dignity of priestly ministry and the grace given to the pastors of the Church:

(This) grace is so exceeding great that were men able to see the glory of this grace, the whole world would wonder at it; but the Lord has veiled it that His servants should not be puffed up but find salvation in humility . . . Truly noble is a priest — the minister at God's altar. Whoever gives offence to him offends the Holy Spirit who lives in him . . . If people could behold in what glory a priest celebrates the divine office they would swoon at the sight; and if the priest could see himself, could see the celestial glory surrounding him as he officiates, he would become a great warrior and devote himself to feats of spiritual endurance, that he might not offend in any way the grace of the Holy Spirit living in him.[81]

In the Orthodox Church, then, priests and bishops are regarded as bearers of divine grace, as instruments through which God himself acts. When receiving a priest's blessing, the faithful kiss his hand as if it were Christ's hand, because it is by Christ's power that he gives the blessing. This sense of holiness and dignity in priestly ministry is weakened in some Christian denominations. In some Protestant communities, for example, the only difference between the laity and the clergy is that the latter have a 'licence to preach'.

If the sacrament of Priesthood is a very special event for the entire community, for the man who has been ordained this day is his personal Pentecost, when the Holy Spirit descends upon him and he receives gifts of divine grace. Some saints are reported to have seen the Holy Spirit in a visible form during their ordination. As the *Life of St Symeon the New Theologian* tells us, when the bishop read the prayer of consecration, Symeon 'saw the Holy Spirit, which descended without form as simple and boundless light and covered his sacred head; he always saw this light when he celebrated the Liturgy throughout the forty-eight years of his priesthood'.[82]

In his autobiographical notes, Father Serge Bulgakov describes his ordinations to the diaconate and to the priesthood as the most memorable mystical experiences of his life:

I was ordained deacon on the day of the Holy Trinity.[83] If the inexpressible can be expressed, I shall say that this first ordination was experienced by me as the most fiery. The most overwhelming aspect of it was my passing, for the first time, through the royal doors and approaching the holy table. It was like passing through fire, burning, illuminating and regenerating. This was entering into another world, into the Kingdom of heaven. This was for me the beginning of a new form of existence, in which I remain till the present . . . The experiences of ordination into priesthood are even more inexpressible than those of the first ordination – 'silence is more suitable' . . .[84]


## MONASTICISM

In the Orthodox Church the rite of monastic tonsure also has a sacramental character. It is called a 'sacrament' ('mystery') by Dionysius the Areopagite and other early Christian authors.[85] It is also called a 'sacrament' in the rite itself. Like Baptism, it is a death to fleshly life and a birth into a new, spiritual mode of existence. Like Chrismation, it is the seal and sign of being elected by God. Like Marriage, it is betrothal with Christ, the heavenly Bridegroom. Like Priesthood, it is a consecration to God for ministry. And like the Eucharist, it is union with Christ. As in Baptism, so in monastic tonsure a person receives a new name and has his sins forgiven. He rejects the sinful life and gives vows of faithfulness to Christ; he takes off a secular robe and puts on a new garment. Being born again, the person assumes infancy anew in order to attain 'to the measure of the stature of the fullness of Christ' (Eph. 4:13).

The main goal of monasticism is the imitation of Christ, whose way of life as described in the gospels was altogether monastic. He was not married, was free from earthly bonds, had no roof over his head, travelled from place to place, lived in poverty, fasted, and spent nights in prayer. Monasticism is an attempt to come as close as possible to this ideal. It is the quest for sanctity, a search for God as the ultimate goal, the rejection of everything that binds one to earth and prevents one from ascending to heaven.

Monasticism is an angelic order and state achieved in an earthly and soiled body. A monk is one who holds only to the commands of God in every time and place and matter. A monk is one who constantly constrains his nature and unceasingly watches over his senses. A monk is he who keeps his body in chastity, his mouth pure and his mind illumined . . . Angels are a light for monks, and the monastic life is a light for all men.[86]

Monasticism is an unusual and exceptional way of life. Not many are called to it. It is a life entirely and integrally *given* to God. Monastic renunciation of the world is not, however, hatred of the world's beauty or of the delights of life. Rather, it is renunciation of sins and passions, of fleshly desires and lusts, in short, of everything that entered human life after the Fall. The aim of monasticism is a return to that primordial chastity and sinlessness which Adam and Eve possessed in Paradise. The Church Fathers called monasticism 'a life according to the Gospel' and 'a true philosophy'. As philosophers sought perfection along the paths of intellectual knowledge, so monks pursue perfection along the paths of ascetical struggle in imitation of Christ.

The entire philosophy of monasticism is expressed in the following words of Christ: 'If you would be perfect, go, sell what you possess and give to the poor, and you will have treasure in heaven; and come, follow me' (Matt. 19:21); 'If any man would come after me, let him deny himself and take up his cross and follow me. For whoever would save his life will lose it, and whoever loses his life for my sake will find it' (Matt. 16:24–5); 'He who loves father or mother more than me is not worthy of me' (Matt. 10:37). Monasticism is for those who want to be perfect, to follow Christ and to give their life for him, to sell everything in order to have heavenly treasure. Like a merchant who goes and sells all his possessions in order to buy a pearl, a monk is ready to deny everything in the world in order to acquire Christ. And the sacrifice is worth making, for the reward is great:

Then Peter said in reply, 'Lo, we have left everything and followed you. What then shall we have?' Jesus said to them, 'Truly, I say to you . . . Every one who has left houses or brothers or sisters or father or mother or children or lands, for my name's sake, will receive a hundredfold, and inherit eternal life.' (Matt. 19:27–9)

Monasticism formed part of the life of the Church from very early times, but it developed significantly in the fourth century, when persecutions ceased. During the first three centuries all adherents to Christianity were potential martyrs, but in the fourth century the new faith became the state religion of the Roman Empire. Now the quest for martyrdom and sacrifice led people deep into deserts, where ascetics created their 'state within the state'. The deserts of Egypt, Syria and Palestine, once fruitless and lifeless, were watered and populated by monks:

Cells arose even in the mountains, and the desert was colonised by
monks, who came forth from their own people, and enrolled themselves
for the citizenship in the heavens . . . So their cells were in the mountains,
filled with holy bands of men who sang psalms, loved reading, fasted, prayed,
rejoiced in the hope of things to come, laboured in almsgiving, and preserved
love and harmony one with another. And truly it was possible, as it were,
to behold a land set by itself, filled with piety and justice. For then there
was neither the evil-doer, nor the injured, nor the reproaches of the tax-
gatherer: but instead a multitude of ascetics; and the one purpose of them
all was to aim at virtue.[87]

There were three types of monasticism in the fourth and fifth centuries: cenobitic, eremitic and sketes. In cenobitic monasteries monks lived together and gathered in church several times a day for the offices. In eremitic communities each monk lived in a separate cell as a hermit. They came to the church once a week in order to receive Communion. In sketes, the monks lived in groups of two or three people. As St John Climacus says, 'The whole monastic state consists of three specific kinds of establishment: either the retirement and solitude of a spiritual athlete, or living in stillness with one or two others, or settling patiently in a community.'[88]

There are three basic vows taken by monastics: obedience, poverty and chastity.

Obedience is a deliberate denial of self-will before God, before the abbot and before every member of the community. The Greek word for obedience, *hypakoe*, literally means hearing, or listening. Monastic obedience is listening to God's will. Human beings suffer greatly from their inability to follow God's will and to accept the world around them as it is. People always tend to think of the circumstances of their lives as less than desirable, and of those close to them as less than perfect. They want to change the world around them and, unable to do so, find no peace. A monk, on the other hand, teaches himself to accept everything as it is and to receive from the hand of God with the same joy and thanksgiving both consolation and sufferings, health and illness, fortune and misfortune. With this attitude the monk obtains an inner, undisturbed peace that no external circumstances can spoil. 'Glory be to God for everything': these were the words of John Chrysostom when he died in exile, in suffering and pain, deprived of his bishopric, driven out of his diocese. Like Christ, who 'humbled himself and became obedient unto death, even death on the cross' (Phil. 2:8), a monk tries to be obedient to God unto the cross, and even to death.

Poverty is a deliberate rejection of every earthly possession. This does not necessarily mean that a monk is totally deprived of all material things, but he must not be attached to anything earthly. Having inwardly rejected material wealth, he attains that spiritual freedom which is higher than any earthly possession.

The word 'chastity' is used in English to render the Greek *sophrosyne*, which literally means wisdom or integrity. Chastity is not synonymous with celibacy. In monasticism the latter is only an element of the former. Chastity as wisdom and integrity, as life according to the Gospel and abstinence from passions and lusts, is also necessary in marriage. To live in chastity means to have one's entire life oriented to God, to check every thought, word and deed against the Gospel's standards.

As far as celibacy is concerned, in the context of monastic life it is a supra-natural form of existence. Loneliness is incompleteness, a deficiency which is overcome in marriage through a common life with one's spouse. Monastics are espoused to God himself. Monasticism, then, is not the opposite of marriage. Rather, it is a different kind of marital union, not between two human beings, but between the human person and God. 'When love is divided between the world and Christ, it is weak; but it is strong when directed at the One', says Gregory the Theologian.[89] Love is found at the very heart of both marriage and monasticism, but the object of love is different. A person cannot become a monk unless his love for God is so deep and ardent that he does not want to direct it towards anyone but him.

Symeon the New Theologian speaks in one of his *Hymns* of monastic life as being with Christ rather than living alone:

> But indeed he who possesses Christ dwelling in him,
> How can he be said to be alone, tell me?
> For the Father and the Spirit are united with my Christ.

How therefore can we speak of being a solitary
When the monk is united with the Three-in-one?
He is the one who is united with God even if he lives alone,
Even if he lives in a desert, even in a cave . . .
He who makes a heaven of his cell through virtue,
Contemplates and looks upon the Creator of heaven and earth,
Installed in his cell.
And he adores Him and is united always with the Light which never
    sets,
The Light without the darkness of evening, the unapproachable
    Light,
Which never leaves him, never completely wanders from him,
Day or night, whether he eats or drinks,
Not even in his sleep or on the road or in moving from place to
    place . . .
So those who by repentance are united with God,
Purify their souls in this world here
And they are considered as solitaries as they are separated from the
    others . . .
They communicate with the Father omnipotent . . .
Their cell is heaven, they indeed are a sun
And the light is on them, the unsetting and divine light . . .
Only such are monks and solitaries,
Those who alone live with God alone.[90]

There is a widespread view of monasticism as a mode of existence which is tough and sombre and deprived of joy. According to the following personal testimony of Archbishop Hilarion (Troitsky), this view is totally misleading:

Monks have a quiet and pure joy, happiness of a pious soul. All that chaos, all that inebriation with life which is commonly called 'delights of life' is something gloomy, something which results in saturation and painful intoxication . . . We monks weep out of joy, out of compunction, and we thank God . . . Every monk knows what tears of compunction are, and all earthly delights seem to him poor and deficient compared to these tears . . . I myself received monastic tonsure and I do not think that I will ever experience again the joy that I experienced then . . . I was full of joy for two months. My soul was so exalted, so gladdened . . . It is not by mere chance that in monastic tonsure, when the abbot clothes a newly tonsured monk in his new robe, the following words are said: 'Our brother . . . is clothed in the robe of joy and spiritual gladness, in order that all his sorrows and perplexity should disappear and be vanquished' . . . The farther one is from passions, the more joy has one in his heart. The purity of heart is deeply connected with gladness.[91]

Monastic tonsure takes place in church. It is normally conducted by a bishop or an abbot. The person who is to be tonsured takes off all his or her ordinary clothes, puts on a long white robe and stands before the abbot. Having made his monastic vows, he listens to the abbot's exhortations, after which he receives a new name, is tonsured, and clothed in black monastic vestments. When the rite has finished, each member of the community comes to him, asking: 'What is your name, brother?' The newly tonsured monk, according to tradition, spends several nights in the church reading the psalter or the gospel.

Monasticism is an inner and hidden life. It is the most radical expression of Christianity as a 'narrow way' leading to the Kingdom of heaven. Monastic detachment and inner concentration do not, however, imply egoism or absence of love for one's neighbour. Having placed himself outside worldly vanity, a monk does not forget his fellow humans, but in the silence of his cell he prays for them. St Silouan of Mount Athos says:

There are people who say that monks ought to be of some use in the world, and not eat bread they have not toiled for; but we have to understand the nature of a monk's service and the way in which he has to help the world. A monk is someone who prays for the whole world, who weeps for the whole world; and in this lies his main work . . . Thanks to monks, prayer continues unceasing on earth, and the whole world profits . . . St Sergius by fasting and prayer helped the Russian people to free themselves from the Tartar yoke. St Seraphim prayed silently, and the Holy Spirit descended on Motovilov.[92] And this is the task of the monk . . . Perhaps you will say that nowadays there are no monks like that, who would pray for the whole world; but I tell you that when there are no men of prayer on the earth, the world will come to an end . . . The world is supported by the prayers of the saints.[93]

The Church Fathers understood that the transfiguration of the world and the happiness of human beings depend not so much on external circumstances but on people's inner condition. True renewal of the world is only possible in the realm of the spiritual life. Thus, neither Christ, nor the apostles, nor the Church Fathers demanded social change. Rather, they all called for the inner spiritual transformation of each particular human being.

Monks do not seek to improve the world. They try to improve themselves in order that the world may be transformed from within. 'Save yourself, and thousands around you will be saved', says St Seraphim of Sarov. These words reflect the ultimate goal of monasticism and of Christianity in general. Needless to say, monasticism is not the only way to salvation, or even the best way. It is one way, like marriage or priesthood, which may lead to salvation and deification, if the path is followed to the end.

### Baptism and the Eucharist in the Early Church

Baptise in the name of the Father, and of the Son, and of the Holy Spirit, in running water. And if you have no running water, baptise in some other water; and if you cannot baptise in cold, baptise in warm water; but if you have neither, pour water three times on the head, in the name of the Father, and of the Son, and of the Holy Spirit. And before the baptism, let him who baptises and him who is baptised fast previously, as well as any others who may be able . . . As far as the Eucharist is concerned, you should give thanks in the following way. First, concerning the cup: 'We thank Thee, our Father, for the holy vine of David, Thy Son, which Thou hast made known unto us through Jesus Christ, Thy Son; to Thee be glory for ever.' And concerning the broken bread: 'We thank Thee, our Father, for the life and knowledge which Thou hast made known unto us through Jesus, Thy Son; to Thee be glory for ever. As this broken bread was once scattered on the mountains, and after it had been brought together became one, so may Thy Church be gathered together from the ends of the earth unto Thy kingdom. For Thine is the glory, and the power, through Jesus Christ, for ever.' And let none eat or drink of your Eucharist except those who have been baptised into the name of the Lord . . . And after it has been completed, pray as follows: 'We thank Thee, holy Father, for Thy holy name, which Thou hast caused to dwell in our hearts, and for the knowledge and faith and immortality which Thou hast made known unto us through Jesus, Thy Son; to Thee be glory for ever.'

*'The Teaching of the Twelve Apostles'*

### The life-giving Flesh

We proclaim the death, in the flesh, of the Only-Begotten Son of God, Jesus Christ, and acknowledge His return to life from the dead and His ascension into heaven, and as we do this we perform the bloodless sacrifice in the churches: and thus we approach the consecrated gifts of the sacrament, and

[ 163 ]

are sanctified by partaking of the holy Flesh and the precious Blood of Christ, the Saviour of us all. We do not receive it as common flesh – God forbid! – nor as the flesh of a mere man, sanctified and linked with the Word in unity of standing, or as enjoying a divine indwelling; we receive it as truly life-giving, as the flesh that belongs to the Word Himself. For as being God He is in His own nature life, and when He became one with the flesh which is His own, He rendered it life-giving.

*St Cyril of Alexandria*

## Christ's real presence in the Eucharist

Christ is now also present ... It is not man who makes the gift of the oblation to become the Body and Blood of Christ, but Christ Himself, Who was crucified for us. The priest stands, fulfilling the original pattern, and speaks these words; but the power and grace come from God. 'This is My Body', he says. This statement transforms the oblations: and as the command, 'Increase and multiply', spoken once, extends through all time, and gives to one human nature the power of reproduction; so the statement, 'This is My Body', uttered once, makes complete the sacrifice at every table in the churches from that time until now, and even till Christ's coming.

*St John Chrysostom*

## The sacrament of love

Marriage is the 'sacrament of love'. As a 'profound mystery' whose prototype is Christ and the Church (and God and the world, and *Yahweh* and Israel), marriage brings two persons into a bond of unity which enhances the distinction and value of each person in direct proportion to the measure in which the 'two become one' in God. The sexual act is an expression of this union in love. When godly, it includes every manner of love. It is an act of *eros*, the passionate yearning for union with the beloved. It includes *friendship* and *affection*. And it is motivated and crowned by *agape* which is the acceptance and affirmation of the other as the other really is through an act totally devoted to the other's wellbeing and happiness.

*Father Thomas Hopko*

## Marriage and monasticism

The two complement each other ... Both are sacraments of love ... It is tempting to make a simple contrast: to say that asceticism and chastity are

the characteristics of monasticism, and love the characteristic of marriage.
Yet the two states cannot be thus opposed. Married people, as well as monks,
are called to the 'narrow way' of ascetic life, to fasting and self-denial; if the
monks are martyrs, then so also are the married, as the crowns and hymns
and the Marriage service plainly indicate. Perfect love is always a crucified
love; yet, for both monks and married Christians, if the cross is voluntarily
accepted, it proves a door to resurrection and new life. In the same way,
chastity — understood in its proper sense of integrity and integration — is a
quality not only of the single but also of the married life. In a sense, marriage
includes within itself the characteristic values of monasticism: the monastic
vows of poverty, chastity, and obedience — when understood, as they should
be, in a positive manner as a way of enabling us to be free to love God
and one another — are also applicable to the married life. And if asceticism
and chastity are marks of the married life, then love . . . is a mark of a true
monk . . . If the monk abstains from marriage, this is not because the married
state is sinful, but because he personally is called to express his love for
God and humankind on a different level . . . St Irenaeus of Lyons . . . speaks
of the Son and the Holy Spirit as the 'two hands' of God the Father . . .
Marriage and monasticism are likewise the 'two hands' of the Church, the
two complementary expressions of one royal priesthood. Each needs
the other, and in her mission the Church uses both her hands together.

*Bishop Kallistos of Diokleia*


## A life in the sacraments

We are called to be united with Christ in order to become in reality parts,
members of His Body, as real as the branch is connected with the vine, as
part of a tree is joined with the whole tree; that is, to be one with Him not
only in soul, not only in a figurative sense, but with the whole of our
being, with the total realness of our lives . . . We are also called to be a
temple of the Holy Spirit, to be His dwelling place . . . We are called to be
united with God in such a way that all of our material being is penetrated
by Him, so that nothing in us — neither our spirit or soul, nor even our
flesh — remains out of the grasp of this presence. We are called ultimately
to burn as the Burning Bush, which burned and never ceased to burn. We
are called to be *partakers of the divine nature* (2 Pet. 1:4). We are called to be
sons, daughters, children of God and the Father. No man can attain any
of this through his own efforts. Neither by our own efforts or by our own
desire can we become a part of the Body of Christ, we cannot be united
with the Holy Spirit through our own efforts, nor likewise can we become

partakers of the divine nature ... The way in which any of this can be realised are the sacraments of the Church. The sacraments are the actions of God within the Church in which God grants us His grace by means of the material world. It is in the sacraments that the Church brings us grace which we cannot acquire by any other means, even at times by a great spiritual feat. She brings grace to us as a gift through the material substance of this world: the water of Baptism, the bread and the wine of the Eucharist, the myrrh of Chrismation. The Early Church spoke of three, five, seven or even twenty-two sacraments ... The material world, even though it is a slave to sin, even though, as St Paul says, it groans in expectation of the glorious liberty of the children of God (cf. Rom. 8:19–22), it is in itself pure and without sin. And God takes this world, this matter, and unites it in an incomprehensible way with Himself, and this material world brings to us the grace which we are unable to raise ourselves up to.

*Metropolitan Anthony of Sourozh*

*Chapter Nine*

# PRAYER

## DIVINE WORSHIP

In the Orthodox tradition there is a distinct and profound interrelationship between dogma and prayer. This is especially close when it comes to liturgical prayer. According to Father Pavel Florensky, a true Orthodox dogmatic theology must be rooted in divine worship.[1] Dogma is based on liturgy, and all lasting dogmatic definitions are born of the liturgical experience of the Church. 'Christianity is a liturgical religion', Father Georges Florovsky wrote. 'The Church is first of all a worshipping community. Worship comes first, doctrine and discipline second.'[2] The Church has not grown out of dogmatic formulae, nor even out of Holy Scripture, but primarily out of the divine Liturgy. In the first years after the Resurrection of Christ, when no gospel was yet written and no dogma formulated, the Liturgy already existed. It was the Liturgy that united Christ's followers into the Church, his mystical body.

The interrelationship between liturgy and doctrine can be seen clearly throughout the history of Orthodox theology. A number of questionable theological opinions advanced at various times have passed unnoticed and eventually been forgotten, but no theological teaching that has contradicted the Church's liturgical experience has been ignored. Theodore of Mopsuestia (d. *c.* 428) put forward a Christology that made a sharp distinction between the two natures of Christ, and yet he died at peace with the Church. His disciple Nestorius, on the other hand, who adopted a quite similar doctrine, was condemned during his lifetime because he refused to give the Virgin Mary the title *Theotokos* (Birth-giver of God). This was contrary to the liturgical practice: Mary had already been named *Theotokos* in the Liturgy. Anselm of Canterbury's theory of Christ's Atonement as the satisfaction of the Father's justice developed in the context of Western culture and might have gone unnoticed in the East, but it was found that a different understanding of the Atonement was implicit in Eastern Liturgy, and so the Latin theory was rejected. Compliance with the Church's liturgical theology is the test for a dogmatic teaching to be true to the Orthodox tradition. The reverse is also true: to teach against the liturgical tradition was enough to be condemned as a heretic.

Orthodox worship is the incarnation of dogmatic truth through the words of prayer. Take, for example, the following hymn from the evening office of Pentecost:

Come, O ye people, let us worship the Godhead in three Persons, the Son in the Father with the Holy Spirit. For the Father before time was begat the Son, who is co-eternal and equally enthroned, and the Holy Spirit, who was in the Father and was glorified together with the Son; one Might, one Essence, one Godhead. Adoring the same let us all say: O Holy God, who by the Son didst make all things through the co-operation of the Holy Spirit; O Holy Mighty, through whom we have known the Father, and through whom the Holy Spirit came into the world; O Holy Immortal, the Spirit of comfort, who proceedest from the Father and restest in the Son; O Holy Trinity, glory to Thee.[3]

Here we find references to all the basic Christian teachings: one God in three Persons; the Son's eternal birth from the Father; the equality, consubstantiality and divinity of the Father, the Son and the Holy Spirit; the creation of the world by the Father through the Son, with the assistance of the Holy Spirit; the coming of the Holy Spirit to the world through the Son; his procession from the Father and his resting in the Son.

Other similar examples are the eight hymns called *dogmatika*. These are dedicated to the Mother of God, and sung in turn on successive Saturday evenings according to the musical tone of the week.[4] This is the *dogmatikon* in Tone 6:

Who is there that does not bless thee, O All-holy Virgin? Who is there that sings not thy undefiled birth-giving? The Only-begotten Son, who shone forth before all ages from the Father, the same came forth from thee, O Pure One, having in wondrous manner become incarnate, being by nature God and becoming by nature man, for our sake; not being divided into two persons, but known in two natures, yet unmerged. Him do thou beseech, O Pure, All-blessed One, that he will have mercy on our souls.[5]

Again, this text expresses Orthodox Christology in its entirety: the eternal birth of the Son; his incarnation from the Virgin; the completeness of both his divine and his human nature, which remain unconfused; and the indivisibility of his Person. The sharpness and clarity of christological formulae is woven into this hymn with poetic beauty and prayerful meditation.

In Orthodox worship, then, dogmas become part of the experience of prayer: we live them in a real and existential manner. A contemporary Russian bishop wrote in his memoirs that for a long time he regarded the Nicene Creed, sung at every Orthodox Liturgy, as a dry and lifeless list of dogmatic statements having no connection with his personal experience of prayer. It was only after many years of celebrating the Divine Liturgy that the importance of the Creed was revealed to him:

The reality which is formulated in these doctrines is the very life of the soul. The soul's life is nothing else than participation in that supernatural life of which the dogmas speak in an abstract manner . . . When the soul understands this by experience, a heartfelt attitude to dogmas is born rather than an intellectual one . . . Knowledge is then transformed into communion. In this state the Creed proves to be not a cool 'acceptance' of dogmas but rather a living 'confession' of faith, a warm testimony of inner communion with God and sincere love of him . . . These dogmatic notions are then able to kindle one with inner fire and to warm up one's heart more than any other means . . . The Creed is then transformed into a prayer even more exalted and dense than many other prayers . . . I have seen many bishops who, having bowed their head under the veil, which was moved above them by the priests,[6] rose then from before the holy table in tears. It was clear that they did not 'think' of dogmatic 'notions' but rather participated in the life, in God . . . [7]

The life of the Orthodox Church is based on the principle: *lex orandi est lex credendi* ('The rule of prayer is the rule of faith'). For this reason, the Church keeps almost unchanged the liturgical rite which evolved in Byzantium at the beginning of the second millennium. This is directly connected with the stability of its dogmatic theology. When a new hymn is composed for liturgical use,[8] it is shaped according to the existing patterns.

Divine worship is a daily school of spiritual life. According to St Ignaty Brianchaninov, the Christian who regularly attends church services and listens to what is sung and read can learn from this 'everything necessary for the journey along the path of faith'.[9] Worship is also a school of prayer: it captures the human heart and mind, and immerses us in the depths where an encounter with the living God takes place. Every service in church, every word of liturgical prayer, has the potential to become an encounter with God. This happens when we pray with attention and concentration, and when the prayer of the Church becomes our own prayer. When our intellect is distracted during prayer, however, the words pass us by and the encounter does not take place. Then we are deprived of the fruits of participation in liturgical prayer.

## SILENCE

'When you pray, go into your room and shut the door and pray to your Father who is in secret; and your Father who sees in secret will reward you. And in praying do not heap up empty phrases as the Gentiles do; for they think that they will be heard for their many words. Do not be like them, for your Father knows what you need before you ask him' (Matt. 6:6–8). These words of Christ often provoke the question: what is the sense of praying if God knows beforehand what we actually need?

In answering this question, we should remember that prayer is not just a request for something; it is above all a personal encounter, a dialogue with the living God. 'Prayer is communion of the intellect with God', according to a classic definition by Evagrius the Solitary.[10] In prayer we encounter the personal God who hears us and responds to us, who is always ready to come to our assistance, and who never betrays us however many times we betray him. In prayer we communicate with the sublime Reality which is the only true Life: compared to this, every other reality is partial and imperfect. Life without communion with God, without prayer, is simply a long pathway towards death. We are alive in so far as we participate in God, and we participate in God through prayer.

Why does Christ command us to avoid too many words in prayer? Precisely because it is not out of words that prayer is born: prayer must be *heard* within one's heart. No true masterpieces of music and poetry were composed out of disconnected letters or sounds: they were first born in the depths of the author's heart, and were made incarnate in words or music. Prayer also is creative work, born not from an excess of words, but out of a deep stillness, out of concentrated and attentive silence. Before embarking on the path of prayer, one must inwardly renounce human words and thoughts; one must *hear silence*:

> Hear, my son, the silence.
> It is an undulating silence.
> A silence where valleys and echoes slide past,
> And which bows faces to the ground.[11]

Our heart, mind, mouth and senses fall silent when we are plunged into the waves of prayer. When we encounter God in the deepest stillness of our heart, words, sounds and worldly impressions disappear, and our face is bowed to the ground. 'Intelligent silence is the mother of prayer', says St John Climacus. 'The friend of silence draws near to God and, by secretly conversing with him, is enlightened by God.'[12] Bishop Kallistos of Diokleia develops this theme in the following way:

To achieve silence: this is of all things the hardest and the most decisive in the art of prayer. Silence is not merely negative – a pause between words, a temporary cessation of speech – but, properly understood, it is highly positive: an attitude of attentive alertness, of vigilance, and above all of listening. The hesychast, the person who has attained hesychia, inner stillness or silence, is *par excellence* the one who listens. He listens to the voice of prayer in his own heart, and he understands that this voice is not his own but that of Another speaking within him.[13]

Like every conversation, prayer is a dialogue, and its aim is not only to express oneself but also to hear another.

'Silence is a mystery of the age to come, but words are instruments of this world', says St Isaac the Syrian.[14] In order to attain silence and stillness, monks deprived themselves of encounters and conversations with people, departed to deep deserts, and hid themselves in mountains and woods.

An ancient story tells of three brothers.[15] One of them decided that his mission would be to bring people to reconciliation, the second decided he would visit the sick, while the third went to the desert to live in silence. The first, finding himself constantly between conflicting sides, and incapable of reconciling adversaries, became deeply afflicted. He visited the second brother, and found him, too, in a state of deep despondency. Together they went to see the third brother and asked him whether he had achieved anything in his desert. Instead of answering, the hermit poured some water into a cup and said, 'Look at the water.' They did so, but it was so disturbed that nothing could be seen in it. After a short time the hermit invited them to look again: the water had settled and become transparent enough for them to see their faces reflected in it. The hermit said to them, 'Someone who lives among the passions and cares of the world will always be perturbed by thoughts, while a hermit contemplates God in stillness.'

An experience of stillness is essential for everyone who wants to learn the art of prayer. It is not necessary to withdraw to the actual desert to achieve this. Yet one does have to put aside some minutes every day, go into one's room, 'shut the door and pray to God who is in secret'. Our usual temptation, or deception, is that we are always very busy and rushing to do something extremely important; we believe that if we spend too much time in prayer, we will not be able to get these important things done. The experience of many people shows that half an hour spent in prayer seldom affects our 'business' negatively, whatever our initial concerns. On the contrary, prayer teaches us concentration and to make the mind more disciplined. As a result, time is won rather than lost.

A lack of taste for solitude and silence is one of the most common illnesses of the contemporary world. Many people are afraid of remaining in stillness, being alone or having free time. They feel more comfortable being constantly occupied; they need words, impressions; they always hurry in order to have the illusion of an abundant and saturated life. But life in God begins when words and thoughts fall silent, when worldly cares are forgotten, and when a place within the human soul is freed to be filled by him.

The Church Fathers, following Jesus Christ himself, emphasise that prayer should be simple and unsophisticated. The state of a person who prays is compared by St John Climacus with that of children speaking to their parents:

Let your prayer be completely simple . . . Do not be over-sophisticated in the words you use when praying, because the simple and unadorned lisping of children has often won the heart of their heavenly Father. Do not try to be verbose when you pray, lest your mind be distracted in searching for words. One word of the publican propitiated God, and one cry of faith saved the thief.[16]

Childlike faith must be combined with deep humility of heart, as St Isaac the Syrian emphasises:

Walk before God in simplicity and not with knowledge . . . When you fall down before God in prayer, become in your thought like an ant, like a creeping thing of the earth, like a leech, and like a tiny lisping child. Do not say anything before Him with knowledge, but with a child's manner of thought draw near to God and walk before Him, that you may be counted worthy of that paternal providence that fathers have for their small children.[17]

Prayer, stillness, silence and humility are deeply connected with repentance: 'A man who loves conversation with Christ, loves to be alone. But he who loves to linger with many is a friend of this world . . . If you love repentance, love stillness also.'[18] Thus, without inner stillness and silence, neither repentance nor prayer are possible.

## WATCHFULNESS

Being alone in a room with the doors shut does not yet constitute stillness. Neither does the avoidance of speech. Stillness implies peace of mind and tranquillity of thought. Yet very often people who are alone and about to pray find turmoil and chaos in their mind. Although they may be reading prayers with their lips, their mind wanders far away.

The Early Fathers call distraction of mind during prayer *meteorismos*, or light-mindedness. The reason for this distraction, they say, is that people are unable to control their thoughts, or the different images and fantasies that appear in their mind. To control our thoughts, we must learn the art of *nepsis* (which means watchfulness, vigilance, alertness, sobriety). This is based on the understanding that any thought captures the human mind gradually. It passes through several stages of development. The first stage is called 'assault', which is a simple conception, or sudden apparition of something in the mind, an image or idea that comes from outside. The second stage is 'converse', or 'conversation': the mind enters into dialogue with the thought. This dialogue may become a 'struggle', when the mind opposes the attacking thought and either rejects or accepts it. The acceptance of the thought by the mind is called 'captivity': it is 'a forcible and involuntary rape of the heart, or a permanent association with what has been encountered'. The last stage of the development of thought is 'passion': 'that which for a long time nestles with persistence in the soul, forming therein a habit, as it were, by the soul's long-standing association with it, since the soul of its own free and proper choice clings to it'.[19]

Every passion begins with a sinful thought: 'No cloud is formed without a breath of wind; and no passion is born without a thought.'[20] The fall of Eve was interpreted by Metropolitan Philaret of Moscow in terms of the development of a thought into a passion. 'When the woman saw that the tree was good for food, and that it was a delight to the eyes, and that the tree was to be desired to make one wise, she took of its fruit and ate' (Gen. 3:6). Her seeing is an assault by a thought; that the tree 'was good' and 'was a delight' are converse and struggle with the thought; the desire is acceptance of the thought, whereby Eve is captured by it; the taking and eating is passion, when the thought is actualised and put into practice. 'A sinful disposition of the soul', wrote St Philaret, 'begins with the powers of the intellect being oriented in a wrong direction ... The multiplicity of one's own desires, which are not centred around the will of God, is connected with one's deviation from the oneness of the divine truth into a multiplicity of one's own thoughts.'[21] In other words, distraction is deviation from primordial simplicity and the state of unification into multiplicity and complexity. Distraction is a consequence of the Fall. The mind's acceptance of sinful thoughts is an illness and a sin of the mind, a 'mental adultery' of the intellect.[22]

The art of *nepsis* is the ability to refuse the sinful thought at the very moment of its first appearance in the mind, before it can develop into a passion. 'The beginning of prayer', says St John Climacus, 'consists in banishing by a single word of prayer the thoughts that assault us at the very moment that they appear.'[23] According to St Hesychios the Priest,

The science of sciences and the art of arts is the mastery of evil thoughts. The best way to master them is to see with spiritual vision the fantasy in which the demonic provocation is concealed and to protect the mind from it. It is just the same as the way in which we protect our bodily eyes, looking sharply about us and doing all we can to prevent anything, however small, from striking them.[24]

Evil thoughts must be 'opposed', they must be 'struggled with'. Therefore prayer is not only a peaceful dialogue with God but also a heavy labour, a fight for the purity of the mind. People who pray must always be watchful over their intellect, memory and fantasy:

Try to make your intellect deaf and dumb during prayer; you will then be able to pray . . . When you pray, keep close watch on your memory, so that it does not distract you . . . For by nature the intellect is apt to be carried away by memories during prayer. While you are praying, the memory brings before you fantasies either of past things, or of recent concerns, or of the face of someone who has irritated you. The demon is very envious of us when we pray, and uses every kind of trick to thwart our purpose. Therefore he is always using our memory to stir up thoughts of various things and our flesh to arouse the passions, in order to obstruct our way of ascent to God . . . Stand on guard and protect your intellect from thoughts while you pray.[25]

## 'INWARD MEDITATION'

A particular form of prayer, known by the technical term *krypte melete* – 'secret occupation' or 'inward meditation' – has developed within the Orthodox tradition. This type of prayer, described since the fifth century, is still very widespread in the Orthodox world and consists of the constant repetition of a short formula, such as the Jesus Prayer: 'Lord Jesus Christ,

Son of God, have mercy upon me, a sinner.' There are also shorter versions: 'Lord Jesus Christ, have mercy upon me', or 'Jesus, Son of God, have mercy on me', or even 'Christ, have mercy' and 'Lord, have mercy'. The entire theory of 'inward meditation' is expressed in the following monastic story from the sixth or seventh century:

A brother named John came from the coast to Father Philimon and, clasping his feet, said to him: 'What shall I do to be saved? For my intellect vacillates to and fro and strays after all the wrong things.' After a pause, the father replied: 'This is one of the outer passions and it stays with you because you still have not acquired a perfect longing for God. The warmth of this longing and of the knowledge of God has not yet come to you.' The brother said to him: 'What shall I do, father?' Abba Philimon replied: 'Meditate inwardly for a while; for this can cleanse your intellect from these things.' The brother, not understanding what was said, asked the Elder: 'What is inward meditation, father?' The Elder replied: 'Keep watch in your heart; and with watchfulness say in your mind with awe and trembling: "Lord Jesus Christ, have mercy upon me." ' The brother departed; and with the help of God and the Elder's prayers he found stillness and for a while was filled with sweetness by this meditation. But then it suddenly left him and he could not practise it or pray watchfully. So he went again to the Elder and told him what had happened. And the Elder said to him: 'You have had a brief taste of stillness and inner work, and have experienced the sweetness that comes from them. This what you should always be doing in your heart: whether eating or drinking, in company or outside your cell, or on a journey, repeat that prayer with a watchful mind and undeflected intellect ... Even when carrying out needful tasks, do not let your intellect be idle but keep it meditating inwardly and praying. For in this way you can ... give unceasing work to the intellect, thus fulfilling the apostolic command: *Pray without ceasing*.[26] Pay strict attention to your heart and watch over it, so that it does not give admittance to thoughts that are evil or in any way vain and useless. Without interruption, whether asleep or awake, eating, drinking, or in company, let your heart inwardly and mentally at all times be meditating on the Psalms, at other times be repeating the prayer, "Lord Jesus Christ, Son of God, have mercy upon me." '[27]

The Jesus Prayer has particular power because the holy name of Jesus is contained within it. It was Jesus himself who commanded his disciples to pray in his name: 'Truly, truly, I say to you, if you ask anything of the Father, he will give it to you in my name. Hitherto you have asked nothing in my name; ask, and you will receive' (John 16:23–4). He also speaks of the miraculous power of his own name: 'In my name they will cast out demons; they will speak in new tongues; they will pick up serpents, and if they drink any deadly thing, it will not hurt them; they will lay their hands on the sick, and they will recover' (Mark 16:17–18). When the apostles Peter and John healed the lame man, they were asked by rulers, elders and scribes: 'By what power or by what name did you do this?' and they replied: 'By the name of Jesus Christ of Nazareth . . . this man is standing before you well . . . For there is no other name under heaven given among men by which we must be saved' (Acts 4:7–12).

There are many references to the name of Jesus in early Christian literature. In the second-century text *The Shepherd of Hermas* we read: 'The name of the Son of God is great and boundless, and upholds the entire universe . . . He supports those who wholeheartedly bear his name. He himself is their foundation and carries them with love because they are not ashamed of bearing his name.'[28]

The practice of prayer in the name of Jesus has lived within the Orthodox tradition throughout its history. St John Climacus in the seventh century, St Gregory of Sinai in the thirteenth century, St Gregory Palamas and other Byzantine Hesychasts in the fourteenth century, St Nicodemos of Holy Mountain in the eighteenth century, St Seraphim of Sarov, St Theophan the Recluse, St John of Kronstadt in the nineteenth century, St Silouan of Mount Athos in the twentieth century – all these authors, and many others, spoke of the Jesus Prayer.[29]

According to ancient tradition, the power and energy of God is present in the holy name of Jesus. At the beginning of the twentieth century Monk Hilarion, a Caucasian hermit, wrote a remarkable book *On the Mountains of the Caucasus*, which includes the following passage: 'The Son of God . . . in the fullness of his divine nature is present both in the Holy Eucharist and in Christian churches. He is also fully and entirely present in his name, with all His perfection and with the entirety of His divinity.'[30] Monk Hilarion quoted St John of Kronstadt: 'Let the name of the Lord . . . be for you instead of the Lord himself . . . The name of the Lord is the Lord himself . . .'[31] Heated arguments arose on Mount Athos in the first decade of the twentieth century about these words and around the teaching of 'the adorers of the Name'. The latter were accused of dogmatic inaccuracy, of confusing the name of God with his essence. Hilarion's book, however, is very much in keeping with the Hesychast tradition of the veneration of the name of Jesus. Regrettably, as a result of the disputes over the name of Jesus, the book came to be regarded as a manifesto of the 'adorers of the Name'. Banned from distribution by the Russian ecclesiastical censors, it has remained virtually unknown.

The most famous book on the Jesus Prayer also comes from Russia. Written during the second half of the nineteenth century, it is known in the English-speaking world as *The Way of a Pilgrim*.[32] The hero and author of this book was a simple Russian peasant, who heard in church the words of St Paul, 'Pray without ceasing' (I Thess. 5:17), and was kindled with the desire to learn this unceasing prayer. For a long time he could not find a spiritual guide. Eventually a *starets* (elder) told him of the practice of the Jesus Prayer and commanded him to repeat it three thousand times a day. The number of repetitions then increased to six and twelve thousand per day, after which the peasant, who was a wandering pilgrim, learned how to pray 'without counting prayers', that is, unceasingly.

And that is how I go about now, and ceaselessly repeat the prayer of Jesus, which is more precious and sweet to me than anything in the world. At times I do as much as 43 or 44 miles a day, and do not feel that I am walking at all. I am aware only of the fact that I am saying my Prayer . . . I thank God that I now understand the meaning of those words I heard in the Epistle: *Pray without ceasing*.[33]

The basic rule which applies to the Jesus Prayer, as well as to other kinds of prayer, is that one should 'enclose one's thoughts within the words of one's prayer'.[34] It has been noticed, however, that when the mind is located in the head, it is very much subject to distraction and cannot concentrate. In order to acquire concentration, it is necessary to relocate the mind in the heart. This ancient method of the descent of the mind into the heart, which was developed in early monasticism, is summed up by St Theophan the Recluse in one of his letters:

You should descend to your heart from your head . . . As far as I remember, you wrote to me that you had a headache from attentive prayer. This happens when one acts only with one's head. But when prayer descends into the heart, there will be no difficulty in prayer, for the head will become empty of thoughts. All the thoughts are in the head, they follow one another, and it is impossible to control them. If you discover your heart and are able to stand within it, then, as soon as thoughts appear, you can descend therein, and the thoughts will disappear . . . The life is in the heart, so you should live in there. Do not think that this applies only to the perfect. No, it applies to everyone who begins to seek out the Lord.[35]

The name of Jesus must become united with the heart of one who prays, as described in a treatise attributed to St John Chrysostom: 'The Lord absorbs the heart and the heart absorbs the Lord, and two become one.'

The author of another treatise, 'The Method of Hesychastic Prayer', attributed to Symeon the New Theologian, writes of prayer of the mind and of the heart, describing three kinds of attention and of prayer. In the first, a man imagines within his spirit the good things of heaven: the angels, the saints, and all that he has read about in the Scriptures. This kind depends on the activity of the imagination. In the second the mind is concentrated on struggle with thoughts, but is not able to overcome them. 'The thoughts vie with each other' and the spirit loses its clarity. In the third, the stillness of the spirit in the depths of the heart is combined with undistracted attention, an absence of worldly concerns, and a pure conscience, free from the passions. This is the only authentic state of prayer.

In order to enable the mind to descend into the heart, the author recommends a special physical technique:[36] to sit in a dark corner on a low chair, close one's eyes, bow one's head, and keep one's breathing light. The mind should find the heart's higher part and, being enclosed there, pray with the prayer of Jesus.[37] This method, however, is not an end in itself. Attentive prayer can also be achieved without special physical techniques, and the spiritual directors of the nineteenth century were very reserved about using them. Theophan the Recluse, when translating the *Method of Sacred Prayer* into Russian, deliberately omitted everything connected with these techniques. 'These external means', he wrote in a special note, 'may scandalise some, may divert others from prayer and may distort the very practice of prayer . . . The essence of them is to get accustomed to holding one's mind within one's heart . . . How to reach this? *Seek, and you will find.*[38] The easiest way to find this is to walk before God and to labour in prayer . . .'[39]

'Walking before God', or 'walking with God', is an expression applied in the Old Testament to righteous people who were faithful to God and observed his commandments.[40] In the Christian context, it points to a congruence between a person's life and the commandments of Christ. To walk before God means to measure every action and thought by the standards of the Gospel, to remember God always, to feel his presence, and not to sin against his truth. Prayer is helpful only when it is combined with a true Christian life according to the Gospel. The Christian ideal is that our whole life should be transformed into an unceasing prayer, so that our every word and deed should be penetrated by it.

## PRAYER AND THEOLOGY

'If you are a theologian, you will pray truly. And if you pray truly, you are a theologian.'[41] These words of Evagrius stress the interrelationship between prayer and theology: one cannot exist without the other. For the Church Fathers, theology was not an abstract theory about 'an unknown God', but a search for personal encounter with him. Genuine theology is not 'about' God but is 'in' God; it does not consider God as an object, but converses with him. Orthodox theology is derived from prayer and mystical experience, and is opposed to an 'objective' scholarship that is detached from God. The purification and stillness of mind which are necessary for prayer are also required for theology:

Discussion of theology is not for everyone . . . It is not for all men, but only for those who . . . have undergone, or at the very least are undergoing, purification of body and soul. For one who is not pure to lay hold on pure things is dangerous, just as it is for weak eyes to look at the sun's brightness. What is the right time (for theology)? Whenever we are free from the mire and noise without, and our commanding faculty[42] is not confused by illusory, wandering images . . . We need actually to be still in order to know God.[43]

Prayer, in turn, derives from theology and is based on it. There can be no true prayer outside true dogma: this is an essential belief of the Orthodox Church. Distortion of dogma leads to distortion of the practice of prayer, and vice versa: wrong forms of prayer give birth to mistaken dogmatic teachings. True prayer is that practised within the context of the Church community, even if it takes place in private. 'Nobody is Christian by himself, but only as a member of the body', wrote Father Georges Florovsky. 'Even in solitude, "in the chamber", a Christian prays as a member of the redeemed community, of the Church.'[44] The personal prayer of individual Christians is not separate from their prayer in church, but is simply a continuation of divine worship. Our entire life as Christians is the Liturgy which we celebrate in our heart and address to God the Trinity, Father, Son and Holy Spirit.

It may be that the practice of prayer is strikingly similar in different religious traditions, but its content varies according to the theological beliefs of those who pray. There are, for example, obvious similarities between the physical techniques of the Jesus Prayer in the Orthodox tradition and those employed in Yoga or Sufism. But neither in Yoga nor in Sufism do we find belief in the Trinity, or in Jesus Christ as God and

Saviour, which lie at the very heart of the Christian prayer. As Bishop Kallistos of Diokleia emphasises:

The essential point in the Jesus Prayer is not the act of repetition in itself, not how we sit or breathe, but *to whom* we speak . . . The Jesus Prayer is not just a device to help us concentrate or relax. It is not simply a piece of 'Christian Yoga', a type of 'Transcendental Meditation', or a 'Christian mantra' . . . It is, on the contrary, an invocation specifically *addressed to another person* – to God made man, Jesus Christ, our personal Saviour and Redeemer . . . The context of the Jesus Prayer is first of all one of *faith*. The invocation of the Name presupposes that the one who says the prayer believes in Jesus Christ as Son of God and Saviour . . . Secondly, the context of the Jesus Prayer is one of *community*. We do not invoke the Name as separate individuals . . . but as members of the community of the Church.[45]

St Paul speaks of the Holy Spirit praying within the Christian's heart (Gal. 4:6). Christian prayer is listening to the voice of God's Spirit. It is not we who pray, but God himself who prays within us. 'Why say more?' exclaims St Gregory of Sinai. 'Prayer is God, who accomplishes everything in everyone,[46] for there is a single action of Father, Son and Holy Spirit, activating all things through Christ Jesus.'[47] If prayer is God the Trinity acting through Christ, there is not much in common between this prayer and that outside the Christian tradition. And if the one who prays truly is a theologian, then there is no true prayer outside the ultimate Truth – the incarnate Christ.

### What is prayer?

Prayer is communion of the intellect with God . . . Prayer is the flower of gentleness and of freedom from anger. Prayer is the fruit of joy and thankfulness. Prayer is the remedy for gloom and despondency . . . Prayer is the ascent of the intellect to God . . . Prayer is the energy which accords with the dignity of the intellect; it is the intellect's true and highest activity . . . Blessed is the intellect that, undistracted in its prayer, acquires an ever greater longing for God. Blessed is the intellect that during prayer is free from materiality and stripped of all possessions. Blessed is the intellect that has acquired complete freedom from sensations during prayer . . . The man who always dedicates his first thoughts to God has perfect prayer . . . As sight is superior to all the other senses, so prayer is more divine than all other virtues.

*Evagrius the Solitary*

## Definitions of prayer

Prayer, by reason of its nature, is the converse and union of man with God, and by reason of its action upholds the world and brings about reconciliation with God; it is . . . a work of angels, the food of the bodiless spirits, future gladness, unending activity, a source of virtues, a means of obtaining graces, invisible progress, food of the soul, enlightenment of the mind, an axe against despair, a demonstration of hope, a cure for sorrow, the wealth of monks, the treasure of hesychasts, the reduction of anger, the mirror of progress . . . a revelation of future things, and a sign of glory. For him who truly prays, prayer is the court, the judgement hall and the tribunal of the Lord before the judgement to come.

*St John Climacus*

## 'To be attentive in your heart'

Prayer should not be the occupation of time but a permanent state . . . This type of prayer is done very simply: keep your intellect in your heart in the presence of the Lord and say 'Jesus Christ, Son of God, have mercy on me' or simply 'Lord, have mercy' . . . All the techniques that are written about (sitting, being bent over and so on) . . . are not for everyone and without the help of a personal teacher can be dangerous. It is better to leave all of this alone. Only one technique is essential – to be attentive in your heart. All the rest is superfluous and adds nothing to the prayer.

*St Theophan the Recluse*

## The name of Jesus

We say 'Jesus', and we rest in a plentitude and totality that can no longer be taken from us. The name of Jesus then becomes a bearer of the whole Christ. It brings us into His total presence. In this total presence are found all the realities towards which the name has served as a means of approach: salvation and pardon, the Incarnation and the Transfiguration, the Church and the Eucharist, the Father and the Spirit. All things then appear to us *gathered together in Christ* (Eph. 1:10) . . . If we cling to the name of Jesus, we shall receive the special blessing that the Scripture promises, *Have mercy on me as is Thy custom toward them that love Thy name* (Ps. 119:132). And may the Lord be pleased to say of us what He said of Saul: *He is a chosen vessel of Mine, to bear My name* (Acts 9:15).

*A Monk of the Eastern Church*

## A conversation with a hermit on the Jesus Prayer

We turned our attention downwards and were surprised to see in the distance a man walking with a large knapsack on his shoulders: with slow and laborious strides and his head cast down he descended along the slope of the mountain into a deep scorched hollow . . . It was astounding and at the same time very moving to see a man in the expanses of this uninhabited country . . . When we looked closer we could see that it was a man belonging to our monastic rank and we were very overjoyed at the hope of being able to learn from him many useful things concerning his life in the wilderness. When he was not far from us we greeted him in the usual monastic fashion: 'Give us your blessing, Father.' 'May God bless you!' . . . He was an elder of advanced years . . . a tall man with a dry body . . . His beard reached his waist, the hair on his head was completely white like the snow in the mountains and fell over his shoulders . . . He bore the visible imprint of spiritual sanctification: the eyes of the elder radiated an inexplicable benevolence and sparkled with goodness, sincerity and a kind disposition of the heart . . . We began to drink tea and dry bread. A remarkable conversation was then struck up between us . . . 'For the sake of the Lord, please tell us what you have acquired best of all in the wilderness?' The elder's face lit up and a spiritual light shone in his eyes . . . He answered: 'I have acquired in my heart the Lord Jesus Christ and in Him, beyond any doubt, eternal life, resounding tangibly and with urgency in my heart' . . . In hearing these unexpected and astounding words, we were greatly amazed, for we had found what we were seeking . . . 'In what way?' I hurriedly asked. The elder answered: 'Through unceasing prayer to the Lord Jesus Christ . . . For almost fifteen years I had been saying a verbal prayer only . . . Then, as a number of years flowed by, this prayer entered my intellect by itself, that is, when my mind became captive of the words of the prayer . . . And then by the grace of God, prayer of the heart was opened up, the essence of which is the closest union of our heart with the Lord Jesus Christ, felt tangibly in His Name. This exalted and supernatural state is the ultimate stage and limit of the aspirations of every reasonable being made in the image of God and which naturally strives for the highest Prototype. Here a union of the heart with God takes place whereby the Lord penetrates our spirit with His presence as a ray of the sun's light penetrates the glass and through this we are given to taste of the inexpressible bliss of sacred communion with God . . . One enters the realm of infinite light and in acquiring freedom we abide in God and God in us.'

'*On the Mountains of the Caucasus*'

### *He who loves God can think of Him day and night*

He who loves the Lord is ever mindful of Him and the thought of God begets prayer . . . The soul that loves the Lord cannot help praying, for she is drawn to Him by the grace she has come to know in prayer. We are given churches to pray in, and in church the holy offices are performed according to books. But we cannot take a church away with us, and books are not always to hand, but interior prayer is always and everywhere possible. The divine office is celebrated in church, and the Spirit of God dwells therein, but the soul is the finest of God's churches, and the man who prays in his heart has the whole world as a church . . . When the soul loses humility, she loses grace and love for God at the same time, and ardent prayer is extinguished. But when the soul stills her passion and grows humble, the Lord gives her His grace, and then she prays for her enemies as for herself, and sheds scalding tears for the whole world.

*St Silouan of Mount Athos*

### Chapter Ten

# DEIFICATION

## THE VISION OF GOD

'The glory of God is the living man, and the life of man is the vision of God', says St Irenaeus.[1]

Orthodox teaching on the vision of God received its dogmatic formulation from St Gregory Palamas and his followers at a number of Local Councils in Constantinople between 1340 and 1360. Based on evidence from Holy Scripture and the writings of the Church Fathers, this teaching was systematically laid out by Vladimir Lossky in his book *The Vision of God*. Lossky shows that both in the Bible and in the patristic tradition we find two kinds of texts dealing with the vision of God that seem contradictory and mutually exclusive: 'Alongside passages ... in which there can be found a formal negation of any vision of God, who is invisible, unknowable, inaccessible to created beings, there are others which encourage us to seek the face of God and promise the vision of God as he is.'[2]

Among the biblical texts in the first group are: 'You cannot see my face, for man cannot see me and live (Exod. 33:20); 'God ... dwells in unapproachable light, whom no man has ever seen or can see' (I Tim. 6:16); and 'No one has ever seen God' (John 1:18). In the second group Lossky includes Genesis 32:30: 'I have seen God face to face, and yet my life is preserved'; the passages in Exodus 33:11 and Deuteronomy 34:10 where God speaks to Moses 'face to face', as one speaks to a friend; and Job 19:27: 'From my flesh I shall see God, whom I shall see for myself.' From the New Testament he cites I John 3:2, 'We shall see him as he is', and I Corinthians 13:12: 'Now we see in a mirror dimly, but then face to face.'

Hence, according to biblical revelation, God is invisible and yet at the same time visible. This apparent contradiction is articulated with great clarity by St Gregory of Nyssa:

*Blessed are the pure in heart: for they shall see God.*[3] God is promised to the vision of those whose heart has been purified. But *no man has ever seen God,* as the great John says.[4] And the sublime mind of Paul confirms this verdict when saying: *Whom no man has seen, nor can see*[5] . . . All possibility of apprehension is taken away by the explicit denial: *No man can see the Lord and remain alive.*[6] Yet to see the Lord is eternal life . . . Do you realise the vertigo of the soul that is drawn to the depths contemplated in these words? If God is life, then the man who does not see Him does not see life. On the other hand, the divinely inspired prophets and apostles testify that God cannot be seen. Is not the hope of man annihilated?[7]

Equally, we find constant reference in the writings of the Church Fathers to both motifs: God's incomprehensibility and invisibility on the one hand, and on the other, the possibility of seeing him. Symeon the New Theologian, in particular, is alert to this dichotomy in Scripture and tradition. He does not hesitate to reflect on the biblical texts which deny the possibility of this vision, but he vigorously refutes those who try to use verses such as John 1:18 in order to prove that the vision of God is impossible for human beings:

[They say:] 'And who would dare to claim that he has seen God or has entirely contemplated him? Away with you! It is written: *No man has seen God at any time.*'[8] O, darkness! Who said this, tell me? '*The Only-begotten Son*', they answer, '*Which is in the bosom of the Father, he declared this.*'[9] You say the truth, and your testimony is true, but it is against your soul. What will you respond if I show you the same Son of God telling you that it is possible? For he said: *He that has seen me has seen the Father.*[10] And he said this not about the vision of his flesh, but about the revelation of his divinity . . . That it is possible for us to see God, as far as our human nature allows, listen to Christ . . . who says again: *Blessed are the pure in heart, for they shall see God.*[11]

For Symeon, the assertion that it is impossible to see God is the worst of heresies, one which contains within it all other heresies.[12] Some of his contemporaries used to say that to see God was possible perhaps for the Old Testament prophets, or for the Lord's apostles, but this vision was certainly not for people in the eleventh century. St Symeon ardently opposed this view: if the vision of God is impossible for us, he argued, it means that the Holy Spirit has departed from the Church. He also refuted the argument that the vision of God is attainable only in the future life and railed against those who interpret Matthew 5:8 as a promise relating to life after death:

[They say:] 'Yes, it is true that the pure in heart shall see God, but it will happen in the age to come and not in this age.' Why and how will it be so, my dear? If it is said that God is seen through purity of heart, it is certain that as soon as purity is attained, the vision follows it ... If purity is here, the vision is also here; and if you say that the vision is only after death, you place purity also after death, and so it happens that you will never see God ... [13]

Symeon was more inspired by visions of God which he himself had experienced throughout his life than by the hope of seeing God after death. This vision begins here, says Symeon, as soon as purity of heart is achieved. The same assertion can be found in Maximos the Confessor. The pure in heart, he declares, 'will see God ... as soon as they purify themselves through love and self-mastery; and the more intensely they strive, the fuller will their vision be'.[14] Therefore, according to both Maximos and Symeon, the promise of Christ can be realised gradually in this life rather than only in the future.

How can the invisible God be seen and how can the Unapproachable One be approached? St Gregory Palamas, following a long tradition in the Orthodox East, answers this question by introducing the distinction between God's invisible and incomprehensible 'essence' (*ousia*) and his 'energies' (*energeiai*),[15] which are 'divine operations, forces proper to and inseparable from God's essence, in which he goes forth from himself, manifests, communicates, and gives himself'.[16] According to Palamas, God's nature is incommunicable and yet at the same time somehow communicable. True Christian devotion, he claims, consists in maintaining that 'the divine nature is communicable not itself but through its energy'.[17] This subtle distinction helps us to understand different aspects of mystical experience without denying the essential incomprehensibility, invisibility and unattainability of God.

It is in this context that we should view the biblical story of Moses ascending Mount Sinai. He could not see God's face, but saw 'the averted figure' of God:

Moses said, 'I pray thee, show me thy glory.' And he said, 'I will make all my goodness pass before you ... But ... you cannot see my face; for man shall not see me and live ... Behold, there is a place by me where you shall stand upon the rock; and while my glory passes by I will put you in a cleft of the rock, and I will cover you with my hand until I have passed by; then I will take away my hand, and you shall see my back; but my face shall not be seen.'

(Exod. 33:18–23)

Here, God's 'face' refers to his essence, which is invisible and unattainable, while to see God's 'back' means to see God in his energies, in his revelation to human beings.

The vision of God in the Old Testament was partial and incomplete, but the Incarnation of Christ opened up a new possibility. People could see him in the person of Christ, God made man. 'No one has ever seen God; the only Son, who is in the bosom of the Father, he has made him known' (John 1:18). In other words, the invisible God the Father became visible through the Lord Jesus. As St Irenaeus says, 'The Father is the invisible of the Son, and the Son is the visible of the Father.'[18]

There are many accounts in the lives of saints and others of occasions in prayer when the spirit has been 'caught up' in mystical rapture and taken to another world, where it contemplates God, the angels, the Celestial Kingdom. St Paul speaks of one such mystical rapture:

I know a man in Christ who fourteen years ago was caught up to the third heaven – whether in the body or out of the body I do not know, God knows. And I know that this man was caught up into Paradise – whether in the body or out of the body I do not know, God knows – and he heard things that cannot be told, which man may not utter.

(2 Cor. 12:2–4)

St Isaac the Syrian describes different kinds of revelation experienced by the saints in prayer. It was during prayer, he says, that an angel appeared to Zacharias and announced the conception of John the Baptist.[19] During prayer at the sixth hour Peter beheld the divine vision.[20] While Cornelius prayed an angel appeared to him.[21]

When the High Priest once a year, during the dread time of prayer, entered the Holy of Holies and cast himself down upon his face . . . he heard the oracles of God through an awesome and ineffable revelation. O how awesome was the mystery which was ministered in this ceremony! So also at the time of prayer were all visions and revelations made manifest to the saints. For what other time is so holy, and by its sanctity is so apt for the reception of gifts, as the time of prayer, wherein a man converses with God? At this time, when we make our petitions and our supplications to God, and we speak with him, a man forcefully gathers together all the movements and deliberations of his soul and converses with God alone, and his heart is abundantly filled with God.[22]

So personal is the experience of the vision of God that it is rarely described in detail. Indeed, the nature of this experience is such that it would be difficult to describe in human language. Note how St Paul limited himself to a few words for this thing about which 'man may not utter'. In this respect, the writings of St Symeon the New Theologian are an exception. He was, perhaps, the only writer in the Byzantine tradition who described his own mystical experience of the vision of God, his encounters with God, and the different revelations which were granted to him. Symeon tells us that during prayer he often saw God as light:

> What is this new marvel which is happening now again?
> Now again does God want to appear to sinners . . .
> The thought of it makes me shudder, how shall I write it out in
>     words?
> What hand would lend its services, what pen would write,
> What word would express, what tongue would articulate,
> What lips would utter what one can see taking place
> In me, happening all day long?
> Much more, even at night, in the midst even of darkness,
> I see Christ – O terror! – opening the heavens for me,
> Christ Himself Who humbles Himself and shows Himself to me
> With the Father and the Spirit, thrice holy light,
> Unique in the three and the three in one single light.
> Most certainly it is They Themselves who are the light
> And the Three are unique light
> Which, more than the sun, enlightens my soul
> And illumines my mind, in darkness until then . . .
> For it is in the light of the Spirit that those who contemplate Him
>     see Him,
> And those who see in this light, it is the Son whom they contemplate,
> But 'the one who has been judged worthy to see the Son, sees the
>     Father',
> And whoever contemplates the Father, assuredly sees Him with the
>     Son.
> That is what, I repeat, is now also taking place in me:
> What the mind cannot understand, I have acquired some
>     knowledge of
> And now I contemplate the invisible beauties from afar,
> The light is inaccessible, the glory is unbearable . . . [23]

In his *Hymns*, Symeon discloses the experience which St Paul either did not want or was unable to disclose:

Again the light illumines me, again it is distinctly seen.
Again it opens the heavens, again it cuts through the night . . .
Again he who is above all heavens,
Whom no human has ever seen,
Without opening the heavens, without destroying the night,
Without leaving the atmosphere or the roof of the house,
Is found invisibly and entirely with me, wretch that I am,
Within my cell, within my mind,
At the centre of my heart, O awesome mystery!
While all things remain as they are,
The light approaches me and carries me above everything.
And as it is at the centre of all things,
It lifts me out of everything.
I do not know whether it is also with my body,
But I arrive there on high, truthfully in one whole,
Where there is only a light, simple,
Which I gaze at, and I become simple and with no evil left in me.[24]

There is nothing in Symeon's teaching that is unknown from earlier Fathers: he was not a 'new theologian' in the sense of putting forward dogmatic innovations. The newness of his theology stems from the fact that he revealed and described an experience about which no one had dared to speak so openly before. The divine light he saw was not a material light, but the uncreated light of the Divinity. It was, as St Gregory Palamas taught three hundred years later, the energy of God. The same light illumined the apostles on Mount Tabor and was revealed to Moses on Mount Sinai as 'darkness'. If we were to compare the light of Tabor and the darkness of Sinai, the difference lies perhaps in the intensity of the experience: the righteous man of the Old Testament was covered by the hand of God and could only see God's 'back', while the apostles contemplated the face of Christ shining with the divine light. The latter was also the experience of St Symeon, as well as that of many other Christians before and after him.

## THE TRANSFIGURATION OF THE PERSON

The Latin word *religio*, according to Lactantius, means 'link', or rather 'recovery of a link' (from the verb *religare*).[25] Many religions have as their aim to establish, or re-establish, a living link between God and humanity. No religion, however, claims the same fullness of communion with God as Christianity. God, who can not only be sought, thirsted for and even encountered, but who can also become *food* for his people – this God is known only to Christians. The Christian God is 'the bread of life' (John 6:35), the 'daily bread' (Matt. 6:11), which 'comes down from heaven, and gives life to the world' (John 6:33). A true life, an 'abundant' life (John 10:10), is only possible in Christ. Outside him, life is incomplete, imperfect; a fading and dying rather than living. Thus St Paul says: 'For to me to live is Christ, and to die is gain' (Phil. 1:21).

The aim of the Christian religion is to reach the fullness of communion with God where we become united to him. In the Eucharist we unite ourselves to God both spiritually and bodily; in prayer we ascend to God with our intellect and heart; in the experience of the vision of God we see him with our 'inner eyes'.

God reveals himself to us as an unspeakable and beautiful light. But he is also a 'fire', the Bible says,[26] a fire which consumes and destroys every evil and which illumines everything that is good, making it even more resplendent. A personal encounter with God is participation in the divine light. But this light can be a burning and painful fire. For some it is deadly, while for others it is salvation. While encounter with God can be transforming for one person, it can be very painful and torturous for another. Divine fire purifies. It does not destroy the sinner; rather, it destroys sin and evil, liberating the individual from them.

This experience of fire is particularly expressed in the Orthodox prayers before and after Communion: 'Behold, I draw near to divine Communion. O Creator, let me not be destroyed thereby; for thou art fire to consume the unworthy. Rather do thou cleanse me from all that defiles.'[27] The fire of the Body and Blood of Christ penetrates the entire person – body, soul and spirit: 'O Thou who didst gladly give me thy flesh for nourishment, who art fire to consume the unworthy: burn me not, O my Creator, but search out my members. Quicken my veins and my heart . . . Purify my soul. Sanctify my thought. Knit firm my bones. Enlighten my senses . . .' This purification by the fire of the Divinity is no less than participation in the divine light, for transfiguration and deification: 'The blood that makes divine, O man, let it be your fear, let it be your dread. Fire is to consume the unworthy. The divine body makes me a partaker of the divine nature,[28] and likewise feeds me; makes the spirit divine and wondrously nourishes the mind.' The Body and Blood of Christ, according to prayers ascribed to St Symeon the New Theologian, make those who truly repent 'partake of the light' and 'share in Christ's divinity'.

In patristic literature, the transfiguration of the person that occurs as a result of union with the Divine is variously called 'assimilation to God', 'transformation into god', 'becoming god', 'divinisation', or 'deification'. The concept of deification is central to the Eastern Orthodox theological and mystical tradition. To confess the true faith, to be a Church member, to observe God's commandments, to pray, to participate in sacraments: all these are necessary primarily because they lead to deification, the ultimate goal of everyone's existence.

God made us so that we might become partakers of the divine nature and sharers in his eternity, and so that we might come to be like him through deification by grace. It is through deification that all things are reconstituted and achieve their permanence; and it is for its sake that what is not is brought into being and given existence.[29]

The patristic doctrine of deification of the person is based on Scripture, though it has certain analogies in ancient Greek philosophy. Christ himself speaks of people as 'gods'.[30] In the Johannine corpus we find ideas of our adoption and likeness to God.[31] The Pauline epistles develop the biblical notion of the divine image and likeness in people,[32] the doctrine of our adoption by God,[33] and the image of the person as a temple of God.[34] St Paul's eschatological vision is characterised by the idea of the glorious state of humankind after the resurrection when it will be transformed and restored under Christ as its head, and when God will be 'all in all'.[35]

The doctrine of deification is summarised by St John of Damascus in the following text:

For John the Theologian said: *Beloved, now are we the sons of God, and it does not yet appear what we shall be, but we know that when he will appear, we shall be like him . . .* [36] For as iron united with light becomes light not by nature, but by union with fire and participation, so what is being deified becomes god not by nature, but by participation.[37]

There are three important characteristics of the approach taken by the Eastern Fathers. First, the deification of the person is viewed in a christological perspective. According to Irenaeus of Lyon, the Word 'became what we are in order to make us what he is'.[38] In other words, through the Incarnation of the Word, we become by adoption what the Son of God is by nature. St Athanasius made this formula even more precise: 'God became man in order that we may become gods.'[39] According to St Gregory the Theologian, there is a direct interdependence between the Incarnation of God the Word and the deification of the person:

Let us recognise our dignity; let us honour our Archetype; let us know . . .

for what Christ died. Let us become like Christ, since Christ became like us. Let us become gods for his sake, since he for ours became man. He assumed the worse that he might give us the better; he became poor that we through his poverty might be rich; he took upon himself the form of a servant that we might receive back our liberty; He came down that we might be exalted; he was tempted that we might conquer; he was dishonoured that he might glorify us; he died that he might save us; he ascended that he might draw to himself us, who were lying low in the fall of sin. Let us give all, offer all, to him who gave himself a ransom and a reconciliation for us. But one can give nothing like oneself, understanding the mystery, and becoming for his sake all that he became for ours.[40]

Secondly, the Fathers frequently place deification within an eschatological framework, as when they speak of the final deification of humankind in the Kingdom of heaven. Gregory the Theologian maintains that in this life we are being trained and prepared, whereas 'elsewhere' we will be deified by our inclination towards God.[41] He understands humanity's final deification as participation in the divine light in the Kingdom of heaven: 'Light is the brilliance there for those who have been purified here, when *the righteous will shine forth as the sun*[42] and God will stand amongst them, gods and kings.'[43] At the same time, deification begins here and now: the one who has surpassed everything earthly, says Maximos, enters the eighth day (that is, the age to come anticipated in the present life) and 'lives the blessed life of God . . . becoming himself god by deification'.[44]

The third important characteristic of the patristic understanding of deification is the notion that the human body itself participates in it. This is one of the concepts that distinguishes the patristic doctrine of deification from its Neo-Platonic counterpart, the idea of 'being god', which we encounter in Plotinus.[45] Macarius of Egypt speaks of the final transfiguration of the bodies of the saints which will be glorified by unspeakable light.[46] St John Climacus states that the bodies of the saints are sanctified during their earthly life, 'and in some way rendered incorruptible through the flame of purity'.[47] When the soul becomes god by participation in divine grace, declares Maximos the Confessor, 'the body is deified along with the soul through its own corresponding participation in the process of deification'.[48] According to St John of Damascus, the saints, who are gods, kings and masters, possess God, who is implanted in their bodies. Referring to I Corinthians 6:19 ('your body is the temple of the Holy Spirit'), he states that the bodies of the saints become 'animated temples of God, animated houses of God'.[49]

Those who achieve divinisation are the most qualified to speak about it. Let us turn again to the writings of Symeon the New Theologian. In his *Hymns* he emphasises that union with God means liberation from the corruptibility of the body, and departure to other worlds, beyond the limits of the visible and the borders of intellectual knowledge:

> O God, O God, Lord all-powerful!
> Who will satiate himself with your invisible beauty?
> Who will be filled with your incomprehensibility?
> Who will walk in a manner worthy of your commandments
> And will see the light of your face?
> Great, admirable light that this sluggish and gloomy world
> Will never know how to contain,
> Light which plucks out of the world the one who sees it
> With his body, oh, strange mystery!
> Who has passed through the rampart of his flesh?
> Who has traversed the darkness of corruption?
> Who has left the entire world and disappeared?
> Alas, how ordinary are our knowledge and our words!
> Indeed, then, where has the one who has crossed the boundaries of
>     the world disappeared to?
> Who has passed outside all that he sees? . . .
> Indeed, as much as the most pure bread surpasses dung
> In value and in fragrance,
> So heavenly realities incomparably surpass
> Earthly realities, for those who taste it wholesome.
> Blush, wisdom of the wise,
> Deprived of all true knowledge!
> Indeed it is the simplicity of our words
> Which as a matter of fact possesses true wisdom,
> By drawing near to God and adoring him,
> This God who gives all life-giving wisdom,
> By which I am re-created, or even divinised,
> Contemplating God for ever and ever.[50]

St Symeon speaks of the participation of the body in deification. God 'embraces' and gives himself to us, and our body, together with our soul, is totally transfigured and renewed:

> And so who would draw nearer to him?
> Or how would he be carried away towards measureless heights?

While I reflect on this, he himself is discovered within myself,
Resplendent in the interior of my miserable heart,
Illuminating me on all sides with his immortal splendour,
Completely intertwined with me, he embraces me totally.
He gives himself to me, the unworthy one,
And I am filled with his love and his beauty,
And I am sated with divine delight and sweetness.
I share in the light, I participate also in the glory,
And my face shines like my Beloved's,
And all my members become bearers of light.
Then I finally become more beautiful than those who are beautiful,
Wealthier than those who are wealthy and more than all the mighty.
I am mighty and greater than kings,
And much more precious that all that is visible,
Not only more than the world or the men of the world, but also
more than Heaven
And all the angels of Heaven, for I possess the Creator of the whole
universe . . .[51]

The Godhead is compared with fire, and human nature with grass; the fire embraces the grass, yet does not consume it:

I suddenly transcended the visible things.
I fell into fear when I saw from what I had been rescued.
I saw truly the things to come, from afar,
And when I desired to understand these things,
The fire of my love flamed up
And little by little the flame was seen,
First in my mind, then in my heart —
And the flame of divine light made tears flow . . .
O what a wonder! It transformed my whole being into flame
And the grass touching the fire was not at all burnt;
But rather the fire surrounding the grass, united with it and made it
completely indestructible . . .
How do you, remaining unchangeable and totally inaccessible,
Preserve without burning the nature of the grass?
Indeed it remains grass yet it is light, but the light is not the grass.
But you, the light, are united without mixture with the grass
And the grass becomes like the light, transfused without a change.[52]

God remains what he is, and human beings remain what they are; straw is not mixed with fire, and fire does not consume the straw; the Divinity is not confused with humanity, and humanity is not dissolved in the Divinity. Yet the union with God is so integral, and participation in the life of the Godhead is so full, that we are entirely changed, are transfigured, and become god by grace. Symeon calls deification 'a wonderful and fearful mystery', of which very few have knowledge. He emphasises, however, that the whole of Scripture speaks of deification, so that those who have attained the highest states of perfection can through their own experience understand everything that is hidden in biblical images and symbols:

> This dark air which David calls the Wall,
> That our Fathers called the Sea of our life,
> He crossed them, he moved beyond them, he came into port
> And all those who arrive there find in it all their blessings.
> That is where paradise is, there, the tree of life,
> There, the bread of sweetness, there, the divine drink,
> There, the inexhaustible richness of the gifts.
> There is where the bush burns without burning away
> And that at once the sandals were unloosed from my feet,
> This is where the sea divides and I cross over alone
> And I see my enemies submerged in the waters.
> There, I see the piece of wood pushed into my heart
> And all that is bitter is changed into sweetness.
> There I sucked the honey which flowed from the rock
> And from that moment my soul no longer experienced any anxiety.
> There, I found Christ, who obtained these blessings for me
> And I followed him with my whole soul.
> There, I ate manna and the bread of angels
> And I no longer desired anything human . . .
> There, my muddy and debauched heart,
> I saw it: pure, holy and virginal,
> And it heard the: 'Hail, full of grace,
> For the Lord is with you and in you forever!'
> There, I heard the: 'Plunge yourself into the pool of tears!'
> I did so and I immediately believed, I recovered my sight.
> There, I was put into the tomb of perfect humility
> And Christ approached me with unbounded mercy
> And he lifted the heavy stone of my malicious deeds
> And said: 'Come, go out of the world as of the tomb!' . . .
> There, I saw the life to come and the immortality

That Christ bestows on those who seek Him
And I discovered that in me was the Kingdom of Heaven,
Which is the Father, the Son and the Holy Spirit,
The Divinity inseparable in three Persons.[53]

Those who have attained true sanctity in their earthly life not only participate in the Kingdom of heaven, but are also united with the light of the
Holy Trinity and are filled with the Godhead. After the universal resurrection and the Last Judgement, however, these saints will experience an even
fuller bliss and a total assimilation to God, unimaginable to us: 'Beloved,
we are God's children now; it does not yet appear what we shall be,
but we know that when he appears we shall be like him, for we shall see
him as he is' (I John 3:2).

## God's essence and energies

To indicate the two 'poles' of God's relationship to us – unknown yet well
known, hidden yet revealed – the Orthodox tradition draws a distinction
between the essence, nature or inner being of God, on the one hand, and
His energies, operations or acts of power, on the other ... By the essence
of God is meant His otherness, by the energies His nearness. Because God
is a mystery beyond our understanding, we shall never know His essence
or inner being, either in this life or in the age to come ... But, while God's
inner essence is for ever beyond our comprehension, His energies, grace, life
and power fill the whole universe, and are directly accessible to us. The
essence, then, signifies the radical transcendence of God; the energies, His
immanence and omnipresence ... By virtue of this distinction between the
divine essence and the divine energies, we are able to affirm the possibility
of a direct or mystical union between man and God – what the Greek
Fathers term the *theosis* of man, his 'deification' – but at the same time we
exclude any pantheistic identification between the two ... There is union,
but no fusion or confusion. Although 'oned' with the divine, man still
remains man; he is not swallowed up or annihilated, but between him and
God there continues always to exist an 'I-Thou' relationship of person to
person. Such, then, is our God: unknowable in His essence, yet known in
His energies; beyond and above all that we can think or express, yet closer
to us than our own heart ...

*Bishop Kallistos of Diokleia*

## The way towards deification

God enlightens our intellect, if it is purified, in the same manner as the speed of lightning enlightens our sight. I think that this is in order to attract us to God by something that is attainable, since what is totally unattainable cannot be an object of hope and attention, and in order to precipitate an admiration by what is unattainable, and to cause greater desire by being admired, and to purify by the desire, and to make divine by purification; and, when we have already become deified, to speak with us as God Who is united with gods and comprehended by them and known by them as also He knows those whom He knows.

*St Gregory the Theologian*

## 'Those who are dark become light'

Brethren and fathers, how great is the condescension and the love of God toward people! Before the unutterable goodness of God I am struck with amazement, I am filled with wonder. So I cry out, 'O wondrous miracle, power of God's commandments, how they change those who practise and observe them!' ... Even I, who am of all human beings most insignificant and useless, have received some of these gifts ... By grace I have received grace, by doing well I have received His kindness, by fire I have been requited with fire, by flame with flame. As I ascended I was given other ascents, at the end of the ascent I was given light, and by the light an even clearer light. In the midst thereof the sun shone brightly and from it a ray shone forth that filled all things ... The divine mind conversed with my own mind and taught me, saying, 'Do you realise what My power has done to you out of love for men because of but a little faith and patience that strengthens your love? Behold, though you are subject to death, you have become immortal, and though you are ruled by corruption you find yourself above it. You live in the world and yet you are with Me; you are clothed with a body and yet you are not weighed down by any of the pleasures of the body' ... To these words I replied with trembling and joy, saying, 'Who am I, O Lord, but a sinner and unclean, that Thou hast at all looked on me and vouchsafed to have converse with me? O Thou Who art undefiled, invisible, and inaccessible to all men, how is it that Thou showest Thyself to me as being accessible and gentle, radiant with beauty through Thy refulgent glory and grace?' These words I heard mystically and in a wondrous way answered. But the supernatural struck me with amazement ... The ineffable beauty of that which appeared to me wounded my heart and attracted me to infinite love . . . I received the certain knowledge of the forgiveness of my sins, yet I saw myself as a greater sinner than all other people. It was impossible for me to disbelieve Him Who spoke to me, yet I was afraid to believe . . . There are times when I, without willing it, mount to the height of contemplation; with my will I am drawn down from it because of the limitations of the human nature and find safety in abasement. I know many things that are unknown to most people, yet I am more ignorant than all others. I rejoice because Christ, Whom I have believed, has bestowed on me an eternal and unshakeable kingdom, yet I constantly weep as one who is unworthy of that which is above . . . When I am abased below all others then I am lifted up above the heavens and am once more united in love with Christ our God. Before Him I hope to stand, once I am rid of the burden of the earthly flesh, and even closer to Him, and in addition be yet more clearly initiated into the eternal joy and exultation of the love that is on high. I have decided to write these things, my brethren, not as one who wishes to pursue glory, for such a person is a fool and a stranger to the glory that is on high! Rather, I have done so in order that you may be aware of God's infinite love for us humans, of the nature of that very light burden of the commandments of Christ our Saviour and God, and of the great price of the gift He bestows. As you learn of it, may you be filled with longing to obtain His love, or else may you fear and tremble at failure to obtain it! . . . Learn also how those people are changed who forsake all things out of love for Him Who has loved us . . . how those who are dark become light in wondrous fashion as they draw near to the Great Light; how those who come from below, even as Moses of old, become gods as they are united to things above.

*St Symeon the New Theologian*

*Chapter Eleven*

# THE LIFE OF THE AGE TO COME

## THE END OF HISTORY

From the beginning, the Christian Church has lived in the expectation of
the Second Coming of Christ. This belief is based on a promise made by
Jesus to his disciples shortly before his death on the Cross:

Take heed that no one leads you astray. For many will come in my name,
saying, 'I am the Christ', and they will lead many astray. And you will hear
of wars and rumours of wars; see that you are not alarmed; for this must
take place, but the end is not yet. For nation will raise against nation, and
kingdom against kingdom, and there will be famines and earthquakes in
various places: all this is but the beginning of the birth-pangs. Then they
will deliver you up to tribulation, and put you to death; and you will be
hated by all nations for my name's sake. And then many will fall away, and
betray one another, and hate one another. And many false prophets will arise
and lead many astray. And because wickedness is multiplied, most men's love
will grow cold ... Then if any one says to you, 'Lo, here is the Christ!' or
'There he is!' do not believe it. For false Christs and false prophets will
arise and show great signs and wonders, so as to lead astray, if possible, even
the elect ... Immediately after the tribulation of those days the sun will
be darkened, and the moon will not give its light, and the stars will fall
from heaven, and the powers of the heavens will be shaken; then will appear
the sign of the Son of man in heaven ... But of that day and hour no one
knows, not even the angels of heaven, nor the Son, but the Father only ...
Watch therefore, for you do not know on what day your Lord is coming.
(Matt. 24:4–13, 23–4, 29–30, 36, 42)

The apostles speak of the Second Coming of Christ in terms that are no
less clear: 'the coming of the Lord is at hand' (Jas. 5:8); 'the end of all
things is at hand' (I Pet. 4:7). Like Jesus, Peter describes the end of the

world as sudden: 'The day of the Lord will come like a thief, and then the heavens will pass away with a loud noise, and the elements will be dissolved with fire, and the earth and the works that are upon it will be burned up ... But according to his promise we wait for new heavens and a new earth in which righteousness dwells' (2 Pet. 3:10, 13). The same unexpectedness is emphasised by St Paul: 'You yourselves know well that the day of the Lord will come like a thief in the night. When people say, "There is peace and security", then sudden destruction will come upon them ... So then, let us not sleep, as others do, but let us keep awake and be sober' (1 Thess. 5:2–3, 6).

It may seem that Paul thought the Second Coming would occur during his own lifetime: 'We shall not all sleep, but we shall all be changed' (1 Cor. 15:54). In the first epistle to the Thessalonians, we find: 'We who are alive, who are left until the coming of the Lord, shall not precede those who have fallen asleep ... The dead in Christ will rise first; then we who are alive, who are left, shall be caught up together with them in the clouds to meet the Lord in the air' (1 Thess. 4:15, 17). The second epistle to the Thessalonians, however, emphasises that the words from the first epistle should not be taken literally in the sense that 'the day of the Lord has come'. Before Christ, the Antichrist will come:

Let no one deceive you in any way; for that day will not come, unless the rebellion comes first, and the man of lawlessness is revealed, the son of perdition, who opposes and exalts himself against every so-called god or object of worship, so that he takes his seat in the temple of God, proclaiming himself to be God ... Then the lawless one will be revealed, and the Lord Jesus will slay him with the breath of his mouth and destroy him by his appearing and his coming. The coming of the lawless one by the activity of Satan will be with all power and with pretended signs and wonders.

(2 Thess. 2:3–4, 8–9)

These are some of the most important New Testament passages relating to the Second Coming and the times that will directly precede it. The teaching they express can be summarised as follows. The 'day of the Lord' will come suddenly. Before this 'day' the world will be subjected to a period of social unrest, natural disasters, wars, and the persecution of Christians. Pseudo-prophets and pseudo-Christs will appear, claiming to be Christ and deceiving many. Next will come the Antichrist, who will gain great power and influence. And finally, the power of the Antichrist will be destroyed by Christ.

Note the highly significant role of the Antichrist just before the end of history. It is his activity, directed against God and the Church, that will lead the world to its last day. Who, then, is this Antichrist? Throughout history many have attempted to describe his characteristics and to predict the time of his coming. Some saw him as a great *religious* leader, a sort of anti-god who would attempt to replace the true faith by some pseudo-religion:[1] he would have people believe in him and not in the true Christ. Others saw in the Antichrist a great *political* leader who would gain power over the entire earth. St Hippolytus of Rome described the Antichrist as someone who would imitate Christ in all aspects of his life and activity:

The deceiver seeks to liken himself in all things to the Son of God. Christ is a lion, so Antichrist is also a lion; Christ is a king, so Antichrist is also a king. The Saviour was manifested as a lamb; so he too, in like manner, will appear as a lamb, though within he is a wolf . . . The Lord sent apostles among all the nations, and he in the same manner will send false apostles. The Saviour gathered together the sheep that were scattered abroad, and he in like manner will bring together a people that is scattered abroad. The Lord gave a seal to those who believed on Him, and he will give one in like manner. The Saviour appeared in the form of a man, and he too will come in the form of a man.[2]

The figure of the Antichrist has consistently attracted attention. Paradoxically, some Christians seem to be more interested in the coming of the Antichrist than in Christ's final victory over him. The *eschaton* is often understood as a realm of fear, global catastrophe and devastation. The end of the world is not awaited with eagerness, as it was in early Christianity, but rather with anxiety and horror.

By contrast, New Testament and patristic eschatology is one of hope and assurance: it is Christ-centred rather than Antichrist-centred. When the apostles speak in their epistles of the nearness of Christ's Second Coming, they do so with great enthusiasm and hopefulness. They were not very much interested in how near the Second Coming might be in time. More importantly, they lived with a constant sense of Christ's presence (the Greek word for 'coming', *parousia*, also means 'presence'). The Early Church, then, did not live in fear of the coming of the Antichrist, but in joyous expectation of the encounter with Christ when the history of the world would end. The eschatological 'last times' began at the very moment of the Incarnation of the Son of God and will continue right up until his Second Coming. The 'mystery of lawlessness', of which St Paul speaks, is already 'at work' (2 Thess. 2:7); it will be more and more clearly revealed in history. Together with the uncovering of evil, however, there will also be the activity of humanity's inner preparation to encounter its Saviour. The battle between Christ and the Antichrist will end with the former's glorious victory.[3] The true Christian vision is directed towards this victory, not to the time of turmoil that will precede it, a time which has in fact already begun, and may continue for a long time to come.

The end of the world will mean the liberation of humanity from evil, suffering and death, and its transformation and movement to another mode of existence, whose nature is not yet known to us. St Paul speaks as follows of this glorious outcome of human history:

Lo! I tell you a mystery. We shall not all sleep, but we shall all be changed, in a moment, in the twinkling of an eye, at the last trumpet. For the trumpet will sound, and the dead will be raised imperishable, and we shall be changed. For this perishable nature must put on the imperishable, and this mortal nature must put on immortality. When the perishable puts on the imperishable, and the mortal puts on immortality, than shall come to pass the saying that is written: 'Death is swallowed up in victory.'

(I Cor. 15:51–4)

## DEATH AND RESURRECTION

'Death is a great mystery', says St Ignaty Brianchaninov. 'It is the birth of the human person from transient life into eternity.'[4] Christianity does not consider death as an end. On the contrary, death is the beginning of a new life, for which earthly life is merely a preparation. We were created for eternity. In Paradise we were fed from the tree of life and were immortal. After the Fall, however, the way to the tree of life was blocked, and we became mortal and subject to time. According to some Church writers, humanity was sentenced to death because God's commandment was broken.[5] Others hold that death was imposed in order to liberate humans from sin and, through death, to open the way to immortality.[6]

What happens to souls after death? According to the traditions of the Orthodox Church, the soul does not leave the earth immediately after its departure from the body. For three days it remains close to the earth and visits the places with which it was associated. Meanwhile, the living show particular consideration to the souls of the deceased by offering memorial prayers and funeral services. During these three days, the personal task of the living is to be reconciled with the departed, to forgive them and to ask their forgiveness.[7]

The traditional teaching on the destiny of the soul after death and on the resurrection of the dead is summarised by Gregory Nazianzen in the following passage:

I believe the words of the wise,[8] that every fair and God-beloved soul, when, set free from the bonds of the body,[9] it departs from here, at once enjoys perception and contemplation of the blessings which await it, inasmuch as that which darkened it has been purged away, or laid aside — I do not know how else to term it — and feels a wondrous pleasure and exultation, and goes rejoicing to meet its Lord, having escaped as it were from the grievous poison of life here, and shaken off the fetters which bound it and held down the wings of the mind, and so enters on the enjoyment of the bliss laid up for it, of which it has even now some conception. Then, a little later, it receives its kindred flesh, which once shared in its pursuits of things above, from the earth which both gave and had been entrusted with it, and in some way known to God, who knit them together and dissolved them, enters with it upon the inheritance of the glory there. And, as it shared, through their close union, in its hardships, so also it bestows upon it a portion of its joys, gathering it up entirely into itself, and becoming with it one spirit, one intellect and one god, the mortal and mutable being swallowed up of life . . . Why am I faint-hearted in my hopes? Why do I behave like a mere creature of a day? I await the voice of the archangel, the last trumpet, the transformation of the heavens, the transfiguration of the earth, the liberation of the elements, the renovation of the universe.[10]

The Christian tradition inherited belief in the resurrection of the dead from the Old Testament, where there are some striking texts devoted to this theme. Many of them emphasise the bodily character of resurrection, describing it in terms of a reunification of soul and body. For example, 'Thy dead shall live, their bodies shall rise' (Isa. 26:19). The Greek version of the book of Job states: 'For I know that my Redeemer lives, and at last he will stand upon the earth; and after my skin has been thus destroyed, then from my flesh I shall see God' (Job 19:25–6; Septuagint). The prophecy of Ezekiel speaks of the bodily resurrection of the 'house of Israel', which is a symbol of entire humanity. In his glorious vision, the resurrection is presented as taking place in three stages: first, many disunited bones appear; then they come together, bone to bone, and finally, breath enters them and they arise (Ezek. 37:1–11). This symbolic picture shows the resurrection as a gradual process, something like the decomposition of the body, perhaps, but in reverse.

Possibly the most remarkable evidence for the Old Testament belief in the resurrection of the dead is the account of the martyrdom of the seven brothers and their mother, recorded in the book of Maccabees. So as not to transgress the Law of Moses, the brothers refuse to obey the king's command to taste the flesh of pigs. For this they are sentenced to death. One of the brothers says to the king: 'Thou like a fury takest us out of this present life, but the King of the world shall raise us up, who have died for his laws.' Another brother, being asked to present his hands so that they can be cut off, holds them out saying: 'These I had from heaven; and for his laws I despise them; and from him I hope to receive them again.' Yet another brother declares before his death: 'It is good, being put to death by men, to look for hope from God, to be raised up again by him.' Finally, their mother, having seen six of her sons tortured and killed, exhorts her remaining son to martyrdom, saying:

I cannot tell how ye came into my womb; for I neither gave you breath nor life, neither was it I that formed the members of every one of you; but doubtless the Creator of the world, who formed the generation of man, and found out the beginning of all things, will also of his own mercy give you breath and life again, as ye now regard not your own selves for his laws' sake.

(2 Macc. 7:1–41)

The words of the martyrs and of their mother show that already in pre-Christian times there was a firm belief in the resurrection among the children of Israel.

The doctrine of resurrection was further clarified in the New Testament. According to the words of Christ, the resurrection will be universal, but for those who have done good it will be 'the resurrection of life', while for those who have done evil it will be 'the resurrection of judgement' (John 5:29). St Paul describes the resurrection of the dead in terms of a great change, when people will receive new bodies to replace their old material ones:

What is sown is perishable, what is raised is imperishable. It is sown in dishonour, it is raised in glory. It is sown in weakness, it is raised in power. It is sown a physical body, it is raised a spiritual body . . . Just as we have borne the image of the man of dust, we shall also bear the image of the man of heaven. I tell you this, brethren: flesh and blood cannot inherit the kingdom of God, nor does the perishable inherit the imperishable.

(I Cor. 15:42–4, 49–50)

These words are fundamental to patristic teaching on the nature of the resurrected body. According to many Church Fathers, the new body will be immaterial and incorruptible, like the body of Christ after his Resurrection.

Gregory of Nyssa, however, claims that there will be an affinity between a person's new immaterial body and the one he or she possessed in earthly life. Gregory sees the proof of this in the parable of the rich man and Lazarus: the former would not have recognised the latter in hell if no physical characteristics remained that allowed people to identify each other. There is what Gregory calls the 'seal' of the former body imprinted on every soul. The appearance of the new incorruptible body will in some fashion resemble the old material body:

The soul has a natural inclination of affection towards the body that has dwelt with it; and it has therefore a disposition, in virtue of this commixture, to recognise the body that belongs to it, as if certain marks had been imprinted by nature, by means of which the community between them remains unconfused, being marked by these distinctive signs. Now since the soul attracts again to itself that which is connected with it and belongs to it, what difficulty, I ask you, would be presented to the divine power to hinder the coming together of the related things which are drawn towards each other by a kind of mysterious natural attraction? The fact that there still remain in the soul some tokens of our composite nature, even after its dissolution, is attested by the dialogue in Hades.[11] For although the bodies had been committed to the tomb, some physical means of identification still attached to the souls, by which Lazarus was recognised, and the rich man was known . . .[12] The form remains in the soul as if by the impression of a seal; and thus it is inevitable that those things which have been impressed by the seal with this stamp should not fail to be recognised by the soul. In fact, at the time of the general restoration the soul inevitably receives back to itself whatever corresponds to the stamp of the form, and clearly all those things which in the beginning were thus stamped by the form would so correspond.[13]

Gregory also maintains that the incorruptible body after the resurrection will bear none of the marks of corruption that characterised the material body, such as mutilation, ageing, and so on.

## PRAYER FOR THE DEPARTED

The practice of prayer for the departed is based on an understanding that the fate of the soul after death is not clear before the final, universal resurrection, and that the situation of the departed might be changed for the better by the prayers of the living.

One of the hymns sung at the Orthodox funeral service is written on behalf of the departed person, who asks the living to pray for him or her:

As ye behold me lie before you all speechless and bereft of breath, weep for me, O friends and brethren, O kinsfolk and acquaintance. For but yesterday I talked with you, and suddenly there came upon me the dread hour of death. But come, all ye who loved me, and kiss me with the last kiss. For nevermore shall I walk or talk with you. For I go hence unto the Judge with whom is no respect of persons. For slave and master stand together before him, king and warrior, the rich and the poor, in honour equal. For according to his deeds shall every man receive glory or be put to shame. But I beg and implore you all, that ye will pray without ceasing unto Christ our God, that I be not doomed according to my sins, unto a place of torment; but that he will appoint unto me a place where is the light of life.[14]

These words reflect what the departed person wants most from his or her friends and relatives: not a splendid funeral, not mourning, but intense prayer, by which the soul is commended into God's hands.

Such prayer is an ancient tradition of the Christian Church. Leaving the body, the person departs from the visible world, but does not depart from the Church. He or she continues to be part of the Church, and it is the duty of those on earth to pray for him or her. The Church believes that prayer can assist the person in the journey after death, and that God accepts prayers not only for the righteous, but also for sinners.

The commemoration of the departed at the Divine Liturgy is particularly important. Liturgical prayer is all-inclusive and universal; it is offered both for the living and the dead. In the words of St Mark of Ephesus:

The departed in faith are definitely assisted by Liturgies celebrated in their memory, as well as prayers and almsgiving . . . Even the souls which are kept in hell and are already assigned to eternal torments . . . can be assisted and given at least a little help, even if not completely liberated . . . The fact that the souls of the dead by prayers are liberated from their imprisonment in hell, as if from a certain penitentiary, is confirmed, among many others, by Theophanes the Confessor, named Graptos . . . In one of his canons for the departed he prays for them in the following way: 'O Saviour, from tears and grief liberate your servants who are in hell.'[15] . . . For, as St Theodore the Studite, himself a confessor and witness of truth, says in the beginning of his Canon for the departed: 'As we celebrate today the memory of the dead from the beginning, let us all entreat Christ to deliver from the everlasting fire those who have fallen asleep in faith and in the hope of eternal life.'[16] . . . Whether the saints are heard by God when they pray for this, it is not our duty to investigate: this was known to them and to the Spirit, which dwelt in them . . . This was equally known to the Lord Christ, who gave the commandment that we should pray for our enemies, Who Himself prayed for those who crucified him and who compelled Stephen to the same, when the latter was stoned. And even if, perhaps, someone would say that when we pray for people of this kind we are not heard by God, yet we do whatever we can. Some of the saints who prayed not only for the faithful but also for the unlawful were heard and by their prayers released them from eternal torment, as, for example . . . the divine Gregory the Dialogos, who is reported to have liberated Trajan. So, for all people of this kind the offerings of prayers and Liturgies are brought by the Church and by us.[17]

These words are of special interest because they deal with the question of prayer for non-Christians, which presents difficulties for some people. In particular, reference is made to a story which is found in some ancient accounts of the life of Gregory the Great. He is said to have prayed for the Emperor Trajan, who was a persecutor of Christians, until he received confirmation from God that his prayer had been heard. The hagiographical sources claim that Trajan's soul was 'baptised' in hell by the tears of St Gregory.

Mark of Ephesus does not seem to make any distinction between the faithful and the 'unlawful' in this context. In some parts of the Orthodox Church today, only departed members are commemorated at public liturgical celebrations, while others are remembered privately. Because of this, some Orthodox have come to believe that they are not allowed to pray at all for the non-Orthodox. A Russian priest wrote in 1905 that prayer for a departed Lutheran would not please this Lutheran since he did not recognise the practice of prayers for the departed and 'at his last hour did not think about converting to Orthodoxy'. The priest made an analogy with certain scientific and economic enterprises and societies that maintain strict 'corporational boundaries'. Orthodox Christians, he argued, 'must educate themselves in the spirit of Orthodox corporation and solidarity' and not pray for the non-Orthodox.

This point of view was firmly opposed at the time by a professor at the Moscow Theological Academy:

In all these comments, one can discern a certain extraordinary callousness, a certain selfish and punctilious care for not doing somebody an additional service and not appearing as someone uninvited. It is completely forgotten here that, in spite of confessional differences, we are all Christians, and therefore out of love for our neighbours we must render them great assistance. Did the departed Lutherans or members of the Reformed Church not believe in prayers for the departed during their lifetime? So what? Are *we* not Orthodox? We do believe that our prayer can be of much help to the departed.

True Orthodoxy, the author concludes, breathes not with 'a spirit of corporation', but rather with a spirit of love and mercy to all people, including those who are or were outside the Orthodox Church.[18]

## THE LAST JUDGEMENT

At the moment of death, the soul leaves the body and enters its new mode of existence. It does not lose its memory or its ability to think or to feel, but departs to the other world loaded with the burdens of this life, with memories of its past and accountability for its sins.

Christian teaching on the Last Judgement is based on the understanding that all sinful actions committed by a person leave traces on his or her soul, and that he or she is to give account for everything before that Absolute Good, with whom no evil or sin can co-exist. The Kingdom of God is incompatible with sin: 'Nothing unclean will enter it, nor any one who practises abomination or falsehood, but only those who are written in the Lamb's book of life' (Rev. 21:27). Every evil for which there was no repentance in the sacrament of confession, every sin which was concealed, every defilement of the soul which was not purified: all of this will be revealed at the Last Judgement. In the words of Christ, 'There is nothing hid, except to be made manifest; nor is anything secret, except to come to light' (Mark 4:22).

From Old Testament times people knew of the Last Judgement. 'Rejoice, O young man, in your youth,' the preacher in Ecclesiastes writes, 'and let your heart cheer you in the days of your youth; walk in the ways of your heart and the sight of your eyes. But know that for all these things God will bring you into judgement' (Eccles. 11:9). Only in the New Testament, however, does the teaching on the Last Judgement receive its final shape. Christ himself describes it in a parable:

When the Son of man comes in his glory, and all the angels with him, then he will sit on his glorious throne. Before him will be gathered all the nations, and he will separate them one from another as a shepherd separates the sheep from the goats, and he will place the sheep at his right hand,

but the goats at the left. Then the King will say to those at his right
hand, 'Come, O blessed of my Father, inherit the kingdom prepared for
you from the foundation of the world; for I was hungry and you gave me
food, I was thirsty and you gave me drink, I was a stranger and you
welcomed me, I was naked and you clothed me, I was sick and you visited
me, I was in prison and you came to me.' Then the righteous will answer
him, 'Lord, when did we see thee hungry and feed thee, or thirsty and give
thee drink? . . .' And the King will answer them, 'Truly, I say to you, as you
did it to one of the least of these my brethren, you did it to me.' Then he
will say to those at his left hand, 'Depart from me, you cursed, into the
eternal fire prepared for the devil and his angels; for I was hungry and you
gave me no food, I was thirsty and you gave me no drink . . .' And they
will go away into eternal punishment, but the righteous into eternal life.

(Matt. 25:31–46)

This parable indicates that for some the Judgement will be a moment of
insight, recognition and conversion, while for others it may turn out to be
a great disappointment and frustration. Those who were sure of their own
salvation may suddenly find themselves condemned, while those who
perhaps did not consciously meet Christ in their earthly life ('when did
we see thee?'), but were merciful towards their neighbour, will be saved.
The King does not ask people about matters of belief, doctrine and
religious practice. He does not ask them whether they went to church, kept
the fasts, or prayed for a long time. He only asks them how they treated
his 'brethren'. The main criteria of Judgement, then, are acts of mercy
performed or not performed by people during their earthly lives.

According to the teaching of the Church, the Last Judgement will be
universal: all people will be present, whether or not they are Christians. If
Christians will be judged by the Gospel's standards, non-Christians will be
judged by the natural law which is 'written in their hearts' (Rom. 2:15).
Christians will take full responsibility for their deeds as those who 'knew'
the will of God, while some non-Christians will be treated less strictly for
they did not know God or his will.[19] The Judgement will 'begin with the
household of the Lord' (1 Pet. 4:17), that is, the Church and its members,
and not with those who did not meet Christ or hear the message of the
Gospel.

Nonetheless, both the New Testament and Orthodox patristic tradition
suggest that all people will appear with some experience of an encounter
with Christ and his message, including those who did not meet him in
their earthly life. In particular, St Peter speaks of Christ's descent into hell

and his preaching there to those sinners who were drowned in the waters of the Flood:

For Christ also died for sins once for all, the righteous for the unrighteous, that he might bring us to God, being put to death in the flesh but made alive in the spirit; in which he went and preached to the spirits in prison, who formerly did not obey, when God's patience waited in the days of Noah, during the building of the ark, in which a few, that is, eight persons, were saved through water. Baptism, which corresponds to this, now saves you . . . through the resurrection of Jesus Christ.

(I Pet. 3:18–21)

If Christ preached in hell, was his message addressed to all people or only to the chosen ones? According to some Church writers, Christ preached only to the Old Testament righteous who were in hell waiting for him. For others, the message of Christ was addressed to all, including those who lived outside the true faith. This view is expressed by Clement of Alexandria:

Does not Scripture tell us without any hesitation or beating about the bush that the Lord proclaimed the Gospel also to those who died in the waters of the Flood, or better, who were fettered and kept in bonds of captivity? I hope, the Saviour will not be deprived of the possibility of saving the pagans also, for the goal of his coming on earth was salvation . . . If the Lord descended into hell – and the fact of his descent is indisputable – his goal was nothing but the proclamation of the Gospel there; in doing this, he converted . . . all the dead. Therefore, all who believed in him will be saved, even if they had been pagans (before) . . . Having been swallowed by hell and kept imprisoned there, they could immediately be converted and accept the faith in Christ, as soon as he appeared there and they heard his divine word and the word of his apostles.[20]

Clement bases his argument on St Peter, who speaks of Christ's coming to those who lived 'in the days of Noah', that is, to those whose 'wickedness' was 'great in the earth', and whose 'imagination of the thoughts' was 'only evil continually' (Gen. 6:5). Christ preached, then, not to the righteous who were to be saved, but to sinners who were condemned for their evil actions. The sinners who were confined in hell must have met the Lord in order to appear before him at the Last Judgement: 'They will give account to him who is ready to judge the living and the dead. For this is why the Gospel was preached even to the dead, that though judged in the flesh like men, they might live in the spirit like God' (I Pet. 4:5–6). Interpreting these words, a Russian bishop wrote at the beginning of the twentieth century:

By 'the dead' we should understand all those dead before the day of Christ's Last Judgement, that is, both those who did hear the word of the Gospel during their earthly life and those who did not . . . Had Christ's Gospel not touched the ears of all the dead, not all the dead would have been subject to Christ's Judgement. This verse gives us the right to think that, in the same manner as those who died before the coming of Christ on earth were instructed by the Gospel's message in hell through Christ, who died and descended into hell, so those who have died after Christ's coming but have not heard the Gospel's message on earth and have not known Christ, will be instructed by this message in hell. Whether this will happen many times or only once, just before Christ's Last Judgement . . . is not revealed by the Apostle. Only this unequivocally derives from the words of the Apostle: that all the dead, including those who have not heard on earth Christ's Gospel, will appear at the Last Judgement of the Lord as those who will have heard it . . . [21]

Can there be an answer here to the complex question of whether or not it is possible for nonbelievers to be saved? Although Orthodox tradition has always asserted that *there is no salvation outside Christ, Baptism and the Church,* not everyone who failed to meet Christ during earthly life is deprived of the possibility of being liberated from hell, for even in hell the message of the Gospel is heard. Having created human beings with free will, God accepted responsibility for the salvation of humanity; and this salvation has been accomplished by Christ. A person who deliberately rejects Christ and the Gospel makes a choice for the devil and becomes guilty of self-condemnation: 'He who does not believe is condemned already, because he has not believed in the name of the only Son of God' (John 3:18). However, how can someone who has not heard the Gospel at all be condemned? 'Imagine that the Gospel was not proclaimed to those who died before Christ's coming', says Clement of Alexandria. 'Then both their salvation and their condemnation is a matter of crying injustice.'[22] In the same way, those who have died after Christ's coming without hearing the Gospel message cannot be treated as if they deliberately rejected him. This is why Christ preached in hell in order that every person created by him could make a choice for good or evil.

The question of the possibility of salvation for non-Christians is particularly important for many of today's Christians whose relatives and friends may have died outside the Christian faith. Modern Orthodox theologians answer it in different ways. A somewhat unexpected answer was given by Metropolitan Anthony of Sourozh to the students of the Moscow Theological Academy in 1966. The Metropolitan was asked, 'Is there the possibility of salvation outside Christ?' He answered, 'I would say yes. Take the words of St Paul about the Gentiles who are instructed by the law written in their heart; that the Jews are instructed by the law of Moses; while Christians follow the law of Christ.'[23] To the further question 'But they must come to Christ?' he answered, 'They might not come, because this is conditioned by historical circumstances. You cannot doubt a person's eternal salvation only because he was born in Central Africa in a period when there were no Christian missionaries. In this case salvation would be conditioned by geography and history . . . It would be no more than God's tyranny: you were born there, therefore you are condemned. There is nothing ethical here: only an occurrence of the evil will of God.' Metropolitan Anthony went on to say that among the people of non-Christian religions there are many who came to such a degree of knowledge of God that only the name of Jesus is missing. Can one imagine, the Metropolitan asked, that when such a person upon his death appears before the Lord, he will not say: 'Here is the One whom I sought throughout the whole of my life, here is the answer to all my questions'?[24] The question, therefore, is no longer about salvation *outside Christ*, but rather about the salvation *in Christ* of those who, for one reason or another, died outside the Christian faith.

## 'WHAT IS HELL?'

'Fathers and teachers! I ask: What is hell? I answer: Suffering on account of the impossibility to love any longer.' These are the words of Elder Zosima, Dostoyevsky's celebrated monk in *The Brothers Karamazov*.

'Why hell?' many people ask. Why does God condemn people to eternal damnation? How can the image of God the Judge be reconciled with the New Testament message of God as love? St Isaac the Syrian answers these questions in the following way: there is no person who would be deprived of God's love, and there is no place which would be devoid of it; all who deliberately choose evil instead of good deprive themselves of God's mercy. The very same divine love which is a source of bliss and consolation for the righteous in Paradise becomes a source of torment for sinners, as they cannot participate in it and they are outside it:

Those who are punished in Gehenna[25] are scourged by the scourge of love.

Nay, what is so bitter and vehement as the torment of love? I mean that those who have become conscious that they have sinned against love suffer greater torment from this than from any fear of punishment. For the sorrow caused in the heart by sin against love is more poignant than any torment. It would be improper for a man to think that sinners in Gehenna are deprived of the love of God. Love . . . is given to all. But the power of love works in two ways: it torments sinners, even as happens here when a friend suffers from a friend; but it becomes a source of joy for those who have observed its duties. Thus I say that this is the torment of Gehenna: bitter regret.[26]

It is not, therefore, that God mercilessly prepares torments, but rather that we ourselves choose evil and then suffer from its consequences. There are people who deliberately refuse to follow the way of love, who do harm to their neighbours: these are the ones who will be unable to reconcile themselves with the Supreme Love when they encounter it face to face. If we are outside love during our earthly life, we will not find a way to be inside it when we depart from the body. We will find ourselves in 'the valley of the shadow of death' (Ps. 23:4), in 'the darkness' and 'the land of forgetfulness' (Ps. 28:12). Jesus called this place, or rather this condition of the soul after death, 'the outer darkness' (Matt. 22:13) or 'the hell of fire' (Matt. 5:22). According to St Basil the Great, hell is 'alienation from God for abundance of sin and disposition opposed to good'.[27] The source of suffering in hell is therefore the subjective awareness of the absence of God. All the images that are traditionally used to describe hell, be they fire or ice, scorching furnaces or burning lakes, are only symbols of the suffering caused by the person's inability to participate fully in God.

It is important to be aware that the notion of hell has been distorted by the coarse and material images in which it was clothed in medieval literature, with its emphasis on satisfaction and punishment. Michelangelo's *Last Judgement* in the Sistine Chapel, for example, depicts Christ hurling into the abyss all who have dared to oppose him. 'This, to be sure, is not how I see Christ', says Archimandrite Sophrony. ' . . . Christ, naturally, must be in the centre, but a different Christ more in keeping with the revelation that we have of him: Christ immensely powerful with the power of unassuming love.'[28] If God is love, he must be full of love even at the moment of the Last Judgement, even when he pronounces sentence.

In Orthodox theology, notions of hell and eternal torment are inseparably linked with the mystery disclosed in the liturgical services of Holy Week and Easter: the mystery of Christ's descent into hell and his liberation of those who were held there under the tyranny of death. The Church teaches that, after his death on the Cross, Christ descended into the abyss in order to annihilate hell and death, and destroy the horrific kingdom of the devil. Just as Christ had sanctified the Jordan at his baptism by descending into its waters, by descending into hell he illumined it entirely with the light of his presence. Unable to tolerate this invasion, hell surrendered: 'Today hell groans and cries aloud: It had been better for me, had I not accepted Mary's Son, for he has come to me and destroyed my power; he has shattered the gates of brass, and as God he has raised up the souls that once I held . . .'[29] In the words of St John Chrysostom, 'Hades[30] was embittered when it met thee face to face below. It was embittered, for it was rendered void. It was embittered, for it was mocked. It was embittered, for it was slain. It was embittered, for it was despoiled. It was embittered, for it was fettered.'[31] This does not mean that in the wake of Christ's descent hell no longer exists. It exists, but it is already sentenced to death.

These liturgical texts reveal a further mystery: they tell us precisely who was rescued from hell by Christ. Without any qualification whatsoever, the hymns speak of the liberation of *all* people, of the whole of humanity:

Christ is risen, releasing from bondage Adam the first-formed man and destroying the power of hell. Be of good courage, all ye dead, for death is slain and hell despoiled; the crucified and risen Christ is King.[32]

O Lord, on the Cross thou hast torn up the record of our sins; numbered among the departed, thou has bound fast the ruler of hell, delivering all from the chains of death by thy Resurrection . . . [33]

Today hell groans and cries aloud: 'My power has been destroyed . . . I held in my power the dead from all the ages; but see, he is raising them all.'[34]

The company of angels was amazed, beholding thee, O Saviour, numbered among the dead, who hast destroyed the power of death and raised up Adam with thyself, setting all men free from hell.[35]

By the Cross having descended into hell, that he might fill all things with himself, he loosed the pains of death: and being risen again the third day, he made a way for all flesh unto the resurrection of the dead.[36]

Let none fear death; for the death of the Saviour has set us free . . . O Death, where is thy sting? O Hades, where is thy victory? Christ is risen and thou art cast down ... Christ is risen, and there is none dead in the tomb.[37]

If only the righteous of the Old Testament had been released from hell while sinners remained eternally damned, Christ's liberation would have been merely a matter of justice, not mercy. It would be the reward for living a godly life rather than the miracle of salvation for all, including those who were unworthy of it. As a prayer ascribed to St John of Damascus says: 'If you save a righteous man, there is nothing great, and if you have mercy on a pure one, there is nothing miraculous; for they are worthy of your mercy.'[38] Why should the Church rejoice about the mystery of Christ's victory and salvation, if nothing mysterious or miraculous happened?

At the same time, it must be pointed out that the liberation of all souls in hell should not be understood as a kind of magic, conferred by Christ against the will of the person. 'God persuades, he does not compel, for violence is alien to him', says an ancient Christian text.[39] 'God's call to salvation comes in the form of an invitation, which we on the human side are free to accept or to reject', claims a contemporary Orthodox theologian.[40] For someone who deliberately refuses to follow Christ and to enter the open gates of Paradise, hell remains the torment of deprivation of God.[41]

While acknowledging the dogmatic importance of the concept of hell, however, the Orthodox Church does not speak of it as the inevitable fate of sinners. On the contrary, the Church prays 'for all those who are held in hell',[42] believing that the salvation of all people is in the hands of God, 'Who desires all to be saved',[43] who is 'not wishing that any should perish, but that all should reach repentance'.[44] Nothing is impossible for God. Through the prayer of the Church and by his own mercy, he can liberate from hell even those who in their lifetime were opposed to him.

In Orthodox theology there is no distinction between the temporary torments of purgatory from which one can be freed, and the eternal punishment of hell from which no liberation is possible. By praying for those in hell, the Orthodox Church demonstrates that it nevertheless believes in the possibility of liberation from hell. The idea of a purifying fire after death, however, found some adherents in the Orthodox East. In particular, St Gregory of Nyssa says:

It is not out of hatred or vengeance for an evil life, in my opinion, that God brings painful conditions upon sinners, when he seeks after and draws to himself whatever has come to birth for his sake; but for a better purpose he draws the soul to himself, who is the fountain of all blessedness. The painful condition necessarily happens as an incidental consequence to the one who is drawn ... When evil is consumed by the purifying fire, the soul which is united to evil must necessarily also be in the fire until the base adulterant material is removed, consumed by the fire.[45]

Here he does not refer, however, to the torments of purgatory, but to the fire of Hell, from which, as St Gregory believes, liberation is possible, since the soul is purified in it from evil and sin.

Thus we have the prayer of the Church for those who are bound in hell, the hope of liberation from their torments, and finally the message of Christ's descent into the abyss to release all those who are held there. These are the things which prevent Orthodox Christians from falling into despair when thinking of hell, giving them both assurance and hope.

## 'THAT GOD MAY BE ALL IN ALL'

We now turn to something which has been the subject of controversy for many centuries: universal salvation. Is it possible that one day the torments of hell will end and all people, both righteous and sinners, will be saved? In considering this question, we will take into account the opinions of ancient Church writers, as well as those of some modern Orthodox theologians. The following presentation is not meant to be exhaustive. These are simply points of view which have found adherents throughout the history of Orthodox Christianity.

In the first century St Paul wrote that, after the resurrection of all and with the final victory of Christ over death, everything will be subjected to God and he will be 'all in all', or 'everything to every one', as the Revised Standard Version renders it:

For as in Adam all die, so also in Christ shall all be made alive ... Then comes the end, when he delivers the kingdom to God the Father after destroying every rule and every authority and power. For he must reign until he has put all his enemies under his feet. The last enemy to be destroyed is death ... When all things are subjected to him, then the Son himself will also be subjected to him who put all things under him, that God may be everything to every one.

(I Cor. 15:22, 24–6, 28)

In the third century, Origen, inspired by both Pauline and Platonic ideas, developed a doctrine of 'the restoration of all' (*apokatastasis ton panton*), according to which all sinners, including demons and the devil himself, will be saved following their submission, for a longer or shorter period, to hell's purifying fire. For Origen, the *apokatastasis* is not the end of world history, but is rather the end of one stage of human history after which another stage will follow. Directly influenced by Plato, Origen believed in the pre-existence of souls and taught that before the present creation, there was another world, and there will be yet another after this one passes away. The entire history of the universe is regarded by Origen as a succession of worlds which appear, develop and come to an end. The events that occur in each of these successive worlds conform to the following pattern: God creates souls which are good by nature, but in time fall away from him. The Incarnation of the Logos then takes place, and because of it all creation gradually ascends to its primordial state. When this state ('the restoration of all') is regained, the possibility for a new falling away opens up. Consequently, God will need to become man again and again in order to take upon himself the sins of the world and to redeem it.[46]

This teaching, together with the idea of the pre-existence of souls (both notions based more on Plato than on St Paul and indeed contradicting the Gospel's message of the uniqueness of Christ's redemptive sacrifice) was condemned by a Local Council in Constantinople in the sixth century.[47] The Church rejected the Origenist understanding of the *apokatastasis* also on the grounds that it attempted to prove rationally what cannot be proved. Mystery hidden within Divine Providence should not become the object of speculation. Objects of hope should not become dogmas. What remains a question must not be promulgated as a doctrine.

Notwithstanding this somewhat fantastic teaching, there is also an Orthodox understanding of the *apokatastasis*,[48] as well as a notion of the non-eternity of hell. Neither has ever been condemned by the Church and both are deeply rooted in the experience of the Paschal mystery of Christ's victory over the powers of darkness. Both of these views are reflected in a hymn sung on Great Saturday:

Hell is king over mortal men, *but not for ever*. Laid in the sepulchre, O mighty Lord, with thy life-giving hand thou has burst asunder the bars of death. To those from every age who slept in the tombs, thou hast proclaimed true deliverance, O Saviour . . .[49]

Hell's power over fallen humanity is, therefore, 'not for ever', not eternal, since Christ destroyed hell by his own death on the Cross.

The teaching that hell is finite was developed by several early Christian theologians, among whom Gregory of Nyssa, one of the fourth-century Cappadocian Fathers, is one of the most important. Unlike Origen, St

Gregory taught that the body will take part in the final restoration.[50] Reflecting on the Pauline concept of the final victory of Christ over death, he described the final restoration of all in the following terms:

Indeed the divine Nature is the source of all virtue. Hence those who are released from evil will be in the divine Nature, so that *God may be all in all* . . . He who becomes all will also be in all. In this the apostle seems to me to teach the complete annihilation of evil. If God will be in everything which exists, evil obviously will not be among the things which exist . . . He has one goal: when the whole fullness of our nature has been perfected in each man, some straightaway even in this life purified from evil, others healed hereafter through fire for the appropriate length of time, and others ignorant of the experience of good and evil in the life here, God intends to set before everyone the participation of the good things in him, which the Scripture says eye has not seen nor ear heard, nor thought attained.[51] This is nothing else, according to my judgement, but to be in God himself . . . The passions resulting from evil become hard for the soul to get rid of, thoroughly mixed up with it, growing onto it, and closely united with it. So when such things are cleansed and purified away by the treatment through fire, each of the better qualities will enter in their place: incorruptibility, life, honour, grace, glory, power, and whatever else of this kind we recognise in God himself and in his image, which is our human nature.[52]

Another great Cappadocian Father, Gregory Nazianzen, who was generally more reserved about eschatological themes, also spoke of the final restoration:

God will be all in all at the time of the 'restoration' (*apokatastaseos*) . . . God will be all in all when we are no longer what we are now, a multiplicity of impulses and emotions, with little or nothing of God in us, but are fully like God, with room for God and God alone. This is the maturity towards which we speed. Paul himself is a special witness here . . . I quote: *Here there cannot be Greek and Jew, circumcised and uncircumcised, barbarian, Scythian, slave, free man, but Christ is all, and in all.*[53]

In the seventh century, Maximus the Confessor spoke of 'the general change and renewal which will take place in the future, at the end of the ages, through God our Saviour; a universal renewal of the whole human race, natural but by grace; a renewal leading from death and decay to immortal and incorruptible life, through the resurrection which we await'.[54] In another passage Maximus mentions 'the time of the hoped-for universal consummation, when the world, like the person, will die to appearances and rise again, a new being from an old, in the instantaneous resurrection which we wait for'; at this moment 'the person such as we – as a part with its whole, and as a small with the great – will rise with the world, receiving the power never to be corruptible again'.[55] As we see, St Maximus spoke of the future renewal of the entire human race, without a single reference to an exception or qualification.[56] When asked to comment on Gregory of Nyssa's understanding of the restoration-*apokatastasis*,[57] Maximus gives three interpretations, which, he claims, are recognised by the Church. The first restoration is the moral regeneration of each individual as a result of virtue; the second is the physical transformation of 'the whole of nature at the resurrection, a restoration to incorruptibility and immortality'; and the third is 'the kind Gregory of Nyssa used more frequently in his writings', which is 'the restoration of powers of the soul, which had fallen under the influence of sin, to the state in which they were created'. It is in the restoration of the third kind that the human soul 'will be restored to its ancient state, and the Creator will be shown not to have been responsible for sin'.[58]

St Maximus, living at a time when the Origenist controversy was more or less over, tried to 'recast and reintegrate' the concept of the *apokatastasis* 'on his own theological grounds'[59] and distance it from Origenism. Instead of pressing the idea that of necessity all will be saved, he more often referred to God's *intention* to save all people. Maximus was indeed within the limits of biblical revelation when referring to God who 'loves all people equally and wants them to be saved and to come to the knowledge of the truth'.[60] It is in this context that he spoke of Christ, who 'accomplished in himself, divinely, the salvation of all'.[61] As B. Daley suggests, St Maximus 'stops short' of the 'conviction that the salvation achieved by Christ will necessarily be realised in every individual', while making clear 'that the overall success of the divine plan does not exclude the possibility of individual failures': in fact, everyone is free to accept or to reject salvation offered by Christ.[62] Salvation will not be compulsory for anyone: it is 'those who wish to follow' Christ who will be saved.[63]

The doctrine of universal salvation is expressed in a very definite and striking manner by Isaac the Syrian, an outstanding mystical writer of the seventh century, whose contribution to Christian eschatology is said to be 'the most important contribution to this subject in the whole of Christian theology'.[64] St Isaac emphasises that, above all else, God is immeasurable and boundless love. In God, Isaac states, there is no revenge or retribution, but only love and mercy. Even when God chastises, he does this out of love and for the sake of salvation, not retribution.[65] Thus it is actually impossible to speak of God's justice, only of a mercy that surpasses all justice.[66] According to St Isaac, the sufferings which a person undergoes in Gehenna have salvation as their goal: these are purifying sufferings which are limited to a fixed period and will be brought to an end when everyone achieves the state of perfection that is necessary for entering the Kingdom of heaven. Most people, states St Isaac, will not experience the sufferings of Gehenna at all; only those who need them will be subjected to them:

Demons will not remain in their demonic state, and sinners will not remain in their sins; rather, he is going to bring them to a single equal state of perfection in relationship to his own Being – in a state in which the holy angels are now, in perfection of love and passionless mind ... Maybe they will be raised to a perfection even greater than that in which the angels now exist; for all are going to exist in a single love, a single purpose, a single will, and a single perfect state of knowledge; they will gaze towards God with the desire of insatiable love, even if some divine dispensation[67] may in the meantime be effected for reasons known to God alone, lasting for a fixed period, decreed by him in accordance with the will of His wisdom ... No part belonging to any single one of all rational beings will be lost, as far as God is concerned, in the preparation of that supernal Kingdom which is prepared for all worlds ... The majority of humankind will enter the Kingdom of heaven without the experience of Gehenna. But this is apart from those who, because of their hardness of heart and utter abandonment to wickedness and the lusts, fail to show remorse in suffering for their faults and their sins ... [68]

In a homily entitled 'Against those who say: If God is good, for what reason has he made these things?', St Isaac opposes a dualistic understanding of the co-eternal existence of good and evil, God and the devil. He bases himself on a teaching commonly accepted in Christian tradition, that God is not the creator of evil and that evil has no substantial existence:

Sin, Gehenna and death do not exist at all with God, for they are effects, not substances. Sin is the fruit of free will. There was a time when sin did not exist, and there will be a time when it will not exist. Gehenna is the fruit of sin. At some point in time it had a beginning, but its end is not known. Death, however, is a dispensation of the wisdom of the Creator. It will rule only a short time over nature; then it will be totally abolished.[69]

Thus, according to St Isaac, the torment of Gehenna will cease and hell will be destroyed; the activity of the devil will be brought to an end, and the power of evil will be subdued. Yet the end of Gehenna is a mystery which goes beyond human understanding. Indeed, St Isaac's opinions go beyond the limits of what is clearly defined in the dogmatic teaching of the Church.

As we can see, there is a certain consensus among several great Fathers of the Church on the idea of universal salvation, though there is no consensus as to when and how it will be worked out. Our excursus has shown that while there is a heretical understanding of universal salvation, there is also its Orthodox interpretation. It would be a heresy to *insist* on the necessity of the salvation of all, as if this were compulsory for both God and human beings, but it is not a heresy to believe in the *possibility* of the salvation of all, and to continue to pray and hope for that. Together with St Paul, Gregory of Nyssa, Maximus the Confessor and Isaac the Syrian, this belief was held also by St John Climacus, who says, 'It is *not impossible for all* to be saved and reconciled with God.'[70]

In our own age, the idea of universal salvation finds much support among Christians, including the Orthodox: it attracts much more attention now than it did in the time of the Early Church. This preoccupation is essentially due to the unprecedented experiences that humanity has undergone in the twentieth century, the most painful epoch in human history so far, with its two world wars, holocausts, and the suffering and death of millions of innocent people. In this context, Christian eschatology's centre of gravity has somehow shifted from ideas of revenge and punishment to notions of forgiveness and reconciliation with God. Some Orthodox philosophers and theologians have suggested that the idea of punishment in general has had a pedagogic rather than a dogmatic significance, and that the pedagogy of fear, which was important for humanity in earlier stages of its development, is less important for contemporary people. Such is the thinking of N. Berdiayev:

Humanity has entered the stage when a frightening and threatening element of religion with cruel penalties contributes only to the success of militant atheism. If formerly the idea of hell retained people in the Church, it now only pushes them away as a sadistic idea, and prevents them from returning to the Church. A juridical religion is no longer suitable for man; man is too much tormented by the world . . . I pray every day for those in the torments of hell, and in doing so I suppose that these torments are not eternal.[71]

In much the same way, Father Alexander Tourintsev, a distinguished Orthodox priest and theologian, reflects upon the mystery of the abolition of hell by the resurrected Christ and makes resolute statements about the pedagogy of fear as being 'out of date' for Christians today:

The Orthodox Church ... prays for all the departed and does not reconcile itself with the idea that some souls will be condemned for ever ... St John Chrysostom, whose inspired sermon finishes Paschal matins, exclaims: 'Hell was embittered when it met Christ.' And then: 'It was embittered, for it was rendered void. It was embittered, for it was mocked. It was embittered, for it was slain. It was embittered, for it was despoiled.' How should one consider these categorical statements of St John Chrysostom ... within the general eschatological context? ... Let us say at once: the idea of eternal hell and eternal torment for someone, and eternal bliss, indifferent to sufferings of the others, for someone else, cannot in a living and renewed Christian consciousness remain the same as it was once depicted in our catechisms and official schoolbooks on theology. This is an obsolete understanding which tries to lean on the Gospel's texts, interpreting them in a literal, brutish and material way ... We cannot admit that the sacrifice of Golgotha was not able to redeem the world and prevail over hell. Otherwise one should say: the whole creation was a complete failure, the exploit of Christ was also a failure. It is high time for all Christians together to witness and disclose their intimate mystical experience in this field, as well as their spiritual hope, and perhaps even their indignation and horror at ... material images of hell and the Last Judgement ... The pedagogy of fear and horror is no longer effective. On the contrary, it bars the way to the Church to many of those who seek the God of love.[72]

At various times, then, theologians have approached the idea of universal salvation in different ways, and there is a continuity between the Early Fathers of the Church and theologians of the twentieth century on this question. It should be emphasised again that both in ancient and modern times this theme has primarily been discussed in the context of hope and prayer, with an emphasis on the boundless love of God who wishes all humanity to be saved.

In this connection, St Silouan of Mount Athos, living in the twentieth century, asserted that an Orthodox Christian must pray for the whole world and for every living creature with the hope for the salvation of all:

We ... must have but this one thought – that all should be saved ...[73]

My soul longs for the whole world to be saved ...[74]

The Lord's love is such that he would have all men to be saved ...[75]

The merciful God . . . makes the heart ache for the whole universe, that all might repent and enter Paradise . . .[76]

In seeking salvation for all men love feels impelled to embrace not only the world of the living but also the world of the dead, the underworld and the world of the as yet unborn – that is, the whole race of Adam.[77]

The Spirit of truth teaches loves towards all, and the soul feels compassion for every being, loves her enemies and pities even devils because they have fallen away from the good.[78]

Once a hermit who was visiting Silouan said: 'God will punish all atheists. They will burn in everlasting fire.' The hermit seemed to be pleased with this idea, but Silouan answered with deep emotion: 'Tell me, supposing you went to Paradise, and there looked down and saw somebody burning in Hell-fire – would you feel happy?' 'It can't be helped', said the hermit. 'It would be their own fault.' Then St Silouan said with sorrow: 'Love could not bear this. We must pray for all.' 'And he did, indeed, pray for all', writes Father Sophrony, St Silouan's biographer. 'His soul was stricken by the realisation that people lived in ignorance of God and his love, and with all his strength he prayed . . . for the living and the dead, for friend and foe, for all mankind.'[79]

As long as the Church lives – and it will live for ever – the prayer of Christians for those outside the Kingdom of heaven will not cease. The heart of the Christian burns with love for all humanity, and for every creature of God. Could Christians really refuse to follow the example of St Gregory the Dialogos who prayed for Trajan, or of St Silouan and many others who prayed and lamented for 'the whole race of Adam'? Could the entire Church truly not cry to God with an assurance of hope that – sooner or later – he will hear her prayer? Every day the Church offers the bloodless sacrifice for all living and departed. She prays for the salvation of the whole world to the most pure Lamb, who took upon himself the sin of the world. And she will pray for the lost and the perished even when time is transformed into eternity and 'we shall all be changed'. She will pray to the Lord for the salvation of all people who were created by him.

## 'A NEW HEAVEN AND A NEW EARTH'

Paradise is not a place, it is rather a state of the soul. Just as hell is a suffering on account of the impossibility to love, Paradise is bliss that derives from the abundance of love and light. Those who have been united to Christ participate completely and integrally in Paradise. The Greek word *paradeisos* signifies both the garden of Eden, where primordial man was placed, and the age to come, where those people who have been redeemed and saved by Christ taste eternal blessing. It can also be applied to the final stage of human history, when all creation will be transformed, and God will be 'all in all'. The blessing of Paradise is also called in Christian tradition 'the Kingdom of heaven', 'the life of the age to come', 'the eighth day', 'a new heaven', 'the heavenly Jerusalem'.

The earliest Christian description of Paradise is found in the Apocalypse of St John, where it is depicted as a holy city coming down from heaven:

Then I saw a new heaven and a new earth; for the first heaven and the first earth had passed away, and the sea was no more. And I saw the holy city, new Jerusalem, coming down out of heaven from God, prepared as a bride adorned for her husband; and I heard a loud voice from the throne saying, 'Behold, the dwelling of God is with men. He will dwell with them, and they shall be his people, and God himself will be with them; he will wipe away every tear from their eyes, and death shall be no more, neither shall there be mourning nor crying nor pain any more, for the former things have passed away.' And he who sat upon the throne said, 'Behold, I make all things new ... It is done! I am the Alpha and the Omega, the beginning and the end. To the thirsty I will give from the fountain of the water of life without payment. He who conquers shall have this heritage, and I will be his God, and he shall be my son. But as for the cowardly, the faithless, the polluted, as for murderers, fornicators, sorcerers, idolaters, and all liars, their lot shall be in the lake that burns with fire and sulphur, which is the second death.' Then came one of the seven angels ... And in the Spirit he carried me away to a great, high mountain, and showed me the holy city Jerusalem coming down out of heaven from God, having the glory of God ... And I saw no temple in the city, for its temple is the Lord God the Almighty and the Lamb. And the city has no need of sun or moon to shine upon it, for the glory of God is its light, and its lamp is the Lamb. By its light shall the nations walk ... But nothing unclean shall enter it, nor any one who practises abomination or falsehood, but only those who are written in the Lamb's book of life.

(Rev. 21:1–27)

In this narrative Father Serge Bulgakov sees the most powerful testimony to the universal *apokatastasis*. 'The eschatology of this prophesy', he says, 'leads us far beyond the limits of God's Judgement with its division into the saved and condemned, into Paradise and hell, with its burning lake in which sinners, "the beast", the pseudo-prophet and Satan himself are burned but not destroyed. This eschatology leads us through the mysterious "ages of ages" to the moment when they are melted in this fire and final spiritual restoration, after which God will be all in all.'[80] The Apocalypse itself, however, leaves open the question of the final restoration of all. Together with 'a new heaven' and 'a new earth' are mentioned 'the burning lake' and 'the second death'. No qualification is made as to whether or not the realm of 'the second death' will co-exist for ever with 'the new heaven', or whether its power will cease.

There are many descriptions of Paradise in hagiographic and patristic literature. Some of them are very picturesque, and include trees, fruit, birds, villages, and so on. Some Byzantine saints, such as Andrew the Fool and Theodora, were 'caught up to the third heaven',[81] and, upon their return, described what they saw there. The authors of their lives, however, emphasise that human words can explain the experience of participation in the Divine only to a limited degree. The concept of Paradise, as that of hell, must be detached from the material images with which it is usually connected. Moreover, the idea of 'many rooms'[82] ought not to be understood too literally: the 'rooms' are not places, but rather different degrees of closeness to God. As St Basil explains, 'Some will be honoured by God with greater privileges, some with lesser, *for star differs from star in glory*.[83] And as there are *many rooms* with the Father, some people will repose in a more supreme and exalted state, and some in a lower state.'[84] According to St Symeon, all images relating to Paradise, be they 'rooms' or 'mansions', woods or fields, rivers or lakes, birds or flowers, are only different symbols of the blessing whose centre is none other than Christ himself:

> You, O Christ, are the Kingdom of heaven;
> You – the land promised to the gentle,
> You – the glazing lands of Paradise,
> You – the hall of the celestial banquet,
> You – the ineffable marriage chamber,
> You – the table set for all,
> You – the bread of life, you – the unheard of drink,
> You – both the urn for the water and life-giving water,
> You, moreover, the inextinguishable lamp for each of the saints . . .

[ 225 ]

They will receive different dwellings and different places:
Their degree of radiance, their extent of love and the vision
That they will have of you, the gauge of the greatness of their glory,
    of their happiness, of their reputation
Will distinguish their abodes, their marvellous dwellings.
Behold the different tents, behold the numerous abodes . . .
And various crowns, stones and the pearls . . .
Behold the beds and the couches, the tables and the thrones,
And all that can procure the sweetest delights:
It was, is and will be to see you, and only to see you.[85]

St Gregory of Nyssa advances a similar idea of God as the sole and integral delight of the Kingdom of heaven. He himself replaces all the transient delights of mortal life:

While we carry on our present life in many different ways, there are many things in which we participate, such as time, air, place, food and drink, clothing, sun, lamplight, and many other necessities of life, of which none is God. The blessedness which we await, however, does not need any of these, but the divine Nature will become everything for us and will replace everything, distributing itself appropriately for every need of that life . . .[86]

Thus, according to St Gregory and to some other Fathers of the Church, the final outcome of our history is going to be glorious and magnificent. After the resurrection of all and the Last Judgement, everything will be centred around God, and nothing will remain outside him. The whole cosmos will be changed and transformed, transfigured and illumined. God will be 'all in all', and Christ will reign in the souls of the people whom he has redeemed. This is the final victory of good over evil, Christ over Antichrist, light over darkness, Paradise over hell. This is the final annihilation of death. Then shall come to pass the saying that is written: 'Death is swallowed up in victory.' 'O death, where is thy victory? O death, where is thy sting? . . . But thanks be to God, who gives us the victory through our Lord Jesus Christ' (I Cor. 15:54–7).

### 'We must long and pray for the reconciliation of all without exception'

There is no terrorism in the Orthodox doctrine of God. Orthodox Christians do not cringe before Him in abject fear, but think of Him as *philanthropos*, the 'lover of men' . . . Hell is not so much a place where God imprisons man, as a place where man, by misusing his free will, chooses to imprison

himself. And even in Hell the wicked are not deprived of the love of God . . .
Hell exists as a final possibility, but several of the Fathers have none the
less believed that in the end all will be reconciled to God. It is heretical to
say that all *must* be saved, for this is to deny free will; but it is legitimate
to hope that all *may* be saved. Until the Last Day comes, we must not despair
of anyone's salvation, but must long and pray for the reconciliation of all
without exception. No one must be excluded from our loving intercession.

*Bishop Kallistos of Diokleia*

## 'That you and everyone will be saved'

It remains spiritually impossible to talk of Hell for others. The theme of
Hell can only be broached in the language of I and Thou. The threats in
the Gospel concern *me*; they form the serious tragic element in *my* spiritual
destiny; they prompt *me* to humility and repentance, because I recognise
them as the diagnosis of *my* state. But for you, the numberless you of my
neighbour, I can only serve, bear witness, and pray that you will experience
the Risen Christ, and that you and everyone will be saved . . .

*Olivier Clément*

## An assurance of hope

The assurance of the salvation of all cannot be an assurance of faith, because
there is no clear and affirmative statement about this in Holy Scripture;
but it can be an assurance of hope, because, knowing God as we know Him,
we have right to hope for everything . . . The text which is always cited is
the Parable of the sheep and the goats (Matt. 25:31–46) . . . But this parable
should be weighed against other parables and sayings of Christ. With the same
authority Christ tells us: counsel with your adversary while you are still on
the way, lest he delivers you to the judge, and the judge to the officer,
and the officer cast you in prison; and you will not depart from there until
you have paid *the very last mite* (Luke 12:58–9). This does not suggest at all
that sin would produce eternal damnation as its result . . . St Paul says that,
when everything will be completed, Christ will subject His power to the
hands of the Father, and God will be *all in all* (1 Cor. 15:28). He says
something very definite here: 'all in all' does not mean 'something in some',
or 'all in a few' . . . And also: the essence of the Kingdom of heaven is love,
while the essence of the kingdom of darkness is absence of love, is hatred
and death to love. Now imagine the Kingdom of heaven into which the
white entered, while the black were left outside, say, sheep and goats. How

would then the sheep feel in the Kingdom of God? When you think theoretically of 'sheep and goats', it does not bother you much . . . But if you imagine a real scene: you are admitted to the Kingdom of God, while your husband, your mother or sister are sentenced to the kingdom of darkness, how would you feel in this Kingdom of God? . . . I think one should also draw one's attention to the following. The Fathers of the Church regard the words from Isaiah: *I will exalt my throne about the stars of God* (Isa. 14:13), as a reference to Satan. Satan's aim is to create a self-sufficient eternal kingdom, which would be independent from God. In this sense, eternal Hell is a victory of Satan: parallel to God, he will achieve what he wanted, he will become a king of an eternal, a co-eternal Hell . . . And now think yourselves on this theme – and hope . . . One passion-bearer wrote before his death: 'It is only a martyr who, on the day of the Last Judgement, will be able to stand before the throne of God and say: O Lord, in Your name and following Your example I have forgiven them; You cannot condemn them!' This is the power to bind and loose which is given to us. It is given to all! Simply think about that. It is not a doctrine, it is a Christian hope, or, in any case, it is the hope of some of us.

*Metropolitan Anthony of Sourozh*

### The mystery of Gehenna

I am of the opinion that He is going to manifest some wonderful outcome, a matter of immense and ineffable compassion on the part of the glorious Creator, with respect to the ordering of this difficult matter of Gehenna's torment . . . It is not the way of the compassionate Maker to create rational beings in order to deliver them over mercilessly to unending affliction in punishment for things of which He knew even before they were fashioned, aware how they would turn out when He created them – and whom nonetheless He created . . . All kinds and manner of chastisements and punishments that come from Him are not brought about in order to requite past actions, but for the sake of the subsequent gain to be gotten in them . . . God is not one who requites evil, but He sets aright evil . . . So then, let us not attribute to God's actions and His dealings with us any idea of requital. Rather, we should speak of fatherly provision, a wise dispensation, a perfect will which is concerned with our good, and complete love . . . That we should further say or think that the matter is not full of love and mingled with compassion would be an opinion full of blasphemy and insult to our Lord God. By saying that He will even hand us over to burning for the sake of sufferings, torment and all sorts of ills, we are attributing to the divine Nature an enmity towards the very rational beings which He created through grace.

*St Isaac the Syrian*

## 'The love of Christ pities all men'

There are people who desire the destruction, the torment in Hell-fire of their enemies, or the enemies of the Church. They think like this because they have not learned divine love from the Holy Spirit, for he who has learned the love of God will shed tears for the whole world. You say that so-and-so is an evil-doer and may he burn in Hell-fire. But I ask you – supposing God were to give you a fair place in Paradise, and you saw burning in the fire the man on whom you had wished the tortures of Hell, even then would you really not feel pity for him, whoever he might be, an enemy of the Church even? Or is it that you have a heart of steel? But there is no place for steel in Paradise. Paradise has need of humility and the love of Christ, which pities all men.

*St Silouan of Mount Athos*

## The resurrection of the whole cosmos

On the Cross, death is swallowed up in life. In Christ, death enters the divinity and there exhausts itself, for 'it does not find a place there'. Redemption thus signifies a struggle of life against death, and the triumph of life. Christ's humanity constitutes the first fruits of the new creation. Through it a force for life is introduced into the cosmos to resurrect and transfigure it in the final destruction of death. Since the Incarnation and the Resurrection, death is enervated, is no longer absolute. Everything converges towards the *apokatastasis ton panton*, that is to say, towards complete restoration of all that is destroyed by death, towards the embracing of the whole cosmos by the glory of God become all in all things, without excluding from this fullness the freedom of each person before that full consciousness of his wretchedness which the light divine will communicate to him . . . Christ is the head of the Church, that is to say, of the new humanity in whose heart no sin, no adverse power can henceforth finally separate man from grace . . . And this work of Christ is valid for the entire assemblage of humanity, even beyond the visible limits of the Church. All faith in the triumph of life over death, every presentiment of the Resurrection, are implicit belief in Christ: for only the power of Christ raises, and will raise, the dead. Since the victory of Christ over death, the Resurrection has become universal law

[ 229 ]

for creation; and not only for humanity, but for the beasts, the plants and the stones, for the whole cosmos . . .

*V. Lossky*

### 'Let our hearts rejoice in the mysteries of the faith which we hold'

Let our hearts rejoice in the mysteries of the faith which we hold, let us exult in God Who is concerned with us . . . Let us rejoice in the hope that has been revealed to us, the children of Christ, in the mystery of the New Covenant which we have received at his hand. How much to be worshipped is the God Who, for our salvation, has done everything in the world to bring us close to Him, before the time when what has been prepared will be revealed, namely the place where we shall receive the good things that are appropriate for the children of God . . . Worthy of all manner of praise, exaltation and glory is the divine Nature which created us and which has given us all these things – and is going to give us others: to Him be worship, honour, and exaltation for eternal ages, amen.

*St Isaac the Syrian*

# NOTES

## Introduction
1  V. Lossky, *The Mystical Theology of the Eastern Church* (New York, 1976), pp. 9–10.
2  'La vie et l'oeuvre de saint Thomas d'Acquin', in Thomas d'Acquin, *Somme théologique*, vol. I (Paris, 1990), p. 24.
3  St Gregory the Theologian, *Oration* 31, 25–6.

## *Chapter 1:* The Search for Faith
1  Cf. Matt.13:45–6.
2  *Confessions* I,1.
3  Here and below the traditional titles of the Orthodox Church are used, for example St Macarius of Egypt (rather than Pseudo-Macarius, or Macarius/Symeon), Dionysius the Areopagite (rather than Pseudo-Dionysius). The discussion of authorship falls beyond the scope of this book.
4  *Homily* 7,5 from the *New Homilies*.
5  Cf. I Cor. 15:10.
6  St Athanasius of Alexandria, *The Life of St Anthony*, 3.
7  I Cor. 9:16.
8  Metropolitan Anthony of Sourozh, *Besedy o vere i Tserkvi* (Moscow, 1991), pp. 308–9 and p. 3.
9  *Timaeus* 28c–30b.
10  *Timaeus* 41a.
11  See, in particular, Chapter 10.
12  Plotinus, *Enneades* 6, 9, 9–11.
13  Cf. Justin Martyr, *Apology* I, 46.
14  *Stromateis* I, 5.

## *Chapter 2:* God
1  *Besedy o vere i Tserkvi*, p. 96.
2  *Oration* 30, 18.
3  See *Letopis' Seraphimo-Diveyevskogo Monastyria* (St Petersburg, 1903), p. 113.
4  *Epistle* 8, 11.
5  *An Exact Exposition of the Orthodox Faith* I, 9.

6   Dionysius the Areopagite, *The Divine Names* 5, 4.
7   See A Monk of the Eastern Church, *The Jesus Prayer* (New York, 1995), p. 24.
8   *Oration* 30, 17.
9   *The Divine Names* 1, 5.
10  *The Divine Names* 1, 5–6.
11  *Oration* 30, 20.
12  Cf. Pss. 24:8; 144:17.
13  St Isaac the Syrian *Homily* 51 (*The Ascetical Homilies*, pp. 250–1).
14  *Oration* 22, 4.
15  See S. Brock, 'Introduction' to St Ephrem the Syrian, *Hymns on Paradise* (New York, 1990), p. 45.
16  *Hymn on Faith* 31, cited in St Ephrem the Syrian, *Hymns on Paradise* (New York, 1990), pp. 45–6.
17  Cf. Thomas Hopko, 'God and Gender: Articulating the Orthodox View', *St Vladimir's Theological Quarterly*, vol. 39, Nos. 2–3, p. 150.
18  *An Exact Exposition* 1, 14.
19  *Oration* 45, 4.
20  *Timaeus* 28c.
21  *Oration* 28, 4.
22  *Letter* 234, to Amphilochius of Iconium.
23  Cited in Socrates, *Ecclesiastical History* 4, 7.
24  Cf. Exod. 33:21–3.
25  Cf Exod. 26:31–3; 36:35–6.
26  Cf. Ps. 8:1 *et al.*
27  *Oration* 28, 3.
28  *Vyzantiyskiye Otsy V-VIII vekov* [The Byzantine Fathers of the fifth to eight centuries] (Paris, 1937), pp. 102–3.
29  Cf. 2 Sam. 22:12.
30  *Dogmatic Poetry* I, 1, 29 (PG 37, 507–8).

*Chapter 3:* **The Trinity**
1   Cf. Bishop Kallistos Ware, *The Orthodox Way*, p. 34.
2   See John 6–8.
3   See John 14:16–17; 15:26.
4   Cf. 2 Cor. 3:15–16.
5   Cf. Ch. Yannaras, *Elements of Faith* (Edinburgh, 1991), p. 26.
6   It is in this sense that the term was used in the New Testament. Cf. Luke 8:43: the woman with the flow of blood had spent all her fortune (*ousia*) on doctors.
7   The Liturgy of St John Chrysostom.
8   *An Exact Exposition* 1, 8.
9   *Oration* 20, 7–10.
10  Cited in G. Florovsky, *Puti russkogo bogosloviya* [The Ways of Russian theology] (Paris, 1937), p. 181.

**Chapter 4: Creation**

1   *Against the Heresies* 4, 20, 1.
2   *On the Holy Spirit* 38.
3   *Against Arians* I, 20 (PG 26, 53).
4   *An Exact Exposition* 2, 2.
5   *An Exact Exposition* 2, 3.
6   The Hebrew term *Shekhina* means 'presence', 'glory'.
7   *Second Part*, Chapter 10, 24.
8   Luke 1:26–8.
9   Matt. 4:11.
10  Luke 22:43.
11  Cf. Matt.18:10.
12  Homily 26 (*Ascetical Homilies*, pp. 131–2).
13  See V. Lossky, *Orthodox Theology*, p. 64.
14  *An Exact Exposition* 2, 4.
15  Cf. St Symeon the New Theologian, *Hymn* 43, 137 (SC 196, p. 66).
16  St Basil the Great, *Hexaemeron*, Homily 2, 4–5.
17  *Creation and Redemption*, Volume Three of the *Collected Works* (Belmont, Massachusetts, 1976), p. 84.
18  V. Lossky, *Orthodox Theology*, p. 80.
19  Cf. Job 1–2.
20  Exod. 4:21; 7:3; 14:4.
21  I Sam.16:14; 19:9.
22  Ezek. 20:25 (in the Hebrew text and Septuagint translation).
23  Rom. 1:24–32.
24  *On Genesis* 11, 4 (PL 34, 431).
25  *On the Soul and Resurrection* 4 (p. 64).
26  See Isaac of Nineveh, *Second Part*, Chapter 39.
27  Cf. Basil the Great, *Hexaemeron*, Homily 1, 6: 'As the beginning of the road is not yet the road . . . so also, the beginning of the time is not yet the time . . . not even the least part of it.'
28  *Timaeus* 38b.
29  *Timaeus* 38b.
30  *On Genesis*, part 1 (ed. Moscow, 1867), p. 6.
31  *Theogony*.
32  *Timaeus* 34b.
33  *Timaeus* 30ac.
34  *Timaeus* 29c.
35  V. Lossky, *Orthodox Theology*, p. 64.
36  Cited in Bishop Kallistos Ware, *The Orthodox Way*, p. 54.

**Chapter 5: The Human Person**

1   *An Exact Exposition of the Orthodox Faith* 2, 30.
2   *That the Origin of Evil is Not in God* 7 (PG 31, 344 C).
3   Ch. Yannaras, *Elements of Faith*, p. 59.

4  *Timaeus* 39e.

5  *De opificio mundi*, 69.

6  *An Exact Exposition* 3, 18.

7  *Discourse On Gratitude* 2 (PG 31, 221 C).

8  *Homily on Ps. 32* (PG 29, 344 B).

9  *Homilies on Genesis* 8, 3–4.

10  *Against Manicheans* 4, 1 (PG 102, 180 B).

11  *Centuries on Theology* I, 11 (*Philokalia* II, p. 116).

12  *Oration against the Greeks* 7 (PG 6, 820 B).

13  *Homily* 46, 5.

14  Cf. St Anastasius the Sinaite, *Questiones* 89; St Photios of Constantinople, *Amphilochia* 253.

15  *An Exact Exposition* 2, 12.

16  *On the Beatitudes* I, 4.

17  *Cratylus* 400c.

18  *Bhagavadgita* 2, 22.

19  *Fragments on Resurrection* 8 (PG 6, 1585 B).

20  *On the Creation of Man* 27. See the full quotation in Chapter 11.

21  *On the Divine Images* 2, 14 (trans. David Anderson, pp. 60–1).

22  *On the Statutes* 11, 2 (PG 49, 116 BC).

23  Gen. 2:7.

24  Gen. 9:4.

25  Lev. 17:11.

26  Gen. 19:17.

27  *Questions to Antiochus* 16 (PG 28, 608 A).

28  *On the Soul and Resurrection* (PG 46, 29 B).

29  *Oration* 14, 7.

30  *Dogmatic poetry* 8, 1 (PG 37, 446 A).

31  *Dogmatic poetry* 8, 73 (PG 37, 452 A).

32  Cf. Ps. 148:8 according to LXX.

33  *On the Character of Man and on the Virtuous Life* 106 (*Philokalia* I, p. 345).

34  2 Cor. 3:3.

35  Macarius the Great, *Homily* 15, 20.

36  Cf. Bishop Kallistos Ware, *The Orthodox Way*, pp. 62–4.

37  *On the Creation of Man* 16.

38  Phil. 2:7.

39  Archimandrite Sophrony, *His Life is Mine* (Crestwood NY, 1977), p. 77.

40  *Dogmatic Poetry* 2, 1, 1 (PG 37, 1004).

41  Archimandrite Sophrony, *His Life is Mine*, p. 78.

42  A. Losev, *Dialektika mifa* [The Dialectics of Myth] (Moscow, 1991), pp. 23–7.

43  *Discourse on Patience and Discernment* 3 (PG 34, 868).

44  Macarius of Egypt, *Homily* 12, 7.

45  A. Losev, *Filosofiya imeni* [The Philosophy of Name] (Moscow, 1990), p. 166.

46  Basil of Seleucia, *Homily* I (PG 85, 40 C–41 A).

47  *An Exact Exposition* 2, 11.

48   On deification, see Chapter 10.

49   Dionysius the Areopagite, *On the Ecclesiastical Hierarchy* I, 3 (*The Complete Works*, p. 198).

50   St John Damascene, *The Life of Barlaam and Joasaph* 7 (PG 96, 908 B).

51   *His Life is Mine*, pp. 32–3.

52   *On the Book of Genesis* 8, 14 (PL 34, 384).

53   *Theol.* I, 357–9 (SC 122, 122).

54   Origen, *Dialogue of Adamantius on the Right Faith in God*, I.

55   *Catechetical Discourse* 5, 175–82 (SC 96, 390–2).

56   St Dorotheos of Gaza, *Instructions* I, I (SC 92, 148).

57   St Symeon the New Theologian, *Ethical Discourse* 13, 63–7 (SC 129, 404).

58   See Gen. 3:14–19.

59   See Rom. 8:19–21.

60   St Symeon the New Theologian, *Catechetical Discourse* 5, 282–310 (SC 96, 400).

61   Sunday of Forgiveness, Vespers, Sticheron, tone 6; *The Lenten Triodion*, translated by Mother Mary and Archimandrite Kallistos Ware (London/Boston, 1978), p. 169.

62   Cf. J. Meyendorff, *Byzantine Theology: Historical Trends and Doctrinal Themes* (New York, 1974), p. 144.

63   One should note that the term 'original sin' is of Western provenance.

64   *On Those Who Think that They are Made Righteous by Works* 120 (*Philokalia* I, p. 135).

65   This is the meaning given, in particular, by the Slavonic recension.

66   *In Romans* 5, 14 (PG 74, 785 A).

67   *Homily* 24, 2.

68   *Discourse on Patience and Discernment* 9 (PG 34, 872–3).

69   Emmanuel Kant's expression.

70   See Isa. 9:6–7.

71   See Isa. 11:1–10; 42:1–7; 61:1.

72   *Aeneid*, Eclogue 4.

73   *Na poroge Novogo Zaveta* [At the Threshold of the New Testament] (Brussels, 1983), p. 507.

## Chapter 6: Christ

1   *Homily on Romans* 10, 1 (*Opera omnia* 8, 520 C).

2   *Oration* 2, 23–5.

3   Cf. John 5:18.

4   See Mark 14:61–4.

5   The Greek word *pathos* means both 'passion' and 'suffering'.

6   L. Tolstoy, *Interpretation of John 5:5–9*.

7   In saying that the gospels are 'inspired by God', we mean the joint creative process of people and the Holy Spirit: their co-operation, or synergy.

8   *Epistle* 39 (to John of Antioch), also known as *The Formula of Reunion* 433 AD.

9   John 1:1.

10   John 1:14.

11   *Tome* by St Leo the Great.

12   The *Horos* of the Council of Chalcedon.

13  *Dogmatic Tome, to Marinus* (PG 91, 77 D-80 A).

14  The *Horos* of the Sixth Ecumenical Council.

15  Cf. Matt. 20:28; 1 Cor. 1:30.

16  Cf. John 8:24.

17  Luke 23:46.

18  *On Matthew* 16, 8 (GCS 40, 498).

19  *Oration* 45, 22.

20  *Great Catechetical Oration* 22–4.

21  *The Catechetical Oration on Easter* ascribed to St John Chrysostom and read in the Orthodox Church during Paschal matins. Cited in Lossky, *Mystical Theology*, p. 248.

22  *Service Book of the Holy Orthodox-Catholic Apostolic Church*, translated from the Church Slavonic by Isabel Hapgood (Englewood, New Jersey, 1983), p. 254.

23  In particular, by Anselm of Canterbury (eleventh century).

24  Much later, in the eighteenth and nineteenth centuries, the theory of satisfaction crept into Russian academic theology, which found itself under the direct influence of Latin scholasticism. Thus, for example, in the *Prostrannyi Christianskiy Catechisis* [The Extensive Christian Catechism], compiled by St Philaret Drozdov (Moscow, 1894), p. 36, we find the following words: 'His [Christ's] voluntary suffering and death on the Cross for us, in being of infinite value and worth as the death of the sinless God-man, is both complete satisfaction for God's justice which has condemned us to death for sin and an infinite merit which has given to Him the right without offending the divine justice to grant forgiveness of the sins of us sinners and grace for the vanquishing of sin.' In this text, the abundance of juridical terms (value, merit, satisfaction, offence, justice, right) makes evident how this understanding of redemption is closer to medieval scholasticism than to the views of the Fathers of the Eastern Church.

25  See A. Mai, *Spicilegium Romanum* 9 (Rome, 1844), p. 70.

26  It was precisely over these words from the Liturgy of St Basil that the Council of 1157 was convoked.

27  *On the Meeting of the Lord* 5 (PG 33, 1192 B).

28  *Hymn* 24, 129–32 (SC 174, 236).

29  St Symeon the New Theologian, *Catechetical Discourse* 5, 413–32 (SC 96, 410–12).

30  *Troparion* of the Hours sung at Easter.

31  St Symeon the New Theologian, *Ethical Discourse* 1, 6, 57–121 (SC 122, 228–32).

32  *Ethical Discourse* 2, 1, 160–3 (SC 122, 322).

33  Cf. 2 Cor. 12:2–4.

34  Cf. John 1:12–13.

35  *Centuries of Various Texts* 1, 74 (*Philokalia* 2, p. 181).

## Chapter 7: The Church

 1  Archbishop Hilarion (Troitsky), *Christianstva net bez tserkvi* [There is no Christianity without the Church] (Montreal, 1986), p. 3.

 2  V. Solovyov, *Dukhovniye osnovy zhizni* [The Spiritual Background of Life] (Paris, 1926), p. 129.

 3  See Chapter 1.

4 Cf. Rom. 3:2.

5 G. Florovsky, *Creation and Redemption*, Volume Three of the *Collected Works* (Belmont, Massachusetts, 1976), pp. 36–7.

6 St Germanus of Constantinople, *On the Divine Liturgy*, Greek text with English translation (Crestwood, New York, 1984), p. 56.

7 The Kontakion for the Ascension of the Lord.

8 Bishop Kallistos of Diokleia, 'Strange Yet Familiar', in *Towards the Authentic Church. Orthodox Christians Discuss Their Conversion: A Collection of Essays*, edited by Thomas Doulis (Minneapolis, Minnesota, 1996).

9 Archbishop Hilarion (Troitsky), *Christianstva net bez tserkvi*, pp. 15–16.

10 *Catechetical Oration* 18, 23.

11 A. S. Khomiakov, *The Church is One* (London, 1968), p. 18.

12 *Epistle* 55, 8 (PL 3, 770).

13 Since an Ecumenical Council has not been convened in the East for twelve centuries, the question of supreme authority in the Orthodox Church, which in fact does not exist, requires urgent attention: 'The problem of central organisation within the Orthodox Church is the burning question of our day', wrote Archbishop Basil Krivocheine in 1972. 'The very life and needs of Orthodoxy pose this question. In a world where everything is organised and co-ordinated, only the Orthodox Church is incapable of remaining without an organisational and co-ordinating centre without incurring great difficulties and harm'; 'Kafolichnost' i struktury Tserkvi' [Catholicity and the Church Structures], *Vestnik Russkogo Zapadno-Evropeiskogo Patriarshego Ekzarkhata* 80 (Paris, 1972), pp. 259–60. In agreement with Archbishop Basil, Father John Meyendorff wrote in the same year: 'We undoubtedly need such a centre ... The Ecumenical Patriarch, heading this centre, would be regarded as an inspirer of the Orthodox Catholicity, if he will be free from political influences from outside and will himself act always *ex consensu ecclesiae*'; 'Kafolichnost' Tserkvi' [Catholicity of the Church], *Vestnik Russkogo Zapadno-Evropeiskogo Patriarshego Ekzarkhata* 80 (Paris, 1972), p. 239. Among the difficulties of Orthodox life today is the problem of the Church calendar as well as the non-recognition by certain local Churches of the legitimacy and independence of others. For example, at present the Church of Constantinople does not recognise the autocephaly of the Orthodox Church in America. Until an Ecumenical (pan-Orthodox) Council is convoked, these problems will remain unsolved.

14 The doctrine of the 'infallibility' of the Church was formulated in reply to the Catholic doctrine of the infallibility (*infallibilitas* in Latin means 'unmistakenness') of the Pope of Rome in questions of faith and morality when he speaks from the apostolic throne (*ex cathedra*). This dogma was adopted in the West in 1870. If in the Western Church the guarantor of infallibility is the Bishop of Rome by virtue of the powers inherited from St Peter, then the guarantor in the Eastern Church is the collective mind of the 'people of God' possessing the 'royal priesthood'.

15 *Epistle I to the Corinthians* 42–4.

16 The Kontakion for Pentecost.

17 See Gen. 11:1–9.

18 See Acts 6:6.

19    The text of the Liturgy does not contain the word 'choir': the Liturgy knows only 'the people'. In present-day liturgical practice the choir represents the people.

20    See A. Louth, *Denys the Areopagite*, pp. 53–4.

21    *Epistle to the Ephesians* 4.

22    *Epistle to the Trallians* 3.

23    Father Thomas Hopko, 'God and Gender: Articulating the Orthodox View', *St Vladimir's Theological Quarterly*, vol. 37, Nos. 2–3 (1993), pp. 172–4.

24    See Bishop Kallistos (Ware), 'Mary Theotokos in the Orthodox Tradition', *Marianum* LII (Rome, 1990), pp. 211–12.

25    Cf. Luke 2:44–6.

26    Cited in Archimandrite Sophrony, *St Silouan*, pp. 391–3.

27    St Symeon the New Theologian, *Chapters* 3, 2–4 (SC 51, 120–2).

28    *Apology* (PL 1, 534).

29    The possibility that they may have been mummified is excluded even on theoretical grounds, as the bodies of the three youths were buried in the earth by their executioners.

30    The famous Shroud of Turin cannot be identified as the Edessa image as it has a different origin and a different picture, namely the image of Christ's body lying in the tomb.

31    See Matt. 9:20–3.

32    *Ecclesiastical History* 7, 18.

33    See Exod. 25:18–20.

34    *On the Divine Images* 1, 8 (trans. D. Anderson, p. 18).

35    *On the Divine Images* 2, 12 (trans. D. Anderson, p. 60).

36    *On the Holy Spirit* 18 (PG 32, 149).

37    *The Post-Nicene Fathers*, t.X: *The Ecumenical Councils*, pp. 548–50.

38    Cf Matt. 24:30.

39    *Homilies on Isaiah* 11, 12.

40    The Exapostilarion for the Exaltation of the Cross.

41    See Num. 10:35–6, where Moses addresses the Ark as 'Lord'.

42    Cf. I Sam. 4:7.

43    *Second Part*, Chapter 11, 4.

44    Cf. Josh. 7:6.

45    *Second Part*, Chapter 11, 4–5.

46    Cf. Exod. 20:4–5; Lev. 26:1; Deut. 5:8.

47    *Second Part*, Chapter 11, 10–11.

48    *Second Part*, Chapter 11, 17–19.

49    *Second Part*, Chapter 11, 24–6.

50    *Second Part*, Chapter 11, 30–4.

51    We heard this story from the late Archimandrite Sophrony (Sakharov).

52    Prayer of the priest after the consecration of the Holy Gifts.

53    *Christianstva net bez Tserkvi*, pp. 79–81.

54    Archbishop Averky (Taushev), *Sovremennost' v svete slova Bozhiya* [Modernity in the Light of God's Word], t.4 (Jordanville, 1976), pp. 371–4. Archbishop Averky was one of the main ideologues of the so-called Russian Orthodox Church in Exile.

55 *Besedy o vere i Tserkvi*, pp. 263–5.
56 *Razgovory mezhdu ispytuyushchim i uverennym v pravoslavii Vostochnoy Greko-Rossiyskoy Tserkvi* [The Dialogues between the One Who Doubts and the One Who is Sure as to the Orthodoxy of the Eastern Greek Orthodox Church of Russia] (Saint-Petersburg, 1815).
57 Cited in Metropolitan Anthony of Sourozh, *Besedy o vere i Tserkvi*, p. 262.
58 *Letter* 113.
59 *Letter* 113.
60 That is, St Athanasius.
61 *Oration* 21, 35–6 (SC 270, 184–8).
62 *On the Trinity* 2, 9; 5, 15.
63 *On the Trinity* 5, 12; 5, 15–17; 8, 1.
64 Some modern theologians prefer to use the Greek word *theologoumenon* ('theological opinion') to designate these 'dogmas of small importance'. The term was introduced by V. Bolotov and was applied by him to the Latin teaching on the procession of the Holy Spirit from both the Father and the Son (the *Filioque*).
65 Cited in Metropolitan Anthony of Sourozh, *Besedy o vere i Tserkvi*, p. 268.

### Chapter 8: The Sacraments
1 *The Ecclesiastical Hierarchy* 2, 1–7, 3.
2 *Epistle* 165 (PG 99, 1524 B).
3 See Meyendorff, *Byzantine Theology*, p. 192.
4 It was, however, written not by the Emperor himself, but by Latin theologians. See M. Jugie, *Theologia dogmatica christianorum orientalium* III (Paris, 1920), p. 16.
5 *On the Sacraments* 33 (PG 155, 177 B).
6 Cited in Meyendorff, *Byzantine Theology*, p. 192.
7 Cited in *The Orthodox Liturgy* (Oxford, 1982), p. 94.
8 Ps. 118/119:126.
9 *On the Holy Spirit* 1, 18.
10 Cf. Isa. 35:6–7; 58:11.
11 Cf. John 4:10–14.
12 Cf. Isa. 1:16.
13 Cf. Acts 8:38 ('they both went down into the water').
14 Cf. *The Doctrine of the Twelve Apostles (Didache)* 7.
15 Cf. *The Doctrine of the Twelve Apostles* 7: 'If you have neither (running cold or warm water), pour water three times on the head . . .'
16 Cf. Acts 10:48 (the baptism of Cornelius and his entire household).
17 *Against the Heresies* 2, 39.
18 Council of Carthage, canon 124.
19 Cf. Mark 16:1 ('He who believes and is baptised will be saved; but he who does not believe will be condemned').
20 *Epistle* 4 (unpublished).
21 See I John 2:20; 2 Cor. 1:21.
22 *Mystagogical Oration* 3, 3–5.
23 *Vodoyu I Duchom* [By the Water and the Spirit] (Paris, 1986), p. 103.

24   *The Orthodox Liturgy* (Oxford, 1982), p. 120. Cf. Gal. 4:5.

25   Cf. A. Louth, *Denys the Areopagite*, p. 60.

26   St Symeon of Thessalonike, *Against the Heresies and on the Divine Temple* 282 (PG 155, 512).

27   *Apology* I, 65–6.

28   Among the ancient Liturgies whose texts have come down to us are those by St James, St Mark, St Basil the Great, St John Chrysostom, St Gregory the Illuminator of Armenia, St Cyril of Alexandria, St Gregory the Theologian, St Ambrose of Milan, St Gregory the Great, and many others. None of these liturgical rites is the creation of the authors with whose names they are associated, although in some cases they may spiritually and even textually originate with them. A gradual unification of the eucharistic rite took place in Byzantium around the twelfth century: as a result, only the Liturgies of St Basil the Great, St John Chrysostom and St Gregory the Great were adopted for Orthodox celebrations; most of the other ancient Liturgies fell into disuse. See Meyendorff, *Byzantine Theology*, p. 117.

29   Cf. the priest's prayer during the singing of the Cherubic Hymn at the Liturgies of St John Chrysostom and of St Basil the Great: *The Orthodox Liturgy* (Oxford, 1982), p. 61.

30   *The Orthodox Liturgy*, p. 89.

31   Great and Holy Saturday, Liturgy, Cherubic Hymn. Cited in *The Orthodox Liturgy*, p. 110.

32   *The Orthodox Liturgy*, pp. 75–6.

33   This Liturgy is still used in the Coptic Church.

34   *He Leitourgia tou hagiou Gregoriou tou Theologou* (Thessalonike, 1981), pp. 19–20.

35   *Epistle to the Smyrneans* 7.

36   *Mystagogical Oration* 4, 3–9.

37   *Hymn* 15, 121–54 (SC 156, 286–90).

38   *Epistle to the Smyrneans* 7. 'To gather for the Eucharist' means to receive Holy Communion, as in Ignatius's time all those present took Communion at the Eucharist.

39   Cf. Matt. 6:11.

40   Cf. St Cyprian of Carthage, *On the Lord's Prayer* 18; St Cyril of Jerusalem, *Mystagogical Orations* 5, 15.

41   Letter 93 (PG 32, 484 B).

42   The 8th Apostolic Canon.

43   *Conferences* 23, 21.

44   Cf Matt. 4:17.

45   See Luke 15:11–24.

46   *The Orthodox Liturgy*, p. 53.

47   *The Ladder of Divine Ascent* 5 (trans. L. Moore, p. 54).

48   *Oration on Mercy* (PG 49, 292).

49   The Rite of Confession: *Service Book* (trans. I. F. Hapgood), p. 288.

50   The Rite of Confession: *Service Book* (trans. I. F. Hapgood), p. 290. This prayer of absolution is of Latin origin.

51   *Dogmatic poetry* 8 (PG 37, 455).

52  Cf. Jas. 1:15 ('... sin when it is full-grown brings forth death').
53  *Symeon tou Neou Theologou eurethenta asketika* (Thessalonike, 1977), pp. 53–4.
54  See Luke 13:16.
55  Literally, presbyters.
56  *For the Life of the World* (Crestwood, NY, 1988), pp. 102–3.
57  *The Spiritual Meadow* 8.
58  Cf. Eph. 5:20–33.
59  *Letter* 3 to Nestorius.
60  St John Chrysostom, *On Marriage*. Quoted in P. Evdokimov, *The Sacrament of Love* (New York, 1985), p. 120.
61  Ibid., p. 118.
62  This understanding is based on a wrong interpretation of 1 Cor. 7:2–9.
63  *Symposium*, Logos 2, 1–2 (pp. 49–50).
64  *Symposium*, Logos 2, 5 (p. 54).
65  *Service Book* (trans. I. F. Hapgood), pp. 295, 299.
66  *The Sacrament of Love*, p. 19.
67  J. Meyendorff, *Byzantine Theology*, p. 198.
68  J. Meyendorff, *Marriage: An Orthodox Perspective* (Crestwood, New York, 1975), p. 17.
69  *Zapisi* [Notes], 6th ed. (Paris, 1990), pp. 34, 58–9.
70  Cf. Matt.19:7–9; Mark 10:11–12; Luke 16:18.
71  St Herman of Alaska used to separate couples temporarily when he failed to bring them to reconciliation. 'It is better for them to live separately', he said, 'than to fight with each other or mistreat each other; it might be dangerous not to separate them as there have been examples of a husband killing his wife or a wife bringing her husband to death.' See *Zhizn' Valaamskogo monacha Germana* (Saint-Petersburg, 1984), p. 10.
72  Cf. Matt. 5:32.
73  In the fifteenth century, for example, the rite of marriage included Communion with the Presanctified Gifts. See St Symeon of Thessalonika, *Against Heresies and on the Divine Temple* 282 (PG 155, 512–13).
74  Cf. Matt. 7:24–7.
75  See also the section on Church hierarchy in Chapter 7.
76  A widowed priest might be ordained a bishop only after he receives monastic tonsure.
77  The Order of Electing and Consecrating a Bishop (*Service Book*, trans. I. F. Hapgood, p. 329).
78  Nowadays, in most Orthodox Churches, bishops are appointed by the Holy Synod; the faithful do not participate in the election.
79  The Church canons forbade the transfer of a bishop from one diocese to another: see the fifteenth canon of the First Ecumenical Council (Nicaea, 325).
80  *Pravoslavnoye pastyrskoye sluzheniye* [Orthodox pastoral ministry] (Paris, 1957), p. 76.
81  Cited in Archimandrite Sophrony, *St Silouan*, pp. 400–4.
82  Nicetas Stéthatos, *Vie de Syméon le Nouveau Théologien* 30, 13–18; ed. I. Hausherr (Roma, 1927).
83  That is, on Pentecost.

84 Archpriest Serge Bulgakov, *Avtobiograficheskiye zametki* [Autobiographical notes] (Paris, 1991), pp. 41–2.

85 See Dionysius the Areopagite, *The Ecclesiastical Hierarchy* 6, 2 ('Mystery of the consecration of a monk'). Cf. J. Meyendorff, *Byzantine Theology*, pp. 191–2.

86 St John Climacus, *The Ladder of Divine Ascent* 1 and 26 (trans. L. Moore, pp. 4, 167).

87 St Athanasius of Alexandria, *The Life of St Anthony* 15 and 44.

88 *The Ladder of Divine Ascent* 1 (trans. L. Moore, p. 10).

89 St Gregory Nazianzen, *Ethical poetry* 1 (PG 37, 563).

90 *Hymn* 27, 18–74 (SC 174, 280). Cf. the words of Plotinus quoted in Chapter 1: 'a flight of alone to the Alone' (*Enn.* 6, 9, 11).

91 Archbishop Hilarion (Troitsky), *Christianstva net bez Tserkvi*, pp. 181–7.

92 See Bishop Kallistos (Ware), *The Orthodox Church*, pp. 131–2.

93 Cited in Archimandrite Sophrony, *St Silouan*, pp. 407–8.

### Chapter 9: Prayer

1 'Filosofiya Kul'ta' [The Philosophy of the Cult], in *Bogoslovskiye Trudy* No. 7 (Moscow, 1977), p. 344.

2 'The Elements of Liturgy in the Orthodox Catholic Church', in *One Church*, vol. XIII, Nos. 1–2 (New York, 1959), p. 24.

3 Pentecost, Vespers, sticheron, Tone One (*Service Book*, trans. I. F. Hapgood, p. 245).

4 Daily and Sunday worship operates within a system of eight 'tones'. Any particular tone designates not only melody but a series of hymns belonging to the tone of the week. The cycle begins at Easter with Tone One, and continues through the cycle of eight, changing every week, until the next Easter.

5 *Service Book*, trans. I. F. Hapgood, p. 586.

6 This ritual takes place during the recital of the Creed in the Orthodox Liturgy.

7 Metropolitan Veniamin (Fedchenkov), 'Liturgiya' [Liturgy], in *The Journal of the Moscow Patriarchate*, No. 1 (Moscow, 1982), p. 77.

8 E.g. a hymn dedicated to a newly canonised saint.

9 *Sochineniya* [Collected Works], vol. 2 (Saint-Petersburg, 1886), pp. 181–2.

10 *On Prayer* 3 (*Philokalia* I, p. 57).

11 F. Garcia Lorca, 'Un silencio'; *Obras completas*, tomo I (Mexico, 1991), p. 160, translated by the author.

12 *The Ladder of Divine Ascent* 11 (trans. L. Moore, p. 92).

13 *The Power of the Name, The Jesus Prayer in Orthodox Spirituality* (Oxford, 1991), p. 1.

14 *Homily* 65 (*Ascetical Homilies*, p. 321).

15 This story is based on the *Apophthegmata patrum* ('The Sayings of the Desert Fathers'). We give it here in the version which we heard from the late Starets Archimandrite Sophrony (Sakharov).

16 *The Ladder of Divine Ascent* 28 (trans. L. Moore, p. 213).

17 *Homily* 72 (*Ascetical Homilies*, p. 351).

18 *Homily* 64 (*Ascetical Homilies*, p. 316).

19 *The Ladder of Divine Ascent* 15 (trans. L. Moore, pp. 115–16). On the technical terms

employed by the Fathers to describe the development of thought into passion see *Philokalia* I, pp. 365–7.

20  St Mark the Ascetic, *On the Spiritual Law* 180 (*Philokalia* I, p. 122).

21  *Zapiski na knigu Bytiya* [Notes on the Book of Genesis], pp. 57–8.

22  Evagrios, *Texts on Discrimination in Respect of Passions and Thoughts* 2 (*Philokalia* I, p. 39).

23  *The Ladder of Divine Ascent* 28 (trans. L. Moore, p. 214).

24  *On Watchfulness and Holiness* 121 (*Philokalia* I, p. 183).

25  Evagrios, *On Prayer* 11, 45–7, 70 (*Philokalia* I, pp. 58–63).

26  Cf. I Thess. 5:17.

27  *A Discourse of Abba Philimon* (*Philokalia* II, pp. 347–8).

28  *The Shepherd*, Similitudes 9, 14.

29  For an outline of their teachings on the Jesus Prayer, see A Monk of the Eastern Church [Archimandrite Lev Gillet], *The Jesus Prayer* (New York, 1995).

30  *Na gorakh Kavkaza* [On the Mountains of the Caucasus] (Batalpashinsk, 1910), p. 16.

31  Cited in *Na gorakh Kavkaza*, p. 16.

32  Its original title is *Otkrovennye rasskazy strannika dukhvnomu svoyemu otzu* [Sincere tales of a pilgrim to his spiritual father] (Kazan, 1884).

33  *The Way of a Pilgrim*, translated by R. M. French (London, 1954), pp. 17–18.

34  *The Ladder of Divine Ascent* 28 (trans. L. Moore, p. 214).

35  Cited in *O molitve Iisusovoy* [On the Jesus Prayer] (Sortavala, 1936), p. 109.

36  For a more detailed discussion of the theme, see Bishop Kallistos of Diokleia, *The Power of the Name*, pp. 20–5.

37  The Greek text is in I. Hausherr, *La Methode d'oraison hesychaste*, *Orientalia Christiana Periodica* 36 (Rome, 1927), pp. 150–72.

38  Cf. Matt. 7:7.

39  A footnote in the Russian translation of the *Writings* by St Symeon the New Theologian, vol. 2 (Moscow, 1990), p. 188.

40  Cf. Gen. 5:24; 6:9; 17:1 *et al.*

41  Evagrios, *On Prayer* 61 (*Philokalia* I, p. 62).

42  That is, the intellect.

43  St Gregory the Theologian, *Oration* 27, 3.

44  Cited in Bishop Kallistos of Diokleia, *The Orthodox Church*, p. 310.

45  *The Power of the Name*, pp. 23–4.

46  Cf. I Cor. 12:6.

47  *On Commandments and Doctrines* . . . 113 (*Philokalia* IV, p. 238).

#### Chapter 10: Deification

1  *Against the Heresies* 4, 20, 7.

2  *The Vision of God*, p. 25.

3  Cf. Matt. 5:8.

4  Cf. John 1:18.

5  Cf. I Tim. 6:16.

6  Cf. Exod. 33:20.

7  *On the Beatitudes* 6 (pp. 137–8).

8   Cf. John 1:18.

9   Cf. John 1:18.

10  Cf. John 14:9.

11  *Ethical Discourse* 5, 88–109. Cf. Matt. 5:8.

12  *Ethical Discourse* 5, 83–95.

13  *Ethical Discourse* 5, 112–24.

14  *Centuries on Love* 4, 72.

15  See J. Meyendorff, *A Study of Gregory Palamas* (New York, 1974), pp. 202–27.

16  Lossky, *Mystical Theology*, p. 70.

17  *Theophanes*, PG 110, 973 D.

18  *Against the Heresies* 4, 6, 6.

19  Cf. Luke 1:10ff.

20  Cf. Acts 10:9ff.

21  Cf. Acts 10:3ff.

22  *Discourse* 23 (Miller, 120–21).

23  *Hymn* 11, 1–82.

24  *Hymn* 40, 1–16.

25  *Divine Institutions* 4, 28, 2; PL 6, 535.

26  Cf. Deut. 4:24; Heb. 12:29.

27  Here and below the prayers are quoted from *The Orthodox Liturgy* (texts translated by the Monastery of St John the Baptist, Tolleshunt Knights, Essex), (Oxford, 1982), pp. 1–16; 211–15.

28  Cf. 2 Pet. 1:4.

29  St Maximus the Confessor, *Centuries of Various Texts* 1, 42 (*Philokalia* 2, p. 173).

30  Cf. John 10:34; Ps. 81/82:6.

31  Cf. 1 John 1:12; 3:2.

32  Cf. Rom. 8:29; 1 Cor. 15:49; 2 Cor. 3:18; Col. 3:10.

33  Cf. Gal. 3:26; 4:5.

34  Cf. 1 Cor. 3:16.

35  Cf. Rom. 8:18–23; Eph. 1:10; 1 Cor. 15:28.

36  Cf. 1 John 3:2.

37  *On Those Who Reject the Holy Images* 1, 19, with reference to Gregory Nazianzen, *Discourse* 40, 6.

38  *Against the Heresies* 5, introduction.

39  *On the Incarnation* 54.

40  *Discourse* 1, 4.

41  *Discourse* 38, 11.

42  Cf. Matt. 13:43.

43  *Discourse* 40, 6.

44  *Centuries on Theology* 1, 54.

45  Cf. *Enneads* 1, 2, 6: 'Man's striving is not to be out of sin, but to be god.'

46  *Homily* 5, 8–9 (the bodies of Christians 'will be glorified by the divine light'). Cf. *Homily* 15, 38 ('all members of the body ... become light, are immersed in light and fire and are transformed').

47  *The Ladder* 30; PG 88, 1157 B.

48  *Centuries on Theology* 2, 88.
49  *Exposition* 4, 15.
50  *Hymn* 9, 1–51.
51  *Hymn* 16, 21–40.
52  *Hymn* 28, 136–66.
53  *Hymn* 19, 107–47.

### Chapter 11: The Life of the Age to Come

1   The literal meaning of the Greek term *antichristos* is 'instead of Christ'.
2   *On Christ and Antichrist* 6.
3   Cf. 2 Thess. 2:8: 'The Lord Jesus will slay him with the breath of his mouth.'
4   Ignaty Brianchaninov, *Sochineniya*, t.V, p. 69.
5   *Sochineniya*, t.5, p. 70.
6   Cf. Theodore of Mopsuestia, *On Genesis* (PG 53, 640).
7   Metropolitan Anthony of Sourozh, *Zhizn, bolezn', smert'* [Life, Illness, Death] (Moscow, 1995), p. 103.
8   Cf. Plato, *Phaedrus* 246a–256a.
9   Cf. the Platonic image of the body as a prison for the soul: Plato, *Phaedo*, 62b; *Kratylus* 400c.
10  *Oration* 7, 21.
11  Cf. Luke 16:23–31.
12  Cf. Irenaeus of Lyons, *Against the Heresies* 2, 34, 1.
13  *On the Creation of Man*, 27.
14  *Service Book* (trans. I. F. Hapgood), p. 391.
15  Saturday, Tone 8, Canon for the Departed, Canticle Six; *Oktoechos*.
16  Saturday of the Dead, Matins, Canon, Canticle One: *Triodion*, p. 129.
17  *The Refutation of the Latin Chapters . . . on the Fire of Purgatory; Patrologia Orientalis* 15, pp. 39–60.
18  The discussion is reported in V. Sokolov, *Mozhno li i dolzhno li nam molitsya v tsesrkvi za nepravoslavnykh?* [Can We or Should We Pray in Church for the Non-Orthodox?] (Sergiyev Possad, 1906), pp. 23–31.
19  Cf. Luke 12:47–8.
20  *Stromateis* 6, 6.
21  Bishop Gregory, *Izyasneniye trudneyshikh mest iz 1-o poslaniya sv. ap. Petra* [Interpretation of the Most Difficult Passages from the 1st Epistle of Peter] (Simpheropol, 1902), p. 10.
22  *Stromata* 6, 6.
23  Cf. Rom. 2:14ff.
24  Metropolitan Anthony of Sourozh, *O vstreche* [On the Encounter] (Saint-Petersburg, 1994), pp. 166–8.
25  *Gehenna* is a Hebrew word meaning 'the Valley of Hinnom'. In the New Testament the word is used for hell, the final place of torment for sinners.
26  *Homily* 28 (*Ascetical Homilies*, p. 141).
27  *Homily on Isaiah* 5, 4.
28  *His Life is Mine* (New York, 1977), p. 32.

29  Holy Saturday, Vespers: *The Lenten Triodion*, pp. 655–6.

30  *Hades* is a Greek word meaning 'hell'.

31  *The Catechetical Oration on Easter* ascribed to St John Chrysostom and read in the Orthodox Church during Paschal matins; cited in Lossky, *Mystical Theology*, p. 248.

32  The Sunday of the Last Judgement, Matins: *Triodion*, p. 139.

33  Holy Friday, Matins: *Triodion*, p. 590.

34  Holy Saturday, Vespers: *Triodion*, p. 656.

35  Holy Saturday, Matins: *Triodion*, p. 645.

36  The anaphora of the Liturgy of St Basil the Great: *The Orthodox Liturgy* (Oxford, 1982), p. 125.

37  *Catechetical Oration on Easter*; cited in Lossky, *Mystical Theology*, pp. 248–9.

38  One of the Orthodox prayers before sleep.

39  *Letter to Diognetus* 7, 4.

40  Bishop Kallistos of Diokleia, ' "We Must Pray for All": Salvation according to St Silouan', *Sobornost* 19:1 (1997), p. 38.

41  The example of Judas and that of the bad thief are pertinent here. We are not told by the Church that Judas was liberated from hell by Christ. Neither are we told that both the good and the bad thieves met the same end: on the contrary, we believe that it was only the former who was taken to Paradise by the Saviour (cf. Luke 23:43). A personal encounter with Christ puts us all in the situation where we can either follow or reject him. This choice can be made in one's earthly life or after death, as in the case of the Old Testament people whom Christ confronted in hell.

42  Vespers of Pentecost, the Third Prayer of Kneeling.

43  Cf. I Tim. 2:4.

44  Cf. 2 Pet. 3:9.

45  *On the Soul and Resurrection* 7 (pp. 83–4).

46  Cf. Origen, *On First Principles* 3, 5, 3.

47  The Origenist teaching on the *apokatastasis* was condemned by the Local Council of 543 in Constantinople. As it now appears, there was no special mention of the *apokatastasis* in the anathemas of the Fifth Ecumenical Council (553) against Origen; see their critical edition: F. Diekamp, *Die origenistischen Streitigkeiten in sechsten Jahrhundert und das funfte allgemeine Konzil* (Munster i.W., 1899), pp. 90–6.

48  The expression *apokatastasis panton* (restoration, or restitution of all) is borrowed from Acts 3:21.

49  *The Lenten Triodion*, p. 649.

50  See Pelikan, *Emergence*, 151.

51  Cf. I Cor. 2:9.

52  *On the Soul and Resurrection* 7–10 (pp. 86–7; 115–16; 121).

53  *Oration* 30, 6. Cf. Col. 3:11.

54  *Exposition on Ps. 59* (PG 90, 857 A).

55  *Mystagogia* 7 (PG 91, 685 BC).

56  Cf. B. Daley, 'Apokatastasis and "honourable silence" in the eschatology of Maximus the Confessor'; *Maximus Confessor: Actes du Symposium sur Maxime le Confesseur*, ed. F. Heinzer and C. von Schonborn (Fribourg, 1982), p. 322.

57 Maximus's engagement with the idea of *apokatastasis* has been interpreted by modern scholars in a variety of ways. H. U. von Baltasaar sees in Maximus an adherent of this teaching: see his *Kosmische Liturgie: das Weltbild Maximus des Bekenners* (Einsiedeln, 1961), pp. 355–9. P. Sherwood, on the contrary, tries to prove that Maximus refuted this idea, at least in its Origenist version: see *The Earlier Ambigua of St Maximus the Confessor and his Refutation of Origenism, Studia Anselmiana* 36 (Rome, 1955), pp. 205–22. The most balanced view on the question is expressed in B. Daley, 'Apokatastasis and "honourable silence" ', pp. 309–39.
58 *Quaestiones et dubia* 13 (PG 90, 796 AC).
59 Daley, 'Apokatastasis', p. 327.
60 *Chapters on Love* I, 61 (PG 90, 973 A).
61 *Ambigua* 31 (PG 91, 1280 A).
62 'Apokatastasis', p. 329–30.
63 *Questions to Thalassios* 63 (PG 90, 668 C).
64 O. Clement, *The Roots of Christian Mysticism* (London-Dublin-Edinburgh, 1993), p. 303.
65 *Homily* 48 (*Ascetical Homilies*, p. 230).
66 *Homily* 51 (*Ascetical Homilies*, p. 244).
67 That is, Gehenna.
68 *Second Part*, Chapter 40, 4–12.
69 *Homily* 27 (*Ascetical Homilies*, p. 133).
70 *The Ladder of the Divine Ascent* 26, 82 (trans. Archimandrite Lazarus Moore, p. 173).
71 *Samopoznaniye* (Self-understanding) (Paris, 1989), p. 354.
72 Quoted from: *'Zhiv Bog'* [God is Alive]. *A Family Catechesis* (London, 1988), pp. 425–6.
73 Archimandrite Sophrony, *St Silouan*, p. 226.
74 *St Silouan*, p. 271.
75 *St Silouan*, p. 368.
76 *St Silouan*, p. 426.
77 *St Silouan*, p. 108.
78 *St Silouan*, p. 469.
79 *St Silouan*, pp. 48–9.
80 S. Bulgakov, *Apokalipsis Ioanna* [The Apocalypse of John] (Moscow, 1991), p. 211.
81 Cf. 2 Cor. 12:2.
82 Cf. John 14:2.
83 Cf. I Cor. 15:41.
84 *Interpretation of Isaiah*, ch. 11.
85 *Hymn* I, 132–59 (SC 156, 168–70).
86 *On the Soul and Resurrection* 7 (p. 86).

# APPENDIX

In studying Orthodox theology, we find ourselves introduced to a community of people who have written and argued about God throughout the ages. Here we give some brief notes on the authors mentioned in this book, and their place in history.

* Names in SMALL CAPITALS indicate a cross-reference to another entry.

**Andrew the Holy Fool** lived in Constantinople, but history cannot say precisely when: the account of his life appeared either between 674 and 695 or between 950 and 959. Supposed foolishness for the sake of Christ (1 Cor. 4:10) was the pattern of his life.

**Apollinarius** (310–390) was Bishop of Laodicea. An advocate of orthodoxy against the Arians, Apollinarius nevertheless explicitly denied the presence of a human mind or soul in Christ. The distinctive feature of Apollinarianism, which was condemned by the Council of Constantinople in 381, is an incompleteness in Christ's humanity.

**Aquinas, Thomas** (1225–1274) was a Dominican monk who spent his life in France and Italy studying and teaching in the famous medieval Universities of Naples and Paris. He is principally known for his *Summa Theologiae*, a major scholastic work which seeks to reconcile reason and science with religion and dogma in a systematic way.

**Arius** (255/280–336) was a priest in Alexandria. He taught that the Son of God was created out of nothing before the rest of creation, and that 'there was when He was not'. The COUNCIL OF NICAEA in 325 condemned Arianism, but it continued to survive for several decades.

**Athanasius of Alexandria** (296–373) was the greatest and most consistent theological opponent of ARIUS at the COUNCIL OF NICAEA in 325 and later. Refusing to compromise with the Arian party, he was exiled five times. He taught that the Son and the Holy Spirit are of one essence (*homoousios*) with the Father.

**Augustine of Hippo** (350–430), born in North Africa, was baptised by Ambrose

[ 249 ]

of Milan in 387 and became Bishop of Hippo in 395. Augustine is one of the most influential Western Christian theologians of all time. He is best known for his writings which include *The City of God*, *Confessions* and many biblical commentaries.

**Basil the Great** (330–379) was Archbishop of Caesarea in Cappadocia, and one of the three CAPPADOCIAN FATHERS. As a defender of Orthodoxy against the Arian heresy he developed and established the principle of consubstantiality of the three divine Persons: Father, Son, and Holy Spirit, existing as one God, the Holy Trinity.

**Bloom, Anthony, Metropolitan of Sourozh** (born 1914), is the founder and head of the Russian Orthodox Diocese of Sourozh in Great Britain. His writings on prayer and spiritual life are known throughout the world. He is recognised as one of the most influential spiritual leaders in the Orthodox Church today.

**Bulgakov, Serge** (1871–1944), an influential Russian theologian, was ordained priest in 1918. Exiled from Russia in 1923, he became one of the key figures of the Paris emigration, and in bringing Russian Orthodoxy to the West. He was a famous religious philosopher and one of the founders of the St Sergius Orthodox Institute in Paris.

**Cappadocian Fathers:** BASIL THE GREAT, GREGORY OF NYSSA, and GREGORY NAZIANZEN (see separate entries)

**Chrysostom, John** (349–407) was born in Antioch, where he trained as a rhetorician under the great pagan teacher Libanios. After his ordination to the priesthood he became famous throughout the Christian East for his extraordinary preaching skills, for which he was given the name 'Golden–mouth'. He was elected Archbishop of Constantinople in 398, but became a victim of political and church intrigues and died on his way to exile. Later his relics were returned to the city with honour.

**Clement of Alexandria** (150–215) was converted to Christianity as an adult and ordained priest around 190. He left a substantial collection of writings including the *Stromateis* and the *Pedagogus* in which he demonstrates both an affectionate devotion to Christ and a deep love of the Hellenic culture.

**Clement of Rome** was Bishop of Rome in the last decade of the first century. He is the author of one or possibly two epistles in which he raises the ecclesiological concerns of his age.

**Climacus, John** (7th century) became a monk in the Monastery of Mount Sinai and spent many years as a solitary. In his old age he wrote *The Ladder of Divine Ascent*, consisting of thirty short treatises on the various stages of spiritual life.

**Council of Chalcedon, the** or the Fourth Ecumenical Council. This took place in 451. During it, more than five hundred bishops reaffirmed the Nicene-Constantinopolitan Creed and clarified christological teaching, according to which Christ is one Person in two natures, divine and human, united 'without confusion, without change, without division and without separation'.

**Council of Nicaea, the** or the First Ecumenical Council. This was convened in

325 by the Emperor Constantine in response to the Arian controversy. The Fathers of the Council declared the Son to be *homoousios* (of one essence) with the Father and condemned the teachings of ARIUS.

**Cyril of Alexandria** (378–444) was the major opponent of NESTORIUS, and the author of numerous treatises on christology, as well as many biblical commentaries. Cyril defended the unity of person in the incarnate Christ and insisted that the term *theotokos* (God-bearer) could be used to refer to Mary as the Mother of the Incarnate God.

**Didache,** or *The Teaching of the Twelve Apostles,* was most probably written in the first half of the second century in Egypt or in Syria. It consists of two parts, of which the first describes Christianity as the way of life opposed to the way of death; the second is concerned with worship and discipline in the Christian community; it also contains one of the earliest records of the *Anaphora* (Eucharistic prayer).

**Dionysius the Areopagite**, an Athenian converted by Paul (Acts 17:34), lived in the first century. His name was used by an anonymous fifth-century writer, author of several treatises and epistles. The author of this corpus of writings (commonly known as *Corpus Areopagiticum*) explores the nature of God, angels and the human soul, using apophatic and cataphatic principles of theology. His teaching became an integral part of Orthodox tradition.

**Ephrem the Syrian** (d. 373), was one of the most famous writers of the Syriac Christian tradition. He spent most of his life in Edessa where he was ordained deacon and established a theological school. The corpus of his writings consists of numerous hymns, poems and orations, which reflect on the mysteries of Christian theology, in particular, on the Incarnation and its implications for human life.

**Eunomius** (330–380/390) was an advocate of subordinationism in christology. As an opponent to the Cappadocians, he insisted that the Son was different in essence from the Father, subordinate to the Father, with the Spirit as his minister. Eunomius's teaching was condemned by the Second Ecumenical Council.

**Eusebius** (260–340) was Bishop of Caesarea and theological adviser to the Emperor Constantine. At the COUNCIL OF NICAEA he showed Arian tendencies, but tried to compromise with ATHANASIUS. He was the author of the first major systematic exposition of church history.

**Evagrios of Pontus** (346–399) was a disciple of BASIL THE GREAT and Gregory NAZIANZEN. In 383 he withdrew to the Egyptian desert, where he wrote systematic treatises on the monastic life. Some aspects of his christology were condemned by the Fifth Ecumenical Council, but he has always been considered as one of the greatest ascetic writers of the Christian East.

**Evdokimov, Paul** (1901–1970) began his theological studies in Kiev shortly before the Russian Revolution of 1917, after which his family emigrated to Paris. There he graduated from the St Sergius Theological Institute, where he studied with SERGE BULGAKOV. A professor at the St Sergius Institute, he was also the author of a number of studies in which modern issues are related to the spiritual and liturgical life of the Orthodox Church.

**Florensky, Paul** (1882–1943), a distinguished mathematician and engineer, was ordained priest in 1911. As a Christian philosopher and theologian he was involved in the pre-revolutionary Russian religious renaissance. In 1933 he was imprisoned by the Soviet authorities. The rest of his life was spent in labour camps, where he died as a martyr.

**Florovsky, Georges** (1893–1970) left Russia in 1920 and taught from 1926 at the St Sergius Institute in Paris. In 1948 he moved to the United States, where he became dean of St Vladimir's Theological Seminary. He also held chairs at Harvard and Princeton. One of the most distinguished Orthodox theologians of the twentieth century, he devoted most of his scholarly works to the systematisation of patristic teaching and church history.

**Germanus of Constantinople** (634–733) was a defender of the veneration of icons in the time of the Emperor Leo III and the author of a symbolic commentary on the Divine Liturgy.

**Gillet, Lev** (1893–1980) pursued an academic career for a few years after World War I, and became a monk and priest in the Roman Catholic Church. He spent some years in ecumenical and pastoral activity in France and in 1928 became an Orthodox priest. From 1938 he lived in Britain, where he was much loved as a priest, theologian and spiritual guide. He was the chaplain to the Fellowship of St Alban and St Sergius. Most of his writings, dedicated to various aspects of the Orthodox Christianity, were published under the name of 'A Monk of the Eastern Church'.

**Gregory of Nyssa** (335–394) was a younger brother of BASIL THE GREAT, one of the three CAPPADOCIAN FATHERS. Having received philosophical education, he became an influential and original theologian who made a substantial contribution to the development of the Christian theological and mystical tradition. Among his most significant writings are twelve treatises including *Against Eunomius*, the *Great Catechetical Oration*, *On the Creation of Man* and *The Life of Moses*.

**Hesychios** most probably lived in the 7th/8th century on Mount Sinai. In the Christian tradition he is known as a contributor to the teaching on the practice of the Jesus Prayer, which he analysed in his writings on watchfulness and devotion to the Name of Jesus.

**Hopko, Thomas, Archpriest**, was a former dean of St Vladimir's Orthodox Theological Seminary in New York.

**Ignatius** (*c*. 35–*c*. 107) was bishop of Antioch and was martyred in Rome. On his journey to Rome he wrote several epistles to various churches, in which he explored the mystical meaning of martyrdom, Church, Eucharist and ecclesiological hierarchy.

**Irenaeus of Lyon** (130–200), a bishop and martyr, was one of the first Christian theologians who withstood Gnosticism and explained Christian doctrine in a systematic form. In his book *Against the Heresies* Irenaeus propounds an early Trinitarian theology in which he describes the nature of Logos and also introduces the theory of 'recapitulation' whereby Christ is seen as the Second Adam.

**Isaac the Syrian** (7th century), a monk and a solitary, spent a short period as Bishop of Nineveh and then withdrew again into the desert. He is the author of numerous ascetical homilies, in which he explores the nature of monasticism and speaks on compassionate love as the main principle of Christian life.

**John of Damascus** (675–749), an official at the court of the Muslim caliph in Damascus, entered a monastery near Jerusalem in around 716. There he wrote a series of treatises and sermons, of which *The Exact Exposition of Christian Faith* is the most popular. He was a staunch defender of the veneration of icons and one of the most famous authors of liturgical poetry.

**John of Kronstadt** (1829–1908) graduated from the St Petersburg Theological Academy. After he was ordained priest in St Petersburg in 1855, he began missionary work among the local citizens, homeless, and criminals, and spent much of his life serving and preaching in Kronstadt near St Petersburg. He was renowned for his outstanding pastoral activity and became an influential spiritual teacher in the Russian Orthodox Church.

**John the Theologian** (1st century) is the title given to John the Apostle, author of the fourth Gospel, three Epistles and the Book of Revelation.

**Justin Martyr** (100/110–165), was the first prominent Christian apologist. He was converted to Christianity through his study of Greek philosophy and his admiration for Christ and his martyrs. He is the author of the two apologias for Christianity, addressed to the Emperor Antonius Pius and the Roman Senate respectively, and of *The Dialogue with Trypho the Jew.*

**Macarius the Great** (4th century) lived in Egypt and was known as a spiritual director and ascetic. Several collections of spiritual homilies, written most probably in South-East Asia or Western Mesopotamia around 370–390, were ascribed to him. The author of the homilies stresses the importance of the spiritual communion with the Holy Spirit, and explores other aspects of mystical life. The homilies exerted enormous influence on many subsequent Christian writers, both in the East and in the West.

**Mani** (216–277) was the founder of Manicheism, a Gnostic sect (to which AUGUSTINE belonged in his youth) which propounded a radical dualism between good and evil, ascribing all the material world to the realm of evil.

**Mark of Ephesus** (15th century), Archbishop and theologian. He represented Orthodoxy at the Council of Florence (1438–9), at which he refused to sign the formula of union with the Roman Catholic Church whereby the Orthodox were to surrender to the Catholic teachings on the primacy of the Pope and the procession of the Holy Spirit from both the Father and the Son (*filioque*).

**Maximus the Confessor** (580–662) was an Orthodox monk and prolific theological writer and the author of many christological and ascetic works. From 540 he stood ground against the Monothelytes, insisting that Christ had both human and divine wills. For his uncompromising position, Maximus was mutilated and exiled, but the Sixth Ecumenical Council in 680 reaffirmed his theology and condemned his opponents.

**Methodius of Patara** (3rd century) was a bishop in Asia Minor and died as a martyr. He is the author of several treatises, in which he expounded Christian theology and moral teaching. He was one of the earliest critics of ORIGEN and an opponent of Gnosticism.

**Meyendorff, John** (1921–1992) was a professor and dean of St Vladimir's Orthodox Theological Seminary in New York where he emerged as a theologian.

**Montanism** was an heretical sect founded by Montanus in the second century. His doctrine placed great emphasis on prophetic revelation in the post-apostolic age.

**Moschos, John** (550–619) entered a monastery near Jerusalem around 575. Subsequently he visited a number of monastic foundations, and wrote the *Pratum Spirituale* which contains many stories about monastic life.

**Nazianzen, Gregory** or Gregory the Theologian (330–389/90), was a friend of BASIL THE GREAT, and one of the most outstanding Christian theologians of all time. As an opponent of Arianism and Apollinarianism, in his orations, letters, and poems, he contributed enormously to the development of the trinitarian theology of the Orthodox Church.

**Nestorius** became Patriarch of Constantinople in 428. Deeply influenced by THEODORE OF MOPSUESTIA, he caused great controversy in Christology by rejecting the term *theotokos* (God-bearer) as applied to Mary the Mother of God. Mary, he maintained, bore a man – Christ later assumed the Logos, since God cannot have a mother. His statements were condemned at the Council of Ephesus in 431 largely through the influence of CYRIL OF ALEXANDRIA. Exiled in 436, Nestorius died some years later.

**Nicodemos of Mount Athos** (1749–1809) was a hesychast monk, author of numerous treatises and compiler of the *Philokalia*, a collection of Christian writings on prayer and asceticism.

**Origen** (185–254/5) lived in Alexandria and Jerusalem and was the author of numerous dogmatic and exegetical works, which contributed greatly to the development of Christian theology. He was posthumously condemned for his christological views, in which clear traces of subordinationism were detected by the Fifth Ecumenical Council, but even after this he continued to be recognised as one of the most outstanding and original writers in the whole history of Christianity.

**Palamas, Gregory** (1296–1359), a monk of Mount Athos and Archbishop of Thessalonike, lived during the decline of the Byzantine Empire. As an opponent of Barlaam of Kalabria, he was a staunch defender of hesychasm – a traditional

Orthodox teaching on inner spiritual life, integral to the theology of the divine energies through which God reveals himself to humans.

**Philaret of Moscow** (1782–1867) was one of the most influential ecclesiastical figures and theologians of nineteenth-century Russia.

**Philo** (30 BC–45 AD) was prominent in the Jewish community of Alexandria, but also drawn to the Greek philosophers, especially Plato. His thought is of particular interest to the Christian tradition because of his method of allegorising Scripture using Greek philosophy. Influenced by the Middle Platonists, he formed a concept of the Logos as God's agent in creation.

**Plato** (429–347 BC) was one of the most original Greek philosophers and the author of many dialogues which greatly influenced Byzantine and Western medieval Christian writers.

**Sabellius** (3rd century) propagated a teaching according to which the three Persons of the Trinity are merged into a monad, the Father being its form or essence, and the Son and Spirit his modes of expression.

**Schmemann, Alexander** (1920–1983) was dean of St Vladimir's Theological Seminary in New York, and the author of numerous books concerning various aspects of Christian life in the modern world. His main study, *The Eucharist*, is dedicated to the explanation of the meaning of the Orthodox Liturgy, which he considers as the most authentic expression of Christian life, spirituality and dogma.

**Seraphim of Sarov** (1759–1833) spent many years as a hermit before becoming a spiritual director to thousands of people from all over Russia. Canonised in 1903, he is one of Russia's best known and most loved saints.

**Sergius of Radonezh** (1314–1392) was a monk and solitary, who later became the founder and first abbot of the Lavra of the Holy Trinity near Moscow, from where monasticism spread to many other places in Russia.

**Silouan of Mount Athos** (1866–1938), born into a Russian peasant family, became a monk on Mount Athos in 1896. His diaries, published with a commentary by his disciple, Archimandrite Sophrony (1896–1993), exerted enormous influence on the Christian spirituality of the second half of the twentieth century.

**Symeon the New Theologian** (949–1022) is one of the most original Christian mystical writers, and author of numerous discourses and hymns. Born into an aristocratic family, he served at the court of the Byzantine Emperor but eventually became a monk and a priest in Constantinople. His teaching on the divine light as the core of mystical life was subject to heated debates during his lifetime and after his death. His writings were 'rediscovered' in the twentieth century, when he acquired enormous popularity both within and outside Orthodox tradition.

**Tatian** (d. 120) was a Christian apologist and disciple of Justin Martyr. In his *Apology to the Greeks* he emphasised the essential unity of the Logos with the Father, and his generation by the Father's will before creation.

**Tertullian** (155–225) studied law and rhetoric at Rome. Having been converted to Christianity around 193 by Christian martyrs, he settled at Carthage. As a theologian he was the first to refer to the Trinity as 'three persons in one essence'; in 207 he embraced MONTANISM and founded his own church community.

**Theodore of Mopsuestia** (d. 428) studied rhetoric together with JOHN CHRYSOSTOM. Later he became a bishop and one of the principal theologians of the school of Antioch. Having been a teacher of NESTORIUS, he was denounced at the Fifth Ecumenical Council in 553, accused of failing to confess the true unity of person of the incarnate Christ.

**Theophan the Recluse** (1815–1894), on graduation from the Theological Academy at Kiev became a monk and priest and later a rector of the St Petersburg Theological Academy. In 1859 he was ordained bishop, but resigned in 1866 and became a recluse in a provincial monastery, where he concentrated on literary work. He is the author of numerous books on Christian ascetical life, translations of patristic texts and letters addressed to the laity. He was canonised by the Russian Orthodox Church in 1988.

**Troitsky, Hilarion, Archbishop of Vereya**, was an influential Russian theologian of the pre-revolutionary period, author of numerous studies on ecclesiology. He died as a martyr in 1937 after a long imprisonment in the Solovetsky labour camp in northern Russia.

**Ware, Kallistos, Bishop of Diokleia** (born 1934), became a Fellow of Pembroke College, Oxford, in 1970, and until 2001 was the Spalding Lecturer in Eastern Christian Studies. His books have brought many to Christianity, and his translations of liturgical texts and the *Philokalia* have greatly contributed to the understanding of the Orthodox worship and spirituality in the English-speaking world.

# BIBLIOGRAPHY

**English translations of patristic writings used in the present study**

Dionysius the Areopagite = Pseudo-Dionysius, *The Complete Works*, translated by C. Luibheid (London, 1987).

Origen, *On First Principles* = Origen, *On First Principles*, translated by G. W. Butterworth (New York, 1966).

*Philokalia* = *The Philokalia*, translated by G. E. H. Palmer, Philip Sherrard, Kallistos Ware, vols I–IV (London, 1979–1995).

St Augustine, *Confessions* = St Augustine, *Confessions*, translated by John K. Ryan (New York, 1960).

St Basil the Great, *On the Hexaemeron* = St Basil the Great, *Exegetic Homilies*, translated by Sister Agnes Clare Way, CDP (Washington DC, 1981), *The Fathers of the Church*, vol. 46, pp. 3–150.

St Gregory the Theologian, *Orations 27–31 (Theological Orations)* = Frederick W. Norris, *Faith Gives Fullness to Reasoning: The Five Theological Orations of Gregory Nazianzen*, translated by Lionel Wickham and Frederick Williams (Leiden – New York, Kobenhavn – Koln, 1991), pp. 217–299.

St Gregory of Nyssa, *On the Soul and the Resurrection* = St Gregory of Nyssa, *On the Soul and the Resurrection*, translated by Catharine P. Roth (New York, 1993).

St Isaac the Syrian, *Homilies* = *The Ascetical Homilies of Saint Isaac the Syrian*, translated by D. Miller, (Boston, Massachusetts, 1984).

St Isaac the Syrian, *Second Part* = Isaac of Nineveh (Isaac the Syrian), 'The Second Part', chapters IV–XLI, translated by Sebastian Brock, *Corpus Scriptorum Christianorum Orientalium* 555, Scriptores syri 225 (Louvain, 1995).

St John Climacus, *The Ladder of Divine Ascent* = St John Climacus, *The Ladder of Divine Ascent*, translated by Archimandrite Lazarus Moore (Brookline, Massachusetts, 1991).

St John Damascene, *An Exact Exposition* = St John Damascene, *An Exact Exposition of the Orthodox Faith*, in St John Damascene, *Writings*, translated by Frederic H. Chase Jr (Washington DC, 1981), *The Fathers of the Church*, vol. 37, pp. 165–406.

St John Damascene, *On the Divine Images* = St John Damascene, *Three Apologies Against Those Who Attack the Divine Images*, translated by David Anderson (Crestwood, New York, 1980).

St Macarius the Great, *Homilies* = Pseudo-Macarius, *The Fifty Spiritual Homilies and the Great Letter*, translated by G. Maloney (Mahwah, New Jersey, 1992).

St Methodius, *The Symposium* = St Methodius, *The Symposium. A Treatise on Chastity*, translated and annotated by Herbert Musurillo, SJ, *Ancient Christian Writers* no. 27 (New York, 1958).

St Silouan of Mount Athos, *Writings* = Archimandrite Sophrony (Sakharov), *St Silouan the Athonite* (Essex, 1991), pp. 269–504.

St Symeon the New Theologian, *Hymns* = *Hymns of Divine Love* by St Symeon the New Theologian, translated by G. Maloney (Denville, New Jersey, s.a.).

St Symeon the New Theologian, *Catechetical Discourses* = Symeon the New Theologian, *The Discourses*, translated by C. J. de Catanzaro (Mahwah, New Jersey, 1980).

## Sources of passages at the end of each chapter

### Chapter 1
St Silouan of Mount Athos = Archimandrite Sophrony, *St Silouan*, pp. 289–290.
Clement of Alexandria = *Stromata* 1, 2–1, 5.
Origen = *On First Principles* 4, 1.
St Augustine = *Confessions* 7, 20–21.
St Paul = *Epistle to the Romans* 8:28–31.
St Symeon the New Theologian = *Ethical Discourse* 2, 7.

### Chapter 2
Clement of Alexandria = *Stromata* 2, 2.
Clement of Alexandria = *Stromata* 5, 12.
Dionysius the Areopagite = *On the Mystical Theology* 1.
Dionysius the Areopagite = *On the Mystical Theology* 4–5.
St John Damascene = *An Exact Exposition of the Orthodox Faith* 1, 4.
St Gregory the Theologian = *Oration* 31, 22.
St Augustine = *Confessions* 1, 4.

### Chapter 3
St Athanasius the Great = *Orations against the Arians* 1, 17–18.
St Gregory the Theologian = *Oration* 31, 13.
St Symeon the New Theologian = *Hymn* 45.
St John Damascene = *An Exact Exposition of the Orthodox Faith* 1, 8.

**Chapter 4**
'Reminiscences of a Priest' = 'Reminiscences of a Priest', in *Nadezhda* no. 13 (Frankfurt on Main, 1986), pp. 269–271.
'On the Mountains of the Caucasus' = Monk Hilarion, *Na gorakh Kavkaza* [On the Mountains of the Caucasus], vol. I (Batalpashinsk, 1910), pp. 4–6.
St Basil the Great = *Homilies on Hexaemeron* I.
Albert Einstein = Cited in *Svet i Zhizn'* [Light and Life], compiled by Father Alexander Men (Brussels, 1990), p. 95.
St Gregory the Theologian = *Oration* 28, 26–31.
St John Damascene = *An Exact Exposition of the Orthodox Faith* 2, 3–4.
St Isaac the Syrian = *The Second Part*, Chapter 10, 18–19.
St Symeon the New Theologian = *Hymn* 38.

**Chapter 5**
Archimandrite Sophrony = *St Silouan*, p. 54.
St Gregory of Nyssa = *On the Creation of Man* 3.
Bishop Kallistos of Diokleia = *The Orthodox Way*, pp. 62–63.
St Dorotheos of Gaza = *Spiritual Discourse* I.
St Macarius the Great = Pseudo-Macarius, *Spiritual Homily* II, 5.
V. Ilyin = *Zapechatannyi grob, Pascha netleniya* [The Sealed Tomb, the Pascha of Incorruption] (Paris, 1926), p. 16.
St Silouan of Mount Athos = Archimandrite Sophrony, *St Silouan*, pp. 448–456.

**Chapter 6**
Origen = *On First Principles* 2, 6.
St Gregory the Theologian = *Letter* 101 (The First Letter to Cledonius).
St Agatho of Rome = *Epistle* to the Sixth Ecumenical Council.
St John Damascene = *An Exact Exposition of the Orthodox Faith* 3, 14–15.
St John Damascene = *An Exact Exposition of the Orthodox Faith* 3, 17.
St Isaac the Syrian = *The Second Part*, Chapter 40, 14.
St Symeon the New Theologian = *Ethical Discourse* 13.
Service for the Nativity of Christ = Vespers, *Sticheron*, Tone 2.

**Chapter 7**
Liturgy of St Basil the Great = *The Orthodox Liturgy* (Oxford, 1982), pp. 129–135.
St Ignatius of Antioch = *Epistle to the Magnesians* 7.
'Letter to Diognetus' = *Letter to Diognetus* 5–6.
St Cyril of Alexandria = *Interpretation of the Gospel according to St John* II, II (PG 74, 560 A-561 B).
Archimandrite Placide Deseille = 'Pravoslavnyi vzgliad na yedinstvo christian' [An Orthodox Understanding of Christian Unity] in *Vestnik RSHD* no. 147 (Paris, 1986), p. 24; with quotations from Gregory Nazianzen's *Orations* 18, 6 and 8, 20.

Metropolitan Anthony of Sourozh = *Besedy o vere i Tserkvi* (Moscow, 1991), pp. 262–275; with an allusion to G. Florovsky, 'The Limits of the Church', in *Church Quarterly Review,* vol. 117, no. 213 (October 1933), pp. 117–131.

### Chapter 8

'The Teaching of the Twelve Apostles' = *Didache* 7, 1–10, 2.
St Cyril of Alexandria = *Epistle* 17 (Third Epistle to Nestorius).
St John Chrysostom = *On the Betrayal of Judas* (Homily on Great Thursday).
Father Thomas Hopko = Thomas Hopko, 'God and Gender: Articulating the Orthodox View', *St Vladimir's Theological Quarterly,* vol. 39, nos. 2–3, p. 163.
Bishop Kallistos of Diokleia = 'The Monastic Life as a Sacrament of Love', *Ekklesia kai Theologia* 2 (1981), pp. 697–699.
Metropolitan Anthony of Sourozh = *Besedy o vere i Tserkvi,* pp. 118–127.

### Chapter 9

St John Climacus = *The Ladder of Divine Ascent* 28 (translated by L. Moore, p. 212).
Evagrius the Solitary = *On Prayer* 3, 14–16, 36, 84, 118–120, 126, 150 (*Philokalia* I, pp. 57–71).
St Theophan the Recluse = Cited in *O molitve Iisusovoy* [On the Jesus Prayer] (Sortavala, 1936), pp. 30–31.
A Monk of the Eastern Church = [Archimandrite Lev Gillet], *The Jesus Prayer* (New York, 1995), p. 106.
'On the Mountains of the Caucasus' = Monk Hilarion, *Na gorakh Kavkaza,* vol. I, pp. 7–10.
St Silouan of Mount Athos = Archimandrite Sophrony, *St Silouan,* pp. 292–297.

### Chapter 10

Bishop Kallistos of Diokleia = *The Orthodox Way* (London-Oxford, 1979), pp. 27–28.
St Gregory the Theologian = *Oration* 37, 8.
St Symeon the New Theologian = *Catechetical Discourse* 17.

### Chapter 11

Bishop Kallistos of Diokleia = *The Orthodox Church* (London, 1987), pp. 266–267.
Olivier Clement = *The Roots of Christian Mysticism* (London-Dublin-Edinburgh, 1993), pp. 301–302.
Metropolitan Anthony of Sourozh = *Chelovek pered Bogom* [Man before God] (Moscow, 1993), pp. 59–65.
St Isaac the Syrian = *The Second Part,* Chapter 39, 6–22.
St Silouan of Mount Athos = Archimandrite Sophrony, *St Silouan,* p. 275.
V. Lossky = *Orthodox Theology. An Introduction* (New York, 1989), pp. 116–118.
St Isaac the Syrian = *The Second Part,* Chapter 11, 32–35.

# INDEX

# THE FELLOWSHIP OF
# ST ALBAN AND ST SERGIUS

(Registered Charity No. 245112)

**Address**

1 Canterbury Road, Oxford OX2 6LU

Tel: 01865 552991 Fax: 01865 316700

Website: www.sobornost.org

E-mail: gensec@sobornost.org

**Presidents**

The Most Revd Archbishop Gregorios of Thyateira and Great Britain

The Rt Revd & Rt Hon. Richard Chartres, Bishop of London

**General Secretary**

The Revd Stephen Platt

The Fellowship exists to work for Christian unity. It provides opportunities for Christians of East and West to meet and to get to know one another, and so to deepen their understanding of each other's theology and worship. It was founded in 1928 at a student conference in St Albans, by clergy and laity of the Church of England and the Orthodox Churches. They found that they could not only talk together but pray together, and that although they could not share the sacrament of the Eucharist, they could worship together. Since then its membership has widened to include Christians from many other traditions. Branches of the Fellowship now exist throughout the world.

**The Aims of the Fellowship**

The Fellowship is a Christian association united in prayer 'for the peace of the whole world, for the stability of the holy Churches of God, and for the union of all' (from the Liturgy of St John Chrysostom). In an atmosphere of trust and openness, growing out of personal friendship, members witness to the truth as

[ 265 ]

they have received it in their own Church, and are ready to share the wealth of their own tradition with others and to learn from them. The Fellowship, as an unofficial body, welcomes official dialogues between the Churches and strives to make their work a reality at a local and parochial level.

## Its Activities

Every member of the Fellowship is entitled to receive its journal *Sobornost* (incorporating *Eastern Churches Review*), published twice a year, and containing important articles on various aspects of Eastern and Western Christian traditions, book reviews, items of news from Eastern Churches and Fellowship reports. All members receive the Fellowship Newsletter, published four times a year. The Fellowship also publishes a small number of books (a list is available from the Fellowship's headquarters).

The annual conference in Great Britain brings together around a hundred members of the Fellowship. During the week that they spend together, participants attend a daily celebration of the Eucharist according to their different rites, emphasising the significance of eucharistic worship as the centre of the Fellowship's activity. They have the opportunity of hearing a variety of speakers and of joining in lively discussion. The conference enables Christians of different traditions and of all ages to meet and become friends in a relaxed and informal setting.

Retreats and study days are held from time to time, and each year an ecumenical pilgrimage is made to St Albans Cathedral as close as possible to the feast of the saint. Central to this is a celebration of the Orthodox Liturgy in honour of the first martyr of Britain.

The Fellowship administers the Zernov Fund, from which it makes a number of grants each year to groups and projects that are in accord with its aims. Through our sponsorship of a wide range of church-related activities, both in Britain and overseas, we are able to form new contacts between Christians of Eastern and Western traditions. Application forms for financial assistance are available from the General Secretary. In addition, the Fellowship has its own programme of activities in several Orthodox countries. These include publications, conferences and exchange visits.

The Fellowship offers an information service for enquirers wishing to know more about the Orthodox Churches and their relationship with Western Christian denominations.

## Headquarters

The Fellowship's administrative office and headquarters are in Oxford, England, in the House of St Gregory and St Macrina. This is a centre for inter-Church meetings and a residence for Christian students, which brings together Orthodox and non-Orthodox in various ways. There is an Orthodox church in the same grounds, and the Fellowship's library is housed in St Theosevia's House, situated on the same site. The library, which holds a varied and unusual collection of

# THE FELLOWSHIP OF ST ALBAN AND ST SERGIUS

*Registered Charity No. 245112*

1 Canterbury Road, Oxford OX2 6LU
Tel: 01865 552991   Fax: 01865 316700
Website: www.sobornost.org   E-mail: gensec@sobornost.org

## APPLICATION FOR MEMBERSHIP

Title (Mr, Mrs, Miss, Dr, Revd, etc) ...........................................................................

Names ...........................................................................................................................

Address .........................................................................................................................

........................................................................................................................................

........................................................................................................................................

Church affiliation ........................................................................................................

Date of birth ................................................................................................................

Occupation ...................................................................................................................

University/College (if student) .................................................................................

I wish to become a member of the Fellowship of St Alban and St Sergius and would like to contribute annually (tick one):

❏ £25.00 (full rate), including one year's subscription to *Sobornost/ECR*.

❏ £15.00 (concessionary rate students, senior citizens, unemployed, members of religious communities), including subscription to *Sobornost/ECR*.

❏ £5.00 (reduced rate), excluding subscription to *Sobornost/ECR*.

I enclose a cheque/bank standing order for the total amount and want the Fellowship of St Alban and St Sergius to reclaim income tax annually on that amount until further notice (please note that you must be paying income tax or capital gains tax in the UK to an amount in excess of 28p for every £1 of contribution. Please also notify us if at any time you cease to pay enough income or capital gains tax to cover tax recoverable on your contribution).

Signed .........................................................................................................................

Date ..............................................................................................................................

---

FOR OFFICE USE ONLY

Date processed ............................................................................................................

Membership no.  .........................................................................................................